What DO You

The Everyday Guide to your Best Self

Colin Bailey

"Our purpose in life is to be happy.
From the very core of our being, we simply desire contentment."

The Dalai Lama

1st Edition Copyright © 2018 Colin Bailey
2nd Edition Copyright © 2020 Colin Bailey
3rd Edition Copyright © 2024 Colin Bailey
Mental Wealth | Resilient Minds UK

No part of this publication may be reproduced, distributed, or transmitted in any form or by any means, including - but not limited to - photocopying, recording, or other electronic or mechanical methods, without the prior written permission of the publisher, except in the case of brief quotations embodied in reviews and certain other non-commercial uses permitted by copyright law.

All rights reserved.

ISBN: 9798333888730

Dedication:

To Megan. Once the woman of my dreams... Now the woman of my reality.

To B, Zach and Abi, The source of my inspiration....
"The holy trinity"[1] - my reason for being. My muses.

To Alison. For always being there. For being the yardstick - and sometimes also the rod!

To Keith. For the gift of brotherly love. For giving me a reason...

To Brent. My doppelganger. My non-biological twin. My adolescent partner in crime.

To Cob and Nik. The rocks from which I built a stronger foundation.

To Rainbow. My No. 1 Fan - Thank you for your support and "encouragement"...

To my parents. I definitely wouldn't be here without you...

To my family, friends and colleagues who keep me grounded, and taught me that "the sky is the limit".

To Bob Proctor, and my friends at The Proctor Gallagher Institute, for the awareness that "the sky is just the beginning".

To each and every one of my "*traveling companions*" - thank you for inviting me on your journeys.

To my fellow writers and motivators, who've supported me with your encouragement and inspiration.

To my supporting cast. You know who you are...

I wouldn't be here without you.

"Goddank vir Klank"

---

[1] "The human family is, in a certain sense, the icon of the Trinity because of the love between its members and the fruitfulness of that love." - Pope Emeritus Benedict XVI

Table of Contents:

"What *DO* You Think?" 4
Prologue – "I am what I am today because of the choices I made yesterday."......6
Your "DO": 16
NLP (Neuro-Linguistic Programming): 28
"Famous Former Failures": 32
DiSC Personality Profiles: 42
Body Language: 50
Relationships: 54
Confidence, and Self-Esteem: 76

~ PART 2 - "THE SCIENTIFIC BIT"… ~

Happiness, Optimism and Gratitude: 92
Mindfulness and Meditation: 118
Motivation: 134
Resilience: 142
"Success": 154
Emotional Intelligence (EQ): 164
Physiology and Energy: 170
Diet and Nutrition: 176
Water and Hydration: 203
Exercise: 214
Rest and Recuperation: 224
Stress: 230
Anxiety, Depression and Fear: 236
Productivity, And Time Management: 244
"My Way": Regrets, and Lessons in Living…..256
Inspirational Quotes: 264
Addendum: Sensory Preference Questionnaire: 266

"What *DO* You Think?"

The average person thinks approximately 50,000 thoughts each day. Research suggests that in certain individuals, that figure could even rise to the lofty heights of 70,000. That equates to 48 thoughts every minute - without even factoring in the hours that you should be spending asleep! The average person is aware of approximately 3,000 thoughts a day, meaning that we think - on average – 47,000 (to potentially 67,000) thoughts of which we are not even aware - every single day...

It should therefore come as no surprise that we sometimes lose ourselves in the turmoil and turbulence of "everyday life" - whatever that may mean to you. Whether you're "working the 9-5"; raising a family; in education; self-employed, or even unemployed - the everyday assault on our senses is an incessant barrage.

- Have you ever experienced the occasional sense of overwhelm, or helplessness - lost at sea with waves of sensory information and distraction constantly breaking around you?

- Do you feel a sense of inadequacy, or a lack of self-confidence when comparing yourself to the "mass perception of perfection" depicted through the airbrushed pages of glossy magazines?

- Do you feel a sense of longing, or perhaps even envy, when viewing the "highlights reels" of your hundreds of "friends" on the hallowed pages of social media - the yardstick by which many of us measure the (relative) quality of our own lives?

- Do you feel that something is missing? That there has to be something "more" to life?

"What *DO* You Think?" has been designed to offer you a number of practical solutions in a concise, and easy to read format. This book does not claim to offer every solution for every individual, but what it does provide, is a veritable smorgasbord of delights for you to consider, and to apply to your everyday life. There is no "One Size Fits All" approach to self-development, but the intention throughout the pages which follow, is for you to select whichever you feel resonates the most with you. As Jim Rohn said, "We need a variety of input and influence and voices".

If you feel that you lack that "elusive something", then **"What *DO* You Think?"** will provide you with everyday tips and tricks you can use to help you to stop comparing yourself with others, and to be the best version of *you* that you can be. It will provide you with valuable insights as to why you sometimes get lost and muddled, and will unlock some of the tools you require to successfully - and confidently - navigate this journey that we call life.

"**What *DO* You Think?**" will also provide inspiration, theories and "life hacks" to energise and motivate you towards your best self, with increased self-confidence, gratitude, and awareness…

As a qualified,[2] professional MasterCoach, NLP Master Practitioner, and founder of Mental Wealth | Resilient Minds (UK) and CS-BCoaching, it is not only my profession - but my passion - to accompany you on your journey to "the island of your dreams". Every day, I help people just like you to gain confidence, clarity and purpose in their lives - as a catalyst for positive and lasting lifestyle transformation…

What *DO* You Think?" is a clear, concise, informal, and informative guide to everyday living with confidence. It is simple, easy to read, and brimming with practical information, supported by research, studies and statistics - carefully selected to help you to make more sense of your life. You will create new habits, experience increased self-confidence, and discover a renewed sense of purpose, or *meaning*, in your daily life.

Don't be the one who misses out on life's opportunities, owing to "analysis paralysis" - if you are truly content with all aspects of your life, or if you are one of the 90% of people who invest in a self-improvement product, and never follow it through to completion[3] - then this book is not for you. If you believe that self-development is a journey of personal evolution, not a destination - or if you are one of the 10% - then please read on…

Take action - your "new you" awaits you inside - "Inaction breeds doubt and fear. Action breeds confidence and courage." *Dale Carnegie.*

"Procrastination is the death of opportunity."

Today is the first day of the rest of your life…

So, **What *DO* You Think?**

---

[2] Qualified with Merit through The Coaching Academy - The world's largest training organisation for coaches, and acknowledged by The Observer as "The number one coach training programme in Britain."

[3] Anthony Robbins' Personal Power Program

Prologue -
"I am what I am today because of the choices I made yesterday."[4]

"Charles has been in an accident. He's in a coma..."

I remember it as though it were yesterday... My best friend had just broken the news – our "third partner in crime" had been involved in a motoring accident. He had been running an errand for his mother's boss - collecting her daughter from school. "Monty" - as he was affectionately known - was a "straight A" student and had only recently dropped out of university as he felt that he wasn't being sufficiently challenged. *En route* back to his mother's office, Monty's beach buggy had veered out of control and he and his passenger had been thrown from the vehicle.

They had crossed in mid-air, and, on impact, Charles' head smashed into the roadside barrier - the force of the impact denting the reinforced metal, designed to withstand and repel the impact of a speeding car. Charles was diagnosed with water on the brain and was scheduled for emergency brain surgery.

We were allowed to visit Monty post-surgery. I can still recall his shaved head - the surgical scars a vivid contrast to his ashen complexion. What I remember the most - more than the plethora of tubes and machines entering and exiting his body - was an overwhelming sense of absolute helplessness and insignificance, as we watched him lying there, motionless - the initial foreboding silence of the room interrupted only by the occasional splutter of his life support.

We were only eighteen - we had officially discarded adolescence and begun to navigate the uncharted waters of adulthood. Only months earlier, I had returned from a "gap year" in London, and "the three musketeers" had been reunited - *"all for one, and one for all"*. We felt invincible. We had our lives ahead of us - nothing could touch us. With the misconceived confidence and naivety of youth, we believed that we were ready to take on anything that the world could throw in our general direction.

How quickly things can change. How suddenly the very things that we take for granted can be thrown into a state of turmoil...

The prognosis wasn't good. Nothing seemed to be working for Monty. The surgeons believed that the operation had been a relative success, but not much was known about neurological damage or head trauma - the information available at the time was sketchy, at best.

---

[4] Stephen Covey, author of "The 7 Habits of Highly Effective People"

The surgeons asked if we would speak to Monty in his coma - they encouraged familiar stimuli, in the hope that it might trigger some sort of response. After a few moments - (we have absolutely no idea of how much time had elapsed) - a nurse burst into the room.

Monty's brain activity was spiking in response to him "hearing" us speaking to him. Noting his reaction to familiar stimuli, the doctors suggested that it could be of great benefit to Monty if we were to compile a cassette (*remember them?*), which could be played continuously at his bedside.

That afternoon, upon arriving home, we set about recording ninety minutes of our favourite music - filling the silences between songs and at each end of the cassette - with our thoughts, best wishes and encouragement for him. What was there to lose?

To cut a long story short, Monty miraculously recovered from his coma - (although I still believe to this day, that it may have been to push the ***"STOP"*** button!) Charles' mother was at his bedside when he "awoke" and had amassed quite a collection of books which had served to pass the time during her devoted vigil. When she did eventually offer some of the books to Charles to read, she was met with the unexpected response of "Thanks mom, but I don't remember how to read…"

That was the day that I learned the true meaning of introspection, and to be truly grateful for each new dawn. It was also when I experienced first-hand just how powerful human will - and mental resolve - can be. The day that I adopted the Sioux battle cry of "*Hokay hey*",[5] living each day to its fullest potential. Life is short, but now, in retrospect, I believe that we simply ***wait too long to start living…*** Seize the day - "*Carpe diem!*"[6]

All too often, life's priorities are revisited in a (retrospective) melancholic sense of regret, brought upon by a major life event, or the receipt of devastating news. (What Bob Proctor would call an "emotional impact", or what Brendon Burchard might term "mortality motivation".) If you were to be told today (God forbid!) that you had six months left to live, would you approach your life any differently? Would you truly *live* each and every day without regret or reservation?

Why wait for the inevitable bombshell? You will never have more time than you do right now…

---

5   "Hokay hey" - "Today is a good day to die".

6   "Pluck the day (as it is ripe)," enjoy the moment.

Brendon Burchard - named by *SUCCESS* magazine as one of the "Top 25 Most Influential Leaders in Personal Growth and Achievement" - chooses to live every day through his philosophy of *"Live. Love. Matter."*

(Coincidentally, Brendon's story also involves a car accident...) Looking down on his bloodied body, and the smoking wreck of his vehicle, he asked himself three questions...

Brendon believes that these are the three questions that we will each ask ourselves as we look back upon our lives:

- *"Did I live?"* Did you live a full life, embracing ***every*** available opportunity, or did you let life slip you by, like grains of sand through your fingers?

- *"Did I love?"* Did you love fully, and to your greatest potential? Did you take every opportunity to serve your significant others to the **best** of your ability? Maybe even something seemingly trivial like letting someone in line ahead of you, or perhaps donating some time, or even loose change, to charity?

- *"Did I matter?"* Did you make a difference, a contribution? Did you realise your purpose, or meaning?

If you can honestly answer "yes" to each of these three questions at the end of every day, I can virtually guarantee that the answer will be a resounding ***"YES!"*** when it comes to your "life review".

Like Brendon Burchard, I chose that day, to live each day to its fullest potential. After being introduced to Brendon's work, and having recently attended his *High Performance Academy* in San Diego, California, I consciously choose every day "to live, to love, and to matter..."

My story begins with my family...

I was born in South Africa, to British parents - although my mother was born in Egypt, within a British Royal Air Force base. Both of my parents were in the medical profession – my father a surgical doctor and my mother a nursing lecturer. My paternal grandfather was a priest who played no small part in translating The Bible into the (South African) language of Afrikaans, and my maternal grandfather a Royal Air Force pilot, who flew Spitfires in the Second World War. My formative years were deeply steeped in the culture of respect, hard work, discipline, humility - and service to others.

Growing up in post-*apartheid* South Africa, I developed a growing curiosity for the political turmoil which engulfed me. I sought a sense of understanding – a sense of reason behind the injustices served by my former generations, and - in my search for meaning - I developed a resolute empathy for my fellow South Africans - on both sides of the "divide".

My parents divorced almost immediately after *yours truly* arrived on the scene, and some of my earliest memories are of me questioning the role that I played in the break-up - "I mean, they loved each other enough to have me, right? Then they didn't? What changed? What was different? Oh! *Me!*" Oh, the logic and naivety of youth...

I grew up constantly questioning my identity, and my purpose. Where did I belong? Was I British, or was I South African? I guess you could say that I was deserving of my adopted Afrikaans slang moniker of "*soutpiel*". To say that I grew up with an identity crisis would be somewhat of an understatement.

My school days passed relatively uneventfully, barring the occasional episodes of playground bullying. I was a reclusive, overweight, bespectacled teenage nerd who drew the inevitable comparisons to "Piggy" when William Golding's "*Lord of the Flies*" reared its ugly head in English Literature classes. Rather than being lauded for an exceptional IQ (it was once recorded as 182 - allegedly in the top 0.1% of the population), I was derided for not being "like the other kids". I think Salvador Dali said it best when he said that "I am not strange. I am just not normal."

I grew up feeling inadequate and confused - a victim of what I later learned was termed "The Tall Poppy Syndrome".[7] A similar saying occurs in Chinese and Japanese culture that translates to "The nail that stands out gets hammered down". Kids can be cruel...

7　　The Tall Poppy Syndrome - a social phenomenon in which people of merit are resented, attacked, or criticised because their talents or achievements elevate them above, or distinguish them from, their peers.

With my father being an extremely popular and successful doctor and surgeon, we didn't get to spend as much time together as I believe that either of us would have liked. We both grew to despise the ring of the 'phone - signifying another patient, or an anticipated house call. We developed our own, personalised take on Pavlov's classical conditioning response, substituting the ring of the 'phone for Pavlov's dinner bell.[8]

Ironically - and I regrettably observed this only in hindsight - he was working hard (ultimately to the detriment of his health) to provide a better quality of life for us, without realising that we valued his company far more than the "life" that his sweat-stained money had brought.

I learned with regret - after his passing - that *presents* are no substitute for *presence*.

I attended M.L. Sultan Hotel School (later incorporated into the Durban University of Technology) where I studied Hotel Management, emerging with a distinction. In the early 1990's, "more than half of the public universities and technikons began facing severe problems caused by financial pressures on students for the payment of fees. Their non-payment led to actions by institutions to exclude them from further enrolment, and also created financial problems for the institutions that were dependent on the student fees to supplement the falling level of subsidy support from government. There were violent student demonstrations that sometimes resulted in senior campus administrators being held hostage."[9]

I was involved in one such "*demonstration*". A handful of students had been excluded from sitting their exams, as a result of them not meeting the minimum attendance criteria, coupled with non-payment of their outstanding student fees. The Students' Union had reacted angrily, and in such a politically charged arena, their "*grievances*" were magnified and intensified. The "racial injustices and discrimination" of the South African higher education system were given credence in the racially volatile cauldron of the M.L. Sultan main campus, where the Director of the campus was taken hostage in his own office. The students refused to attend any further lectures until the victims of the discrimination had been re-instated and were allowed to sit their exams - as was believed to be their "democratic right".

As students of the Hotel School campus we felt removed and dissociated from the events unfolding on the main campus - but not for long…

---

[8] During the 1890's Russian physiologist Ivan Pavlov observed salivation in dogs in response to being fed. He would ring a bell when bringing the food, and he noticed that his dogs would begin to salivate whenever he rang the bell, even when he was not bringing them food.

[9] Richard Fehnel, Private Higher Education, CHET.org.za

The effectiveness of any given protest is directly proportional to the number of participants lending their support to said protest. As much as we supported the democratic right to a peaceful protest, we also believed in our democratic right to an education - especially to one to which we continued to contribute, not only in terms of attendance and studies, but also through substantial financial contributions...

One morning, *"demonstrators"* burst into our Hotel School kitchen, proclaiming that *"you're either with us, or against us"*. When we unanimously declined their kind offer to participate in the "peaceful protest", we were militantly marched out of our kitchens at the sharp end of our own kitchen knives!

We decided then to take action of our own. Following a number of discussions with a few of our lecturers to determine what options might be available to us, we were advised that a petition with 1,200 signatures would be sufficient to *"persuade"* the Students' Union to accept our desire to exercise our right *not* to protest, and to continue our education, irrespective of their grievances.

The resultant petition read (roughly) as follows – (faded slightly by memory):

"We, the undersigned, as students of M.L. Sultan Technikon hereby wish to exercise our democratic right to an education. As much as we acknowledge the right to a *peaceful* protest, we acknowledge also the right not to protest, and the right to an unhindered education, free from the threat of violence or retribution."

The petition soon gained a certain level of notoriety amongst the students and was even featured on the second page of Natal's provincial newspaper - our *ripples* had become *waves*.

One particularly memorable day, when canvassing the main campus for signatures, I was approached by a group of young male students. I naively suspected nothing - it was not unusual for students to approach me to lend their support to the petition.

Before I became aware of what was unfolding around me, I had become surrounded by eight students, demanding my copies of the petition. I backed into a wall, to protect my backpack, which contained all of the original copies of the petition. I was not willing to let all of our hard work slip away. I refused, stating that I was not willing to endanger any of the signatories - to whom I had promised anonymity. To relinquish the documents would be in direct contravention of the agreement between myself and said signatories.

"The petition's racist! We've been watching you, and none of the black students have signed your petition. Show us the papers, we want to see how many black signatures you've got!" the *"ringleader"* demanded. Not for the first time during the course of the "peaceful protest", I found myself at the wrong end of a knife...

Again, I refused. "I can't tell you how many of the ***signatures*** are black, other than those signed in black ink. Each signature belongs to an individual, regardless of race. I do not see the signatures on this petition by the colour of the signatories' skin. Like yourselves they desire an education. *Unlike* yourselves, they are not willing to *deny* others their rights. And the reason that you have not seen a "black student" sign the petition is *because* of the fact that you have been watching - they're scared. Of all the signatures collected, not one has been coerced into signing - if they don't want to sign, they don't have to. They have freedom of choice - and *I have no need for a knife to reinforce my opinion…"*

I tip my hat to the playground bullies of my school days. If it weren't for the lessons learned from them, I'm certain that I would not have walked away from that mob - at least not with the petition. "Out of life's school of war: What does not destroy me, makes me stronger". *Friedrich Nietzsche*

We had amassed 1,467 signatures by the time the dispute was *"amicably resolved…"*

A requirement of the Hotel Management qualification process is that the students are required to complete two six-month periods of practical hotel placements. I was blessed with the opportunity to be placed at *The Wild Coast Sun Hotel and Casino* resort in the Transkei.[10] It was at The Wild Coast Sun that I was honoured and humbled to personally meet Nelson Mandela.

Following his release from insufferable incarceration - and prior to his historic inauguration, in May 1994, as South Africa's first truly democratically elected president - Mandela had been invited to stay at the resort, in his homeland - the Transkei. As a Hotel School student, I had the absolute honour of cooking him breakfast one morning. He shook my hand, and *he* thanked *me* - that was the moment that my life truly slipped into perspective, and that my journey towards self-development and self-acceptance truly gained momentum.

My second period of practical experience was completed at The Holiday Inn, GreenMarket Square, in Cape Town, whereafter I was fortunate to be offered a contract to extend my employment through to the end of the 1995 Rugby World Cup – which was held in South Africa. I served on "The Holiday Inn Rugby World Cup Troubleshooting Committee" and witnessed the birth of "The Rainbow Nation" with the equivalent of a "backstage pass".

Not only was I one of only 19,726,579 South Africans to cast their vote in South Africa's first-ever truly democratic elections, on the historic day of April 27th, 1994 - but I was also blessed to have been involved "behind-the-scenes" in another of South Africa's historic chapters.

---

10   The Tanskei - the first of four territories surrounded by South Africa, to be declared independent of South Africa.

To say that I feel privileged to have been merely involved in the shaping of a malleable country - rising phoenix-like from the tumultuous ashes of *apartheid* - would be the mother of all understatements.

After the Rugby World Cup, I once again left the security of my family, and my homeland, to emigrate to England to pursue my dreams. Unlike the "gap year" a few years previously, this time it was *"for good"* - I had no intention to return (other than the occasional holiday…) With my life condensed into a 20kg backpack, I boarded the plane to see the world - or at least Europe! My journey took me to working in pubs - the epitome of "backpackers' employment" in Britain.

I was initially employed as an Assistant Manager, and within six months, had progressed to Relief Manager for Whitbread Inns, in the Medway region of South-East England. I was essentially providing interim management cover within the area - covering managers' holidays and temporary vacancies - whilst simultaneously demonstrating my competence in preparation for a management role to call my own.

My first *"relief"* was at *The Black Horse*, in Ilford, where, on my very first day, I was "glassed" from behind, by what transpired to be one of the regulars - the boyfriend of one of the barmaids, to be honest! Talk about a baptism of fire!

I was sitting at the bar at the time, and he just walked up behind me, totally "out of the blue". He had taken exception to the fact that I was a "white South African", and when I turned to face him, he wasted no time in enlightening me to the fact that I had "killed many of his brothers". He then invited me outside so that he could "finish the job". (All his words.) At this point, with some of the other patrons attempting to restrain him, I rose to my feet, the remnants of his pint trickling down my neck and face. (Fortunately, I had been struck over the back of my head with his glass, rather than stabbed with it - *there's always a silver lining!*)

I'm not a fighter - Nelson Mandela and Mahatma Gandhi have taught me everything about dignified restraint in adversity. I guess the Hotel school experience with the petition, also served to aid my (surprising) composure - (nobody was more surprised than I was!) I refused his offer to step outside, rejected his claim of being a mass murderer incarnate, and then proceeded to calmly ask him which of the two of us was the racist… Me - minding my own business, in a pub - with no concern or judgement for the colour of the patrons' skin; or him - cowardly glassing me from behind - without any forewarning or prior interaction - based purely on the colour of my skin, and my ethnicity?

He was forcibly ejected from the establishment - by his peers and fellow patrons - four of whom later offered to buy me a drink out of a sense of new-found respect…

I was once told that "everything happens for a reason…" I prefer "It is in your moments of decision that your destiny is shaped." *Tony Robbins.*

"I am not a product of my circumstances. I am a product of my decisions."
Stephen Covey.

What follows is the product of my decisions to date…

Your "DO":

Take a moment to ask yourself just what it is that you are looking to gain, from reading this book? What is your goal? Your focus? Your aspirations? Your *Desired Outcome* (*DO*)?

"If you don't design your own life plan, chances are you'll fall into someone else's plan. And guess what they have planned for you? Not much..." says Jim Rohn. "To accomplish great things, we must not only act, but also dream; not only plan, but also believe." *Anatole France*. Viktor Frankl - a survivor of the Auschwitz concentration camp - and author of *"Man's Search For Meaning,"* wrote that "What man actually needs is not a tensionless state, but rather the striving and struggling for some goal worthy of him."

Write it down - make a note in your phone, on your tablet, your laptop - or preferably "old school" pen and paper... Neuroscientific research suggests that it can actually be more beneficial to physically write down your *DO* - as opposed to digitally - but, of course, make use of what works best for you...

When you write something out that takes deep thought, you build over 10,000 new neural pathways in your brain. When you type your goals out on a computer, you are only building 600 new neural pathways. You create 16.6 times more new neural pathways when you write down your goals, compared to typing them on a computer. If "we become what we think about all day long", how much more likely are your goals to materialise if you have written them down?

My mentor, Bob Proctor, frequently stressed the importance of meaningful goals. In a *LinkedIn* article, Bob is quoted as saying that "this is a subject that you would have great difficulty placing too much emphasis upon". "The people who have goals, achieve and enjoy far more than those who do not, and those who have written goals achieve the most of all."

According to Bob Proctor, a study of Harvard University alumni determined that "83% had no goals. 14% had specific goals which were not written down, and they were earning three times the income that the 83% were earning. The remaining 3% had specific goals, clearly written to read and review, and were earning 10 times the income of the 83% who had no goals. Maxwell Maltz - author of *"Psycho-Cybernetics"* - once said that "you and I function akin to bicycles. Unless we are moving forward toward an objective, we will fall and fail."

"J.C. Penny, founder of the retail store chain that bears his name said, "Give me a stock clerk with a goal, and I'll give you a person who will make history. Give me a person without a goal and I'll give you a stock clerk."

A professor at the Dominican University of California found that "people who wrote down their goals, shared them with others, and maintained accountability for their goals were 33% more likely to achieve them, versus those who just formulated goals."

The physical act of writing has been shown to stimulate your Reticular Activating System (RAS) - responsible for filtering the information or stimuli that your brain processes, assigning greater importance to what you're actively focusing on at the time.

In *"Write It Down, Make It Happen"*, author Henriette Anne Klauser says that "writing triggers the RAS, which in turn sends a signal to the cerebral cortex: "Wake up! Pay attention! Don't miss this detail!" Once you write down a goal, your brain will be working overtime to see you get it and will alert you to the signs and signals that… were there all along."

Linguistics professor Naomi Baron, in researching her book - *"Words Onscreen: The Fate of Reading in a Digital World"* - surveyed the reading preferences of more than 300 university students from America, Japan, Slovakia and Germany. "When given a choice between media ranging from printouts to smartphones, laptops, e-readers and desktops, 92% of respondents replied that it was hard copy that best allowed them to concentrate."

Now take a moment to *really* visualise your **DO** - taste it, smell it, feel its rich texture, experience it in glorious high definition technicolour. Associate the benefits of achieving the outcome - what does it feel like? What does it look like? What benefits does it give to you? "If you are working on something that you really care about, you don't have to be pushed. The vision pulls you". *Steve Jobs*

Ensure that your **DO** is framed in the positive - your mind works best working towards a **DO**, rather than away from a negative association. The brain will procrastinate towards processing a **DO** of "wanting to lose weight", for example - that's a negative association, and the brain will subliminally protect you from losing *anything*. Your brain is hard-wired to avoid any type of loss - behavioural theorists call this "loss aversion". A positively framed **DO** such as "I want to reach my target weight of…" is much more appealing to your overprotective (selfish?) subconscious.

Ensure also that your **DO** is *your* **DO**. By that, I mean that *you* need to be in control of the **DO** - your **DO** can't be that you want little Jimmy - ("the names have been changed to protect the innocent") - to be better behaved, or George to be more considerate - that's a **DO** for little Jimmy, and George, respectively - that's not *your* **DO**. You can't change other people; you can only influence them…

Also if your **DO** is something that you believe that you *should* do, then it's probably somebody else's **DO** - why do you believe that you *should* do it? Is it your perception of what (or how) you believe that other people expect you to be, or do? Or do you really want it for yourself?

Stop *"shoulding on"* yourself, and instead, go after the goal which you simply *must* achieve. When you add necessity to your goals, your likelihood of achieving them is far greater - desperation can be motivation! (Ever heard the phrase, "necessity is the mother of invention"?)

Heed the advice of Kenneth Blanchard, "There's a difference between interest and commitment. When you're *interested* in doing something, you do it only when it's convenient. When you're *committed* to something, you accept no excuses - only results."

Now that you have a clear visualisation of your **DO**, you are already one step closer to it. You need to be able to see your target to be able to aim at it. (It is a common practice for top athletes to visually enhance (or enlarge) the target in their minds to be able to see it with greater detail and clarity.) Consider the analogy of a satellite-navigation system - the more detailed the co-ordinates that you input, the closer that you will find yourself to your "destination", and you will find that you can then plot your route with greater clarity, and ease.

Let's take London's "Big Ben" for example. If you were to type "London" into your hypothetical *sat-nav*, it would take some considerable effort to find *Big Ben*, especially if you had never previously visited London, which - incidentally - comprises an area of 1 572km². Type in "Westminster", and you would have a much greater chance of success. If, however, you were to type in the actual postcode of Big Ben (SW1A 0AA for you *information addicts*) you would find it extremely difficult *not* to emerge into the shadows of one of London's most iconic landmarks.

The more specific your destination - or target - the greater your chance of success in reaching it, and the more precisely and accurately you can then navigate your route. T. Harv Eker proposes that 90% of people aren't living the lives that they desire, simply because they do not know *what* they desire - they simply lack the clarity of their **DO**.

What resources do you already have at your disposal to aid you towards your **DO**? What additional resources do you feel that you might need? In keeping with the *Big Ben* analogy, by what means will you get there? Bus? Car? Taxi? London Underground? You might perhaps need a train, or even a 'plane just to get into London - or even the United Kingdom? And the latter would necessitate opening the can of worms associated with international travel documents - passports, visas, and the like. All of these factors need to be incorporated into your action plan – your "how". "If you fail to plan, you are planning to fail". *Benjamin Franklin.*

Your **DO** is no different - the better that you plan and make use of your available - and required - resources, the more fruitful that your outcome is likely to be.

You may even choose to see Buckingham Palace, Piccadilly Circus, Trafalgar Square, St. Paul's Cathedral, Westminster Abbey, Harrods, Covent Garden, or even Camden along the way! And that is by no means an exhaustive list. After all, who travels to London "just" to see *Big Ben*?

You may find it beneficial to seek the advice of people with a degree of specialist knowledge. If you get lost - or lose GPS signal, for example, would you be more likely to ask a fellow (lost?) tourist for directions, or a local? A perceived "expert"? If you're planning to book a holiday abroad, do you ask a knowledgeable travel agent to help you to plan the itinerary? Or do you at least conduct a certain degree of research yourself, before booking the holiday? Do you enjoy the journey and embrace the opportunities to see the sights along the way?

The same applies if your **DO** is to increase your knowledge - or competence - in a particular field. If you want to grow, you not only need to share the knowledge you have with people, but you also need to be comfortable in learning from others. Seek out someone who is already doing - or has done - what it is that you want to be doing, and learn from them…

Tony Robbins suggests that if you want to be successful, there are three "secrets for turning your dreams and goals into reality"…

1. Model someone who is already successful.
2. Ask someone who can help you. Somebody who has already discovered how to do it can save you time and pain with their knowledge and experience.
3. Success leaves clues.

Ask yourself how much do you want your **DO**? On a scale of 1-10? Is it a "*should*"? or is it a "*must*"? Is it your **DO**, or have you borrowed it from somebody else's perceived expectations of you? Is it a "*déjà vu*" **DO** - one that you've been putting off for some time? One that regularly reappears, but you never take action on it? If so, why haven't you taken action? What's stopping you? How much do you really want it? Are you *interested*, or are you *committed*?

Now ask yourself:

- ✓ "What will happen if I achieve it?"
- ✗ "What won't happen if I achieve it?"
- ✓ "What will happen if I don't achieve it?"
- ✗ "What won't happen if I don't achieve it?"

Now take a few minutes to really think about what motivates you. "Are you pushed by your problems, or led by your dreams?" *Ralph Waldo Emerson.*

If your **DO** is a little overwhelming, that's great! The best **DO**'s are ones that take you out of your comfort zone, and that challenge you into some form of action. After all, if you're comfortable doing it, then where's the challenge? And where's the sense of satisfaction and achievement when you do achieve it?

Your *DO* should simultaneously scare and excite you! It will excite you because you *really* want it, but it will also scare you as your brain has no reference point of comparison and will trigger your anxious reptilian brain which craves routine and predictability. (Your reptilian brain is hard-wired to protect you, and where are you most protected from any perceived threat or danger? Your comfort zone.)

The primary objective or benefit of your *DO* should be to grow - we are growth-oriented organisms, and according to the law of polarity - a law of opposites - if you're not creating, you're disintegrating. Or, as Tony Robbins says, "If you're not growing, you're dying."

Many of you may be perfectly comfortable with the position in which you currently find yourselves. If you're comfortable with your bank balance, for example, then what's driving you towards financial success? Academically, if you're satisfied with a *B*, then why invest all that time and effort to strive for that *A*?

If you're comfortable in *all* aspects of your life, then ask yourself, just why are you reading this book?

Step out of your comfort zone, and embrace your "stretch zone"… "The cave that you fear to enter holds the treasure that you seek." *Joseph Campbell*.

If your *DO* is simply too overwhelming, then break it down into bite-sized chunks, and approach it one step at a time. One of my favourite quotes to emerge from my time with The Coaching Academy was "How do you eat an elephant?" The answer - "One bite at a time".

You will have long-term *DO*'s and short-term *DO*'s - the important thing is to ensure that your short-term *DO*'s are aligned with your longer-term *DO*'s. Take daily action to improve yourself. You don't need to take massive action or make radical adjustments in order to change your life for the better. Small daily improvements are the key to staggering long-term results.

I find that the analogy of a hot-air balloon works for the overwhelming majority of my clients…

Picture your long-term *DO* as a hot-air balloon, and anchor it over on the horizon. Up close, the balloon is enormous - it occupies all of your focus and attention, and it obscures your view - you simply can't see anything else. You "can't see the wood for the trees". But over there on the horizon, the balloon doesn't seem quite so overwhelming now, does it?

It's still there, you can still see it, and work towards it, but it's not quite as daunting as when it was right in front of you. You can now also see what's around you, and what's between you and the balloon... Not just the path that you've now revealed towards it, but the obstacles and barriers along that path that you must overcome in order to reach it. You have a much greater sense of *perspective*.

Oprah suggests that "the key to realising a dream is to focus, not on success, but significance - and then even the small steps and little victories along your path will take on greater meaning."

Focus on the daily steps, watch your footing, and be aware of your surroundings - all the while keeping the balloon - your **DO** - on your horizon, in the knowledge that each step you take is another step closer. "The journey of a thousand miles begins with a single step." *Lao Tzu.*

Now set a realistic timescale within which to achieve your **DO** - your **DO** is now a dream with a date.

Be realistic, but remember to challenge complacency - step out of your comfort zone. Revisit what you wrote down earlier, and now add the date to your original **DO**.

Now phrase your **DO** in the present tense, such as "I am" or "I have". Let's take the previous example of "losing weight"... Add some emotion now as well. Remember before, when you were really visualising the benefits associated with realising your **DO**. Try "I am so happy and grateful now that I am..."

Framing your **DO** in the positive, "losing weight" became "I want to reach my target weight of..." Now that we also have a date, and framing the **DO** in the present tense, the **DO** now becomes something akin to "I am so happy and grateful now that it is January, 1st, 202x, and I have reached my target weight of ..." (for example.)

To your subliminal overprotective brain, the statement of "I have now" is far easier to work towards, compared with "I will be" and again, the positive affirmation is far more powerful. The brain - rather than leading you towards a hypothetical result of which it has no recollection, or tangible reference point - is now leading you directly towards your target weight of... something which the brain can now process with the greatest of ease.

Try a little exercise... Try saying these two differently phrased **DO**'s out loud. Not such a great idea if you're reading this on the commute in to work, but it's important that you do read it out loud to gain the full benefit of the exercise. (Neuroscience suggests that 43% of people aren't aware of what they're thinking, until they hear it out loud.)

It can wait until you get home...

"By January, 202x, I will have lost 10 kilograms",

or…

"I am so happy and grateful now that it is January, 1st, 202x, and I now weigh 70.2 kilograms (woman), or 83.6 kilograms (man)"[11] (*Feel free to insert your own target weight here…*)

Which one sounded better to you? Which of the two did you actually **believe**?

In summary, GREAT *DO*'s should be positive, personal, framed in the present, and - most of all - be possible for you to achieve - albeit challenging. The best *DO*'s should both excite you and scare you at the same time. You should be excited at the prospect of what realising your *DO* will bring you, but also somewhat naturally apprehensive, or scared, as your mind hasn't yet got the answers - and your reptilian brain will always look for a point of reference, or reassurance.

Neuroscience supports the suggestion that your brain is hard-wired to protect you.

Your reptilian brain (that we touched on earlier) is responsible for the primary "*fight or flight*" response - either aiding your swift escape (*flight*) from whatever the perceived danger may be, or preparing your attack (*fight*) - "offence being the best form of defence".

Your brain sees the fact that you are comfortable as your ultimate protection. To put it simply, if you are comfortable, then you are not threatened - you are "safe" - wrapped in cotton wool, so to speak. As far as your brain is concerned, keeping you in your respective comfort zone is simply "mission accomplished".

"Life will only change when you become more committed to your dreams than you are to your comfort zone." *Billy Cox.*

The brain is also designed to conserve energy and is therefore constantly looking for shortcuts. Again, in terms of "*fight or flight*", it is essential to have energy in reserve if it were to be required. It takes a lot less energy to perform a routine - or predictable - task, which is why we tend to develop habits, and paradigms. (A paradigm after all, is essentially just a collection of habits.) Your mind is constantly looking to "fill in the gaps" or "join the dots" with regards to predictability. Allow me to demonstrate…

Take the following paragraph for example:

---

[11] According to the Office for National Statics, at the time of writing, the average woman in the UK weighed 70.2kg, and the average man 83.6kg

"Aoccdrnig to a rscheearch at Cmabrigde Uinervtisy, it dseno't mtaetr in waht oerdr the ltteres in a wrod are, the olny iproamtnt tihng is taht the frsit and lstat ltteer be in the rghit pclae. The rset can be a taotl mses and you can sitll raed it whotuit a pboerlm. Tihs is bcuseae the huamn mnid deos not raed ervey lteter by istlef, but the wrod as a wlohe."

Allegedly, only 55 people in every 100 will be able to read - and make sense of - the paragraph, but, honestly, I have not yet encountered someone who could *not* extrapolate the meaning…

Maxwell Maltz, in *"Psycho Cybernetics"*, proposes that our mind is akin to a thermostat - a cybernetic control mechanism. Just as a thermostat regulates the predetermined temperature of a room, for example, so our thoughts regulate - or control - our results.

Our habits - our paradigms - are the results of our *"thermostatic"* setting. Or, from a slightly different perspective, take the example of an aeroplane's auto-pilot. As the 'plane is buffeted slightly off-course, the cybernetics "kick in" and the route is recalculated - or re-calibrated - to compensate for the slight deviation.

Our comfort zone - our "here and now" - is our current calibration, it's the point to which our mind constantly returns us. It's our point of reference - our yardstick - for how we live our lives. You might even think of it as your predetermined flight path.

Think about it for a second, why do you keep doing what you're currently doing, even if you're not happy with the results?

At The Proctor Gallagher Institute, we term this the "knowing-doing gap" - you know what you want, you're not happy with your results, but yet you doggedly continue with the same behaviour and (stubborn?) mindset. You therefore continue to return the same results - if do what you've always done, you'll get what you've always gotten.

Einstein suggests that "doing the same thing over and over and over again, and expecting a different result" is actually the definition of insanity. There is a chasm of difference between *knowing* what you want, and *doing* what is necessary to change your "*pyscho-cybernetics*".

The good news is that you can actually change your results - you *can* recalibrate your "*thermostat*". You can reprogram your cybernetics.

If you're not happy with your results, you need to change your behaviour, and it's your thoughts which ultimately determine your behaviour. As Ralph Waldo Emerson said, "we become what we think about all day long". Wayne Dyer said that "If you change the way you look at things, the things you look at change."

Change your thinking, change your life!

It won't be an "overnight" transformation, though - your new habits and new paradigms need to be bedded-in and nurtured, so that they grow and develop; and as they develop and strengthen, so will the "old" habits and paradigms diminish and weaken. Your new habits will then become your new cybernetic calibration - your revised thermostat setting. You can't just change your paradigms, you need to create a new model which makes the old one obsolete. But - with the right programming - it can be done.

It's never too late to start to live the life of your dreams - to plant the seed. You just need to know how… There's a Chinese proverb that says "The best time to plant a tree was twenty years ago. The second-best time to plant a tree is now." Plant the seed - take control of your life - take charge of your thermostat. Don't live your life on auto-pilot.

Not to be confused with sowing seeds and planting trees, Bob Proctor believes that the most important benefit associated with achieving goals (*DO*'s) is *growth*. "We are growth-oriented - we *need* to grow. If we're not creating, we're disintegrating." In a similar vein, Tony Robbins says that "if you're not facing fear every day, you're getting weaker, not stronger".

Feed your mind… Read books, take a class, attend a lecture or seminar; listen to - and learn from - people, and the world around you. "Growth can be taking a chance, a risk, or pushing yourself to reach for the unknown, rather than settling for the comfort zone of "the known".

John Assaraf's *Neurogym* programme suggests that "your biggest growth will come from overcoming your moments of greatest resistance and negative self-talk". Growth may also be stretching yourself and trying to find new ways to become a better version of yourself every single day".

As Leo Tolstoy is quoted as saying, "Each person's task in life is to become an increasingly better person". Zig Ziglar reinforces this through saying that "what you get by reaching your destination is not nearly as important as who you will become by reaching your destination".

Growth can come in many forms. But growth creates the most impact when it leads to mastery, which Tony Robbins believes has three levels: intellectual, emotional and physical.

"Repetition is the mother of skill, which is why for so many of us growth is truly addictive. The more you grow, the more you're able to master. The more you master, the more you grow. How's that for a positive feedback cycle?" asks Robbins. "And the more you bring growth into your body, the less you have to think about it. Make growth a priority - and a habit - and it will make your life one of dynamic improvement."

With your *DO* in your mind, and in your heart, start to take *action*. As Dr Henry Link said, "We generate fears while we sit. We overcome them by action". Tony Robbins proffers that "The path to success is to take massive, determined action," and that "execution trumps knowledge every day of the week".

Don't wait for the perfect opportunity - "take imperfect action towards your goals and dreams". *Bill Baren.* Lucy Johnson suggests that "7/10 is the new perfect". Mark Victor Hansen proposes "Don't wait until everything is just right. It will never be perfect. There will always be challenges, obstacles and less than perfect conditions. So what? Get started now. With each step you take, you will grow stronger and stronger, more and more skilled, more and more self-confident and more and more successful."

If you don't leap, you'll never know what it's like to fly…

Make a decision. Take the first step today, and ignite your momentum - the distance between your dreams and reality is called action. "It doesn't matter how slowly you go as long as you do not stop." *Confucius.*

You can't accelerate if you haven't started moving…

"A real decision is measured by the fact that you've taken a new action. If there's no action, you haven't truly decided." *Tony Robbins.*

Remember that small daily improvements are the key to staggering long-term results and remember also that "the journey of a thousand miles begins with a single step."

Start moving…

"If you think you are too small to make a difference, try sleeping with a mosquito." *The Dalai Lama.*

Seize the day!

The underlying principle of this book is succinctly also one of the proverbs by which I choose to live my life - "Give a man a fish and you feed him for a day; teach a man to fish and you feed him for a lifetime."

The following chapters are intended to aid your understanding - their contents are by no means exhaustive, nor do they claim to be comprehensive. I can only hope that this book will serve to whet your appetite and generate your thirst to further develop your understanding - particularly in the areas which appeal the most to you. "**What DO You Think?**" is merely the tip of your personal-development iceberg. The intention herein, is to supplement your new-found thirst for knowledge with samples of core principles, and nuggets of insightful information to reinforce, motivate, and inspire you towards your best self.

The second part of the book is brimming with research, studies and statistics to underpin many of the concepts contained within, and to satisfy your curiosity. One of my philosophies is that it's better to have it and not need it, than to need it and not have it… As mentioned previously, coaching is not a "One Size Fits All" concept. My intention is to cater for everybody. This buffet welcomes all…

To borrow from Robin Sharma - author of "*The Monk Who Sold His Ferrari*" - "I'm just an ordinary guy who happened to have learned ideas and tools that have helped many human beings reach their best lives… I'm no different from you. I have my struggles, my frustrations and my own fears - along with my hopes, goals and dreams. I've had good seasons and some deeply painful ones. I've made some spectacularly good choices and some outrageously bad mistakes. I'm very human - a work in progress. I'm no guru".

"Why are you so uncomfortable being called a guru? "*Gu*" simply means "darkness" in Sanskrit and "*rus*" simply means "dispel". So the word "guru" simply speaks of one who dispels the darkness and brings more understanding and light. Made me think". *Robin Sharma, The Greatness Guide.*

Your best self is not a destination - it's a wondrous journey…

NLP (Neuro-Linguistic Programming):

NLP was founded in the early 1970's, with the collaboration of Richard Bandler and John Grinder at the University of California. Bandler and Grinder proposed that there was a direct correlation between our neurological processes - the mind and the sensory organs with which we receive and filter information through our five senses ("neuro"); our language - the way that we communicate and interpret experience, including words, body language, images, sounds, feelings, tastes and smells ("linguistic"); and our individual behavioural patterns which we have adopted through experience - the way that we construct personal "programmes" of communication, thought, and behaviour ("programming").

At the heart of NLP lies the "modeling" of human excellence. Bandler and Grinder believed that through studying, analysing, and modeling experts in their field, and then copying their critical success elements, you would then be able to achieve the same results. "NLP is about getting the best procedure from the people who have succeeded the best at any task and teaching other people to do it." *Dr Richard Bandler* - who I had the honour of working with in 2017.

There is *substantially* more content to the theories of NLP, than exist in this chapter. I have purposely chosen to expand on only a few key presuppositions to support your learning. I wholeheartedly recommend pursuing a more detailed insight into NLP, but that's a different book for a different time...

"Bandler and Grinder's work revealed that our experience of the world is purely subjective, and that it conforms to a structure - how we think about something affects how we experience it."[12] In NLP we make a clear distinction between the actual *"territory"* - the physical world itself - and the unique internal *"map"* - our *perspective* - or *perception* - of the *territory*, subject to our own unique personalisation, through our filters of deletion, distortion and generalisation. This is often referred to as *"the map is not the territory"*.

In a nutshell, we experience our world through our five senses: visual (sight), auditory (hearing), kinaesthetic (touch), olfactory (smell) and gustatory (taste). Our senses are constantly bombarded with so much information that we (consciously and unconsciously) delete what we don't wish to pay attention to. (Remember the 50,000 thoughts that we think each day?) How many times have you "lost" moments of your day? "Daydreaming"? Have you ever left your house in the morning, and arrived at your destination - but recall nothing of the events in between. The journey existed - you left, you arrived - it's almost as if you were in *"auto-pilot"*.

---

12   Alfred Korzybski, "Science and Sanity."

When driving - how many times have you "missed" an important road sign? It *was* there… The details of the journey have been deleted - the data lost in the automatic, subliminal "cleanup" of your internal hard-drive.

The remaining data is then consciously filtered, through our past experiences, values and beliefs. The outcome is therefore often incomplete and inaccurate, owing to the fact that some of the original input no longer exists, and what remains has been subjected to our personal generalisations or distortions.

This filtered information forms our internal "map", which will influence our physiology and "*state*". This in turn affects our reactions to certain situations - our behaviour, and therefore our results, which are then manifested in our choice of action - or inaction ("*fight, flight or freeze*").

NLP suggests that we can never share the same "map" as not only do our filters of values, beliefs, and culture differ from person to person, but the core information that we have subjected to our filters will differ also – having been subjected to deletions. It therefore stands to reason, that we will never see things from other people's perspectives - we can never *truly* experience their *perception* of their reality.

"Everything we hear is an opinion, not a fact. Everything we see is a perspective, not the truth." *Marcus Aurelius*

To put it simply, how many times have you watched a movie with a friend, or read the same book, but held *totally* contrasting opinions? How can one piece of music truly inspire and motivate someone, whereas the self-same piece of music can drive someone else to despair? The associations and filters are different - the source, however, is the same… "You never really know a man until you understand things from his point of view, until you climb into his skin and walk around in it." *Harper Lee, "To Kill a Mockingbird"*.

So why do we judge others? "There is nothing noble in being superior to your fellow man; true nobility is being superior to your former self." *Ernest Hemingway*. "Before you criticise a man, walk a mile in his shoes. That way, when you do criticise him, you'll be a mile away and have his shoes." *Steve Martin*. And why do we allow ourselves to be judged by others? "Care about what other people think and you will always be their prisoner." *Lao Tzu*.

A key presupposition[13] of NLP is that "all behaviour is the best choice currently available". The behaviour that you choose in any given moment is "the best choice available to you at the time when considering your personal history, beliefs, knowledge, resources and your frame of reference".[14]

---

13   Presupposition: A thing tacitly assumed beforehand at the beginning of a line of argument or course of action.

Essentially, when we review our actions - or decisions - or judge somebody else's - generally with some negative connotation - the decision that was made, was the best decision that was available - ***at that time***.

We may regret the action, but hindsight is blessed with 20/20 vision. Taking into account all of the factors which influenced our action, it was the best decision available *at that time*. Those factors can never again be *perfectly* replicated - "No man ever steps in the same river twice, for it's not the same river and he's not the same man." *Heraclitus.*

You did the best you could with what was readily available - don't beat yourself up, don't dwell in regret, as long as there was learning derived from it. "Don't sweat the small stuff". Something that my father used to tell me when I was growing up was that "the only mistakes that you make are the ones from which you didn't learn…"

Another key presupposition of NLP is that "there is no failure, only feedback". This presupposition is a little contentious, but can be extremely powerful and invigorating, when placed in the correct context. It's *OK* to "*fail*". Try it on for size… Take a moment, stop what you're doing and tell yourself out loud that it's "OK to fail!"(Again, it can wait until you get home…)

"Don't let your failures define you, let them teach you." *Barrack Obama.* Or, similarly, "I never lose. I either win or learn." *Nelson Mandela.*

Now I'm not advising you to fail your exams, beat up your boss, or not complete *necessary* tasks. We're all big enough, old enough, and wise enough to know that there are consequences to our actions… There is a law of cause and effect. What I am advocating is that it's OK to mess up sometimes, AS LONG as you take the learning from it! To put it simply, the more "*failures*" that you experience, the more that you will learn from them.

On the pages which follow, you will learn of some "famous former failures" - as I like to call them - including J.K Rowling… "By every usual standard, I was the biggest failure I knew." *J.K. Rowling.*

The perfect example to underline this presupposition is that of *Thomas Edison*, who once famously said, "I am not discouraged, because every wrong attempt discarded is another step forward." Through the process of eliminating which materials didn't work, Edison was able to identify the appropriate materials, thereby inventing the incandescent light bulb.

Rather than becoming disheartened with each "*failed*" attempt, he considered each one a relative success in that each attempt reduced the number of remaining alternatives.

"We must trust that everyone in life is here to learn different lessons at different times, that good and bad experiences are only the perceptions of man... Success truly is the result of good judgement. Good judgement is the result of experience, and experience is often the result of bad judgement!" *Tony Robbins.*

"Famous Former Failures":

"A person who never made a mistake never tried anything new." Albert Einstein.

"The more you study great people in history, the more you realise you just can't give up." Brendon Burchard.

George Orwell, Animal Farm

In 1945, Knopf Publishers, rejected George Orwell's *"Animal Farm"* as a "stupid and pointless fable". By 1973, the book had sold in excess of 9 million copies, and *Time* magazine selec*ted the book as one of the 100 best English-language novels (1923 to 2005.) *Animal Farm* also featured at number 31 on The Modern Library List of Best 20th-Century Novels; won a Retrospective Hugo Award in 1996, and is also included in the "Great Books of the Western World" selection.

Rudyard Kipling

Rudyard Kipling was fired from *The San Francisco Examiner*, in 1889. His editor allegedly told him, "I'm sorry, Mr Kipling, but you just don't know how to use the English language."

Kipling's works include *"The Jungle Book"*, *"Mandalay"*, and *"If-"*. Henry James once said that "Kipling strikes me personally as the most complete man of genius (as distinct from fine intelligence) that I have ever known." In 1907, he was awarded *The Nobel Prize in Literature* - the first English-language writer to receive the prize, and its youngest recipient to date. He was also approached for the British Poet Laureateship, and for a knighthood - both of which he declined.

J.K. Rowling

J.K. Rowling was allegedly fired from the London office of *Amnesty International*, for "writing stories on her work computer". Her first *Harry Potter* book, *"Harry Potter and the Philosopher's Stone"*, was allegedly rejected by 15 different publishers before *Bloomsbury Publishing Company*. Its acceptance by Bloomsbury has been accredited to the fact that the editor's eight-year-old daughter enjoyed the story so much, that she begged her father to read the story through to the end. Even after the book had been accepted for publishing, Rowling was advised to "get a day job, because she wouldn't make any money writing children's books".

The *Harry Potter* series of books has been translated into 73 different languages, sold millions of copies, and accumulated over £14 billion through sponsorships, and movie adaptations. J.K. Rowling is the first woman to become a billionaire author.

"It's impossible to live without failing at something, unless you live so cautiously that you might as well not have lived at all - in which case, you fail by default." *J.K. Rowling.*

Stephen King

Stephen King's first published novel, "*Carrie*", was allegedly rejected thirty times. One such rejection letter read, "We are not interested in science fiction which deals with negative utopias. They do not sell." *Carrie* was actually King's fourth novel, but it was the first one to be published. It was written - while he was living in a trailer - on his wife Tabitha's portable typewriter (on which he also wrote *Misery*).

Carrie began as a short story intended for *Cavalier* magazine. "I did three single-spaced pages of a first draft, then crumpled them up in disgust and threw them away," King recalls. Tabitha rescued the pages, encouraged him to finish the story, and advised him to expand it into a novel. King later said, "My considered opinion was that I had written the world's all-time loser."

Stephen King's books have sold more than 350 million copies, many of which have been adapted into feature films, miniseries, television shows, and comic books. King has published 54 novels, and six non-fiction books. His novella "*Rita Hayworth and Shawshank Redemption*" was the basis for the movie "*The Shawshank Redemption*" which is widely regarded as one of the greatest films of all time.

He has also received awards for his contribution to literature, such as *The World Fantasy Award for Life Achievement* (2004), *The Canadian Booksellers Association Lifetime Achievement Award* (2007), and The Grand Master Award from *The Mystery Writers of America* (2007). In 2015, King was awarded with a National Medal of Arts from *The United States National Endowment for the Arts* for his contributions to literature.

Elvis Presley

In 1954, Elvis Presley failed an audition for a local vocal quartet, "*The Songfellows*". He later told his father that, "They told me I couldn't sing". *Songfellow* Jim Hamill is quoted as saying that Elvis "did not demonstrate an ear for harmony".

Elvis began working as a truck driver for the Crown Electric company, where he was advised by a friend to contact Eddie Bond, leader of his friend's professional band. Bond allegedly rejected him after an audition, advising Elvis to "stick to truck driving because you're never going to make it as a singer".

Elvis Presley went on to become one of the "most celebrated and influential musicians of the 20th century". He is the best-selling solo artist in the history of recorded music, with estimated record sales of around 600 million units worldwide, winning three Grammy awards, receiving *The Grammy Lifetime Achievement Award* at the age of 36. Elvis has also been inducted into multiple music halls of fame.

The Beatles

The Beatles were infamously rejected by *Decca Records*, after auditioning on New Year's Day, 1962. *Decca* executive, Dick Rowe was quoted as saying that "guitar groups are on the way out". The Beatles were also told that "they had no future in showbusiness".

The Recording Industry Association of America ranks The Beatles as the best-selling music artists in the United States, with 178 million certified units. The Beatles have had more number-one albums on the British charts and sold more singles in the UK than any other act.

In 2008, the group topped *Billboard Magazine*'s list of the all-time most successful "*Hot 100*" artists. As of 2015, they held the record for most number-one hits (20) on the *Hot 100* chart. They have received ten Grammy Awards, an Academy Award for Best Original Song Score and fifteen Ivor Novello Awards.

Collectively included in *Time Magazine*'s compilation of the twentieth century's 100 most influential people, they are the best-selling band in history, with estimated sales of over 600 million records worldwide. The group was inducted into the Rock and Roll Hall of Fame in 1988, with all four members also being inducted individually between 1994 and 2015.

U2

U2 were rejected by *RSO Records* in May, 1979, with the written rejection, "we have listened with careful consideration, but feel it is not suitable for us at present".

U2 have released 14 studio albums to date - from "*Boy*" in 1980, to "*Songs of Experience*" in 2017. "They are one of the world's best-selling music artists, having sold more than 170 million records worldwide. They have won 22 Grammy Awards - more than any other band, and were inducted into *The Rock and Roll Hall of Fame* in their first year of eligibility. *Rolling Stone* ranked U2 at number 22 in "The 100 Greatest Artists of All Time" and labeled them "The Biggest Band in the World".

Socrates

During his lifetime, he was described as an "immoral corrupter of youth" and was sentenced to death, owing to his "*radical*" ideas. He ultimately poisoned himself.

Albert Einstein

Albert Einstein reportedly didn't speak until he was four, and didn't read until he was seven. He was expelled from school, and was refused admission to the Zurich Polytechnic School.

Thomas Edison

Thomas Edison was fired from Western Union in 1867, after spilling acid on the floor… He also "*failed*" an estimated 10 000 times in creating the incandescent lightbulb. "I have not failed. I've just found 10 000 ways that won't work." *Thomas Edison*

Alexander Graham Bell

In 1876, William Orton of Western Union allegedly declined to pay $100, 000 for Alexander Graham Bell's patent for the telephone. He is reported as saying, "While it is a very interesting novelty, we have come to the conclusion that it has no commercial possibilities."

Alexander Graham Bell was ranked 57th among the 100 Greatest Britons in an official BBC nationwide poll, and among the Top Ten Greatest Canadians, and the 100 Greatest Americans. In 2006 Bell was also named as one of the 10 greatest Scottish scientists in history after having been listed in the National Library of Scotland's "Scottish Science Hall of Fame". (And, to think that growing up, I thought that *I* had an identity crisis!)

In 2006, there were estimated to be 20 fixed telephone lines for every 100 people in the world. That was 1 fixed-line telephone for every 5 people on the planet! In 2001, in developed nations, there were estimated to be 57 fixed lines per 100 people.

According to *TIME* magazine, a recent United Nations study revealed that more people have access to mobile phones, than have access to toilets… Out of the world's estimated 7 billion people, 6 billion had access to mobile phones. Only 4.5 billion had access to working toilets.

Interestingly, Bell considered his most famous invention "an intrusion on his real work as a scientist and refused to have a telephone in his study".

Babe Ruth

Babe Ruth, best known for his home runs, at one stage also held the record for a total of 1,330 *strikeouts*. In a similar vein to Thomas Edison's philosophy, Ruth claimed that "Every strike brings me closer to the next home run."

Ruth became such a symbol of the United States during his lifetime that - during World War II - Japanese soldiers allegedly yelled in English, "To hell with Babe Ruth", to infuriate American soldiers.

Ruth has been named the greatest baseball player of all time in various surveys and rankings. In 1998, The Sporting News ranked him number one on the list of "Baseball's 100 Greatest Players". In 1999, baseball fans voted Ruth into the Major League Baseball All-Century Team. In 1969, he was named baseball's Greatest Player Ever in a ballot commemorating the 100th anniversary of professional baseball.

The Associated Press reported in 1993 that Muhammad Ali was tied with Babe Ruth as the most recognised athlete(s) in America. In a 1999 ESPN poll, he was ranked as the second-greatest U.S. athlete of the century, behind Michael Jordan.

Michael Jordan

"I have missed over 9,000 shots in my career. I have lost almost 300 games. On 26 occasions I have been entrusted to take the game-winning shot, and I have missed. I have failed over and over and over again in my life. And that is why I succeed". *Michael Jordan.*

Michael Jordan's individual accolades and accomplishments include five Most Valuable Player (MVP) Awards, ten All-NBA First Team designations, nine All-Defensive First Team honours, fourteen NBA All-Star Game appearances, three All-Star Game MVP Awards, ten scoring titles, three steals titles, six NBA Finals MVP Awards, and the 1988 NBA Defensive Player of the Year Award.

Jordan holds the NBA records for highest career regular season scoring average (30.12 points per game) and highest career playoff scoring average (33.45 points per game). In 1999, he was named the greatest North American athlete of the 20th century by ESPN, and was second only to Babe Ruth (*more on Babe Ruth on the following page*) on the *Associated Press'* list of athletes of the century. Jordan is a two-time inductee into the Basketball Hall of Fame - in 2009 for his individual career, and again in 2010 as part of the group induction of the 1992 United States men's Olympic basketball team ("*The Dream Team*").

In addition to lending his success to Nike's *Air Jordan* trainers - introduced in 1985 - Jordan also starred, as himself, in the 1996 feature film *Space Jam*. In 2015, Jordan became the first billionaire NBA player in history.

Marilyn Monroe

At the outset of her modeling career, modeling agencies advised her that she should "consider becoming a secretary". Marilyn went on to became one of the most popular sex symbols of the 1950's, emblematic of the era's attitudes towards sexuality. She was a top-billed actress for only a decade, before her unexpected death, in 1962 - by which time her films had grossed $200 million. Today, she continues to be considered a "major popular culture icon".

Walt Disney

In 1919, Walt Disney was fired from *The Kansas City Star* - his editor said that he "lacked imagination, and had no good ideas". The following is extracted from *The Kansas City Star* website, "*Our Famous Employees*"...

"For six years as a boy, Walt Disney delivered copies of *The Kansas City Star* and (morning) *Kansas City Times* with his father, who was a newspaper carrier. He applied for a permanent job with *The Star* as a cartoonist, clerk and even truck driver - but the newspaper turned him down each time.

Disney based Mickey Mouse on a little rodent he befriended while working in his small animation studio in Kansas City. After his studio failed, he left nearly penniless on a train for Hollywood. He told fellow passengers he was going to make animated cartoons. The reaction, Disney recalled, "was like saying I swept out latrines".

Walt Disney's animation/motion picture studios and theme parks have developed into a multi-billion-dollar television, motion picture, vacation destination and media corporation that carry his name. Among other assets, The Walt Disney Company owns five vacation resorts, eleven theme parks, two water parks, thirty-nine hotels, eight motion picture studios, six record labels, eleven cable television networks, and one terrestrial television network.

The company operates through four major business "segments". Its parks segment is by far the world's largest operator of theme parks in terms of guest attendance per year, its merchandising segment is the world's largest licensor in terms of annual retail sales of licensed merchandise, and its motion picture segment is one of the six major film studios in Hollywood." As of 2013, the company had annual revenues of over $45 billion and employed approximately 175,000 people.

Steven Spielberg

Spielberg was rejected by *The University of Southern California School of Theatre, Film and Television* - on three separate occasions.

Spielberg is regarded as one of the most popular directors and producers in film history. He co-founded DreamWorks Studios and has twice won The Academy Award for Best Director – *Schindler's List* (1993) and *Saving Private Ryan* (1998). *Jaws* (1975), *E.T. The Extra-Terrestrial* (1982), and *Jurassic Park* (1993) - each returned their own box office records. The unadjusted gross of all Spielberg-directed films exceeds $9 billion worldwide, making him the highest-grossing director in history. His personal net worth is estimated to be more than $3 billion.

Sylvester Stallone - The *Rocky* Road To Success

Owing to complications which his mother suffered during labour, the lower left side of Sylvester Stallone's face is paralysed – including parts of his lip, tongue, and chin. This accounts for Stallone's trademark snarling look and slightly slurred speech. As a child, Stallone was constantly in and out of foster homes and his odd features made him an outcast in school. Stallone was often suspended for behavioural problems, including fighting – and poor test results.

Stallone's parents divorced when he was 11 years old, and he was sent to a high school for "troubled kids", where he was voted "most likely to end up in the electric chair". His own father even told him, "You're not going to get into the movies, so you might as well do some gymnastics or something, and get paid doing that!"

In the mid 1970's, Stallone moved to New York to pursue his dream of becoming an actor. He suffered repeated rejections - "They looked at me and said, you're stupid looking, do something else, you're never going to be a star in the movies… Who's going to hire someone who talks at the side of their mouth?"

At one point, Stallone was so poor, that he even resorted to pawning his wife's jewellery – contributing in no small part to the collapse of their marriage. Stallone was later evicted and lived rough on the streets. He reveals that he sheltered at New York's Port Authority Bus Terminal for three weeks. On "the worst day of his life" - out of pure desperation - Stallone was faced with no option but to sell his most prized possession, his beloved dog, Butkus. He simply could not afford to feed "the only soul that gave me unconditional love". By his own admission, Stallone had "hit emotional rock bottom".

Two weeks later Stallone chanced upon a boxing match on television - Muhammad Ali vs Chuck Wepner. Stallone was inspired with the thought of a "nobody" being given a chance at the world title. "There was this one moment, where a *nobody* had stayed on his feet and knocked down the greatest boxer that the world has ever known." After three days, and 20 straight hours,[15] Stallone had completed the script for "*Rocky*". He attempted to sell the script to a few different studios, with the intention of playing the lead character himself.

Irwin Winkler and Robert Chartoff became interested and offered Stallone $100,000 for the movie rights, but on the condition that they cast their own lead - allegedly rumoured to have been either Robert Redford, or Burt Reynolds – both massive stars at the time. Stallone was adamant that he would be *Rocky*.

---

15   Tony Robbins Interview, Youtube

They raised their offer to $125,000, with the ultimatum to either sell the script, or forget the offer. Stallone left with his script. He could not afford the rent on his "*seedy*" apartment (his words) and only weeks previously, Stallone had resorted to selling his dog, because he couldn't afford to feed it...

And here he was, walking away from $125,000.

A few weeks later, Cartoff and Winkler invited Stallone back to a meeting, wherein they offered him $250,000 to sell the script. Again, he refused. They offered Stallone $325 000, and then (another) "final" amount of $360 000 for the script. Stallone repeatedly declined.

Finally, they agreed to let Stallone play the lead, and to pay him $35 000 with additional investment rights linked to the release.

Stallone agreed.

It was never about the money - only Stallone would be able to project the character of *Rocky* to a point which would make this movie such a success. Stallone had realised his **DO.** He was - and remains - *Rocky Balboa*.

The first thing Stallone did after leaving the studio with his $35,000, was to go back to the store where he had sold his dog. He returned unsuccessfully for three days, before he saw the man to whom he had sold Butkus. The man refused to sell. Stallone kept increasing his offer, but still the man refused, claiming that he too had "now developed an affection" for the dog. Ultimately, Stallone succeeded in buying back "*his*" dog - costing him $15,000 and a part in the movie. (Butkus is in the movie too.)

It reportedly cost $1 million to produce *Rocky*, and it grossed in excess of $200 million. *Rocky* was nominated for ten Academy Awards, including Best Actor and Best Original Screenplay nominations for Stallone. The film won the 1977 Academy Awards for Best Picture, Best Director, and Best Film Editing.

Rocky grossed $5 million during its opening weekend and eventually reached $117 million at the North American box office and returning a worldwide box office accumulation of $225 million. Adjusting for inflation, *Rocky* earned nearly $460 million in North America (at 2015 prices.)

With its production budget of $1 million, *Rocky* returned a worldwide percentage return of over 11,000%. It was the highest-grossing film of 1976 in the United States. The original *Rocky* series - excluding "*Creed*" - the only *Rocky* not to be penned by Stallone - has grossed a total of $1,271,222,322 to date. According to a *New York Times* profile, when the original movie premiered, Stallone "had $106 in the bank". Stallone claimed that before the success of *Rocky*, he was "kicked out of agents offices over 1,500 times".

"You, me, or nobody is gonna hit as hard as life, but it ain't about how hard you hit, it's about how hard you can get hit and keep moving forward, how much you can take and keep moving forward. That's how winning is done".

"Now if you know what you are worth, go out and get what you are worth, but you gotta be willing to take the hits and not pointing fingers, saying you ain't where you want to be because of him or her or anybody. Cowards do that, and that ain't you. You're better than that". *Rocky Balboa, "Creed"*.

DiSC Personality Profiles:

DiSC personality profiling can be an extremely beneficial tool in helping you to increase your inter-personal knowledge, communication, and self-awareness. DiSC profiling can help to reveal your motivational drives, your responses to conflict, and your stressors, to name but a few benefits.

Through developing an understanding of the different personality types - and an increased awareness of their associated personality criteria - it will also become significantly easier for you to negotiate, to compromise, and to influence your communication styles within your interpersonal relationships.

DiSC is an acronym for the four proposed personality profiles - Dominance (or Directing), Influence, Steady, and Compliance (or Cautious.) Remember that each of us is unique - *"the map is not the territory"*. It is essential, therefore, to be mindful of the fact that DiSC profiling is not about "pigeon-holing" people, or about putting them into boxes - different people will go about the same tasks in different ways. DiSC is not a personality assessment, but rather an assessment of behaviour in given circumstances.

Your own profile will change with your external stressors - you can be a *"D"*, an *"I"*, an *"S"* or a *"C"*, (or any combination thereof) at any given time, largely dependent on the environment in which you find yourself. Take your "home you", your "work you", and your "social you" for example; I'll bet that they don't exhibit the same personality traits.

"There are, however, core characteristics that generally remain consistent – especially when under pressure. It is valuable to understand these styles because they help us to understand "how people tick". When we stop labeling characteristics as either "wrong" or "right", then we begin to understand the world from other people's perspectives. The DiSC philosophy is "wherever there is agreement there is power".[16]

As much as I can only recommend that you embrace the opportunity to complete a DiSC profile questionnaire to satisfy your curiosity - the quintessence of DiSC can be gleaned from William Moulton Marston's *Behavioural Model*, reproduced on the following page. (Incidentally, Marston (1893-1947) was also a lawyer, and invented the first functional lie-detecting polygraph. A man of many talents, he is also responsible for the character of *"Wonder Woman"* - for which he was posthumously inducted into the Comic Book Hall of Fame, in 2006.)

---

16   Dave Pill, *"Click or Clash"*

Marston's model is divided into four quadrants, and split between two axes - *Outgoing* or *Reserved*, and *Task-Oriented* or *People-Oriented*. The *Outgoing* quadrant is generally epitomised by positive, enthusiastic, optimistic, and energetic personality traits. *Reserved* personality characteristics are associated more with creative, reflective, conscientious and cautious attributes.

The *People* quadrant is relational - focusing on our interactions with others - including empathy, understanding, compassion and emotions; whereas the *Task* segment is concerned primarily with procedures, plans, projects and processes.

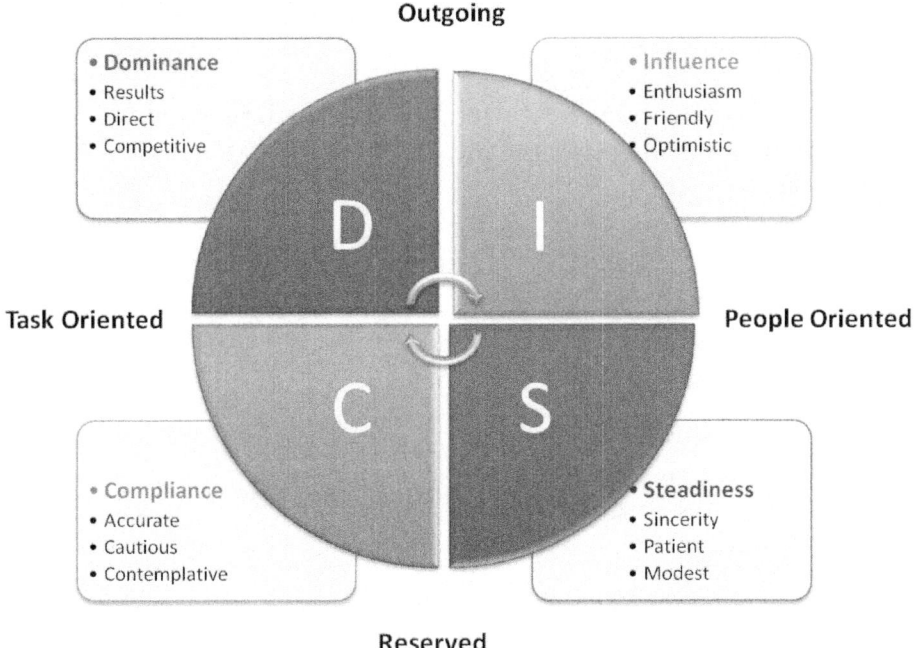

The *"Dominance"* or *"Directing"* personality type is a blend of *Outgoing* and *Task-Oriented* - generally being results driven, competitive, and direct.
The *"Influence"* personality type is a blend of *Outgoing* and *People-Oriented* - generally being enthusiastic, friendly and optimistic.
The *"Steady"* personality type is a blend of *Reserved* and *People-Oriented* - generally being sincere, patient and modest.
The *"Compliance"* or *"Cautious"* personality type is a blend of *Reserved* and *Task-Oriented* - generally being contemplative and accurate.

---

17   Image reproduced courtesy of John-Fallon - YouTube

As I mentioned earlier, through using DiSC to identify their dominant personality traits, your communication with other people - and in turn, your relationships - can only improve. If you can extract their personality type, you can use the following generalisations to formulate a basis, or foundation, for your interaction.

Remember that we are all different, with different perspectives - deletions, distortions, generalisations, values, beliefs, and sensory preferences - and now different personality preferences too!

Conflict does not always have to be personal - sometimes it's merely born of frustration - a *distortion* based on miscommunication through different preferences, or personality types.

It's no surprise that we sometimes get it wrong, leading to confusion, frustration, misunderstanding, and sometimes the inevitable conflict - even if the intention wasn't there to begin with!

Dominant Style: (Outgoing + Task) - *"The Tellers"*

D-style personality types are competitive.

They are results-driven and they thrive on decision-making, as well as focusing on long-term, strategic goals. They prefer to be judged by their results rather than their methods.

They communicate very directly - they "say it as it is" and do not often consider the impact on other people's feelings. They may be best described as blunt. They like explanations to be brief and to the point. Written communication tends to be in short paragraphs and bullet-points, with the emphasis on headings and critical information. In essence, "short and to the point, just do it!"

Demanding, Decisive, Determined, Domineering, Driven, Delegator

Greatest Fear:	Fear of failure, Fear of being taken advantage of
Driving Passion:	Winning
Preferred Communication Style:	Directing, Telling
When under pressure:	Finds comfort in taking action
Famous *D-style* personalities:	Simon Cowell, Madonna, Margaret Thatcher

Influential Style (Outgoing + People) - *"The Sellers"*

I-style personality types thrive on praise and recognition.

They are often creative and may become easily distracted, finding it easy to initiate projects, but much harder to see them through to completion. They can be over-optimistic and are generally very friendly - sometimes confident and theatrical.

To the *I-style*, it's all about having fun.

Influential, Inspirational, Interactive, Impulsive, Impressionable

Greatest Fear:	Fear of rejection, Loss of popularity
Driving passion:	Recognition
Preferred Communication Style:	Collaborating, Selling, Influencing
When under pressure:	Finds comfort in talking
Famous *I-style* personalities:	Muhammad Ali, Will Smith, Jonathan Ross

Steady Style (Reserved + People) - *"The Listeners"*

S-style personality types crave clarity of purpose.

They prefer the structure of completing one task at a time and like to see tasks through to completion. They are great listeners and work well within teams. They need time to adapt to change and seek rationalisation and reassurance before committing to the change, preferring the safer options of routine and security.

They are generally calm, considered and empathetic - being concerned with people's feelings, and basing their decisions on the needs of others.

They are motivated by peace, harmony and security.

Sensitive, Secure, Self-sacrificing, Stable, Supportive, Sympathetic

Greatest Fear:	Fear of change, Loss of security
Driving passion:	Harmony
Preferred Communication Style:	Co-operation, Listening
When under pressure:	Finds comfort in working with a team
Famous *S-style* personalities:	Princess Diana, Mother Theresa, Ghandi

Compliant Style (Reserved + Task) - *"The Perfectionists"*

C-style personality types are often perfectionists.

They are obsessed with quality and may be slower to make decisions because they require all of the information before starting to take action. They will analyse and understand - focusing on the facts, details and logic.

Conscientious, Careful, Consistent, Creative, Competent, Cautious, "Cold"

Greatest Fear:	Fear of getting it wrong, Unvalidated criticism
Driving passion:	Perfection
Preferred Communication Style:	Written - prefer to "go it alone"
When under pressure:	Revert to trusted systems and procedures
Famous *C-style* personalities:	Albert Einstein, Bill Gates, Stephen Hawkins

Now that we have a greater level of insight into the four personality types, it's considerably easier to understand how easily conflict through "personality clashes" can arise. A *D-style* person, for example, may make decisions without listening to others' feedback, generating the perception that their input was not valued. This could cause offence, particularly to an *I-style* individual, who fears rejection.

Similarly, an *I-style* person will dominate a conversation with a *C-style* "perfectionist", who would be unwilling to contribute to the conversation, until they have assessed all of the information - culminating in a sense of overwhelm, or possibly even intimidation - which was definitely not the intention of the *I-style* personality type. A *C-style* character may present information using excessive detail, which will only serve to frustrate a blunt, "get to the point" *D-type* personality. The list is endless...

You can be a "D", an "I", an "S" or a "C", (or any degree of combination thereof) at any given time - you may even concurrently display a combination, or "blend", of more than one of the personality traits. I'll use the analogy of a cup of coffee... (*Insert beverage of choice here.*)

Personally - in case you hadn't noticed – I am a dominant "I". So let's begin with a cup of strong, black coffee - in my case, that's the "I". If you add milk, it's still a cup of coffee, but with a different appearance, and different characteristics - a blend. In my own personal "*DiSC Starbucks*", (*I bow to no sponsor...*) I would be a "*High I*" with dashes of "D" and "S" - I'm still a dominant "I", but I also happen to have a strong representation of "D" and "S" in my profile.

You can substitute the milk for cream, or dairy for soya? Latte? Cappuccino? Espresso? Mocha? Different blends, still coffee... Then if you add sugar, whipped cream, syrup, or extra "shots" - it's still a cup of coffee, but you see, the personalised combinations influence the blend - the distinctive variations in flavour, texture and aroma. Arguably, it's possible for you - the "*DiSC barista*" - to produce virtually any blend of "D, I, S or C".

In keeping with effective communication, another presupposition of NLP is that "the meaning of your communication is in the response that you get" - in essence, regardless of what you meant to say, the meaning comes from how the recipient "hears" and responds to it. The *meaning* that they attach to it. Remember also, "the map is not the territory"...

As Dave Pill[18] reveals in the Coaching Academy's DiSC practical training delivery accelerator day, the key to effectively applying the principles of DiSC, is "short-term modification to manage". Like an "old-school" graphic equaliser, or *EQ* (*Google* it if you're not old enough...) - used to change the frequency, bass, treble, or tone of a sound, song, or instrument - you can basically "dial up" or "dial down" your personality traits to gain better harmony in your communication with others, and therefore also in your relationships.

We like people who are like us, so - in NLP terms - if we are able to successfully "mirror" their behaviour, and language - in terms of personality, tone, pace and pitch - then we are far more likely to communicate successfully with them. I like to view the art of communication as a dance – one leads, the other follows... The beauty of "the dance" lies in the symmetry, rhythm and synchronised interaction of the participants.

Effective communication is just that - a meaningful interaction between two (or more) interested, and engaged, parties – a rhythmic ebb and flow.

---

18   DiSC Personality Profiling - The Coaching Academy

Body Language:

It has been proffered that 55% of communication is non-verbal. (Of the remaining 45%, a mere 7% can be attributed to the actual words - or language - being used, and the remaining 38% lies in the tone, or emotion, of the communication.) It therefore stands to reason that in order to communicate effectively - "the meaning of your communication is in the response that you get" - it is necessary to have a basic understanding of body language.

Body language is also crucial in terms of your self-image and confidence.

Ask yourself - whether it be in a social or corporate environment - are you more likely to be swayed by somebody who speaks with an air of authority, and who projects a positive body image - head held high, chest puffed out - also known as the "power pose"? Or are you more likely to be influenced by someone who holds regular conversations with their shoes, mumbling incoherently? And which would you believe to be the more confident of the two individuals?

Again, remember that we are all unique. You may be perfectly confident standing up and delivering a presentation to hundreds - or thousands - of people, or the mere thought of it may turn you into a quivering wreck - (think "*human jelly*".) Like DiSC, your level of confidence is variable, but is generally directly proportional to your perception - or fear - of the task. I like to view fear as an acronym - *False Expectations Appearing Real*. (More about that later…) Now, back to body language, have you ever heard the phrase "Fake it 'til you make it?"

Here's another exercise for you to try at home - this time in front of your mirror - a full-length mirror, if possible, please. (The mirror is not *essential*, but it definitely adds to the experience…) Stand in front of your mirror and adopt a "high power" pose. Open your body up, push your shoulders back, lift your head up, puff out your chest and suck in your stomach. Place your feet approximately shoulder-width apart, and for good measure, place your hands on your hips. Hold that pose for about two minutes, whilst observing yourself in the mirror. Just notice what you notice. How did that make you feel?

Now try a "low power" pose. Feet together, shoulders hunched, chin down, looking down at the floor (but just enough so that you are still able to see yourself in the mirror.) Cross your arms protectively across your chest, and you can slightly turn your shoulder away if you'd prefer. Hold that for about two minutes again please. How did that make you feel?

"Fake it 'til you make it…"

Now for the scientific reveal…

Amy Cuddy, a social psychologist, and professor at Harvard Business School, and listed in *Businessinsider.com*'s *"50 Women Who Are Changing The World"* - gave an interesting talk on body language, and "faking it 'til you make it" in a "TED talk" a few years ago.

Professor Cuddy maintained that one of the most important elements of body language is the "power pose". A pose typically associated with power and dominance would be that of Milton's *Wonder Woman* - an extremely open body pose, exuding power and confidence - sometimes also referred to as "The Harvard Power Pose" - legs apart, shoulders back, chest puffed out and - more often than not - hands on hips.

When under stress, or struggling with low levels of confidence - "low power" people tend to close up, and disassociate themselves from others, seeking protection from their vulnerability.

Picture someone with arms crossed - usually across the chest - shoulders hunched - maybe even totally withdrawn into the foetal position. People may also turn away, giving rise to what is commonly referred to as "the cold shoulder".

This logic can also be easily transferred to simple movements - broad, extravagant gestures are often associated with confidence, authority and power - as is the length of stride whilst walking, hence confident people tend to exhibit "a spring in their step".

In her presentation, Professor Cuddy maintained that certain "power poses" don't just alter other people's perceptions of you, but that power poses immediately alter your body chemistry, as well as influencing your interactions with other people.

Quoting her own research, professor Cuddy revealed a dramatic change in body chemistry within test subjects following a brief observation. The research involved test subjects adopting a "high power pose" for two minutes and then - a little later - a "low power pose" for a further two minutes. She found that the levels of testosterone - the "dominance" hormone - rose by 20% in the "high power" posers. The levels of testosterone, which professor Cuddy also associated with what she termed "risk tolerance" - within the "low power" group fell by 10%.

Another chemical associated with "power" is cortisol. A drop in cortisol levels is typically associated with better handling of stressful situations. After the 2-minute poses, the cortisol levels of the "high power" group had drastically reduced, whereas the cortisol levels of the "low-power" group, had increased significantly.

Professor Cuddy then experimented with power poses in preparation for interviews. The "interviewers" were conditioned to be completely passive during the interviews, being instructed to give no responses whatsoever.

Rather than have the candidates adopt power poses during the interviews and therefore be perceived to be arrogant or over-confident, Cuddy asked the candidates to adopt high power poses - in private - in the bathrooms immediately before their interview. Other candidates were asked to prepare for their interviews by assuming low-power poses in the waiting room area.

The "high-power" posers were unanimously the ones that the "interviewers" would have chosen to hire. Interestingly, based on their feedback, what the candidates actually said in the interviews was irrelevant - it was all due to their "presence". Body language was everything.

To add a different perspective to the evidence above, here's a bit of information regarding Professor Amy Cuddy's background...

At the age of 19, Amy Cuddy was seriously injured in a car accident. (*It's starting to develop into a bit of a theme through this book...*) Regaining consciousness in the head-trauma ward, she was told that her *IQ* had dropped by "two standard deviations", and that she would never complete her college degree.

Through hard work and persistence, she graduated - four years after the rest of her class, but she graduated. Then she persuaded Princeton to accept her, where - by her own admission - she says that she felt like an impostor.

Amy Cuddy "faked it". She "faked it" through Princeton, and Northwestern, and Harvard. She "faked it" until she forgot that she was actually "faking it". Professor Cuddy had not just "faked it 'til she made it", she had faked it until she *became* it.

Relationships:

Relationships are not merely confined to the common, rose-tinted perception of romance. At any given point in your life, you will undoubtedly have had a relationship with your parents, friends, colleagues, fellow students or even possibly sibling(s). Whatever your standing in life - or your current situation - you will be an integral part of a relationship - your actions directly influence somebody else around you.

Having said that, where better to start a chapter on relationships than with the Hollywood notion of romance, and perhaps the quintessence of modern romance - marriage? Marriage is one of the most discussed relationship dynamics of today. *The New York Times*, calls it "one of the best endeavours that you can embark on in life", adding that "being married tends to make people happier and more content with their lives, particularly if they are experiencing stressful periods of their life".

According to Tony Robbins, "One of the most important things in life is love. When you're in an intimate, passionate, connected relationship and you anticipate your partner's needs, it's an experience of pure ecstasy and joy – but it's an experience most people never have."

I read an article in which marriage was likened to a river. At first, it can be rather turbulent, but as you journey further down the river, the water flows deeper. The turbulent whitewater rapids have forged a smoother, stronger current. A relationship can be easy to give up on when times are tough, but through commitment we can experience a deeper level of love and understanding that we might otherwise not have known, if we hadn't chosen to persevere with it – if we hadn't chosen to brave the rapids.

I recently read another wonderful analogy regarding marriage - that most people get married believing in the myth that marriage is a beautiful box full of all of the things they have longed for - such as companionship, intimacy, and friendship, for example.

In all honesty, marriage begins as an *empty* box - you must first put something in before you can expect to take anything out. "There is no love in marriage, love is in people, and people put love in marriage. There is no romance in marriage, you have to infuse it into your marriage. A couple must learn the art, and form the habit of giving, loving, serving, praising, of keeping the box full. If you take out more than you put in, the box will be empty."

If you believe that the union of marriage will magically deliver everything that is missing from your life – such as love, happiness, friendship and companionship, then ultimately you will only find disappointment…

Relationships aren't about making an unhappy person happy, nor are they about making an unloved person feel loved. Relationships are about sharing the love and happiness that is already present within you with one another - growing, improving and evolving together, both emotionally and spiritually.

If you enter into any relationship with an expectation to become complete simply by being in it - expecting to "take from the box" without giving anything back in return, you will end up feeling resentful and disappointed. As the box empties, you will have many regrets - not just about marriage, but also about your life in general.

"The way I see it, there's nothing wrong with marriage. Marriage is not the problem. The problem comes from the expectations people have when it comes to marriage," says Luminita Saviuc, otherwise known as *"purposefairy"*. "There is no love in relationships, love is in people. It's the people who put love in relationships. It's the people who put love, happiness, romance and passion in marriage", she adds.

And now - in the famous words of Monty Python - for something completely different...

Where better to gain advice on romance, than divorce attorneys? Who better to reflect on what causes marriages - one of society's most hallowed relationships - to crumble, and therefore, to advise on potential marital pitfalls to avoid? To learn from their "failures"? (feedback?)

Brittany Wong, Divorce Editor of *The Huffington Post*, interviewed eleven divorce attorneys - each of whom contributed one valuable insight, which she collated in her article, "Marriage Truths From Divorce Attorneys"...

1. A sustainable marriage is not about love, it's about tolerance.
2. Give your spouse the benefit of the doubt.
3. Don't be afraid to feed your spouse's ego now and then.
4. Put your spouse before your kids.
5. Don't wait until it's too late to work on your marriage.
6. When you need to discuss something important, timing is everything.
7. Know that you can't change your partner.
8. Love is about the little things.
9. Communication really is the cornerstone of every solid relationship.
10. Be an active listener.
11. Marriage doesn't get easier the second or third time around.

Since 1938, Harvard University has been conducting a longitudinal study of human development. Spanning more than three quarters of a century, the Grant Study has followed the lives of graduates of Harvard University, including President John F. Kennedy.

Psychiatrist Dr. Robert Waldinger has overseen the Grant Study since 2003 and shared his findings in a recent *TED* talk. "The lessons aren't about wealth or fame or working harder and harder", says Waldinger. "The clearest message that we get from this 75-year study is this: Good relationships keep us happier and healthier." In his *TED* talk, Waldinger reveals three key findings about relationships that he believes serve as reliable predictors of the future levels of health and happiness in the subjects:

1. Loneliness. "People who are more isolated than they want to be from others find that they are less happy, their health declines earlier in midlife, their brain functioning declines sooner, and they live shorter lives than people who are not lonely", claims Waldinger. According to statistics released by Age UK – the UK's largest charity for older people - 1.9 million older people "often feel ignored or invisible".[19] More than one in five Americans will – at some time - report that they're lonely.

2. The *quality* of relationships. "Living in the midst of conflict is really bad for our health", adds Waldinger. "High-conflict marriages, for example, without much affection, turn out to be very bad for our health, perhaps worse than getting divorced. And living in the midst of good, warm relationships is protective."

3. "Dependence". "People who are in relationships where they really feel they can count on the other person in times of need, those people's memories stay sharper longer", claims Waldinger. "And the people in relationships where they feel they really can't count on the other one, those are the people who experience earlier memory decline", he adds.

Arthur Aron - Professor of Social Psychology at *The State University of New York* - recommends that married couples try new things together, to visit new places, or try different foods, for example. New experiences flood the brain with dopamine and norepinephrine - the same chemicals that are associated with "new romance".

New experiences can recreate and replicate the chemical impulses of new love. New, different experiences encourage the brain towards different thought patterns, rather than the predictable, routine and possibly even mundane thought patterns favoured by your reptilian brain - hardwired to save energy and seek out shortcuts and traditional patterns of habit.

"Mix it up a little" - try something new. Try something different, fresh and spontaneous. In my humble opinion, *predictability* is fatal to romance…

---

[19]   Age UK "Loneliness in Figures"

What brings people together? What tears them apart? Tony Robbins proposes that there are six stressors - or triggers - in a relationship that can create tremendous uncertainty and stress.

i. Competing priorities. "We often compete for focus, attention, energy and time," says Tony. "It is essential to feel not just loved, but significant, in the eyes of our significant others."

ii. Stress demands/Expectations. "We all have expectations of our intimate partners – and they have expectations of us," he says, adding that "Stress is anything that is seen as preventing, reducing or threatening to limit any certainty, significance, connection, variety, growth or contribution."

iii. Failure to meet core timelines. "Relationship crisis or stress can occur when one person believes (that) they are not where they "must" be in their relationship, career or finances", Robbins suggests.

iv. Physical fluctuations. "These two most important parts of our lives – our health and our relationships – are inextricably linked," says Tony. "Lack of energy and vitality can be fatal to a relationship", he warns.

v. Loss / Inner conflict. "If your relationship were to end, do you know what actions you would take in response? If you're experiencing inner conflicts that cloud your perspective on your relationship," asks Robbins, "how can you get a clear picture on exactly how things are right now?"

vi. Language that triggers emotions and meanings from the past. "People who are successful in their relationships – and in every other aspect of their lives – know (that) they should divorce their pasts and marry their futures," says Robbins.

In *"Seven Questions Which Reveal The Truth About Your Marriage"*, relationship coach Allison Reiner may perhaps have the answer to Tony's question, "… how can you get a clear picture on exactly how things are right now?"

Reiner says that "When I could get truthful about the state of my marriage I was then able to uncover the reasons why, and begin the inner work required to make a shift in my self-belief great enough to change the dynamic in my marriage." She believes that there are seven questions which you should ask yourself, which may indicate a potential "phase of instability", as she calls it…

Her suggestion? Read each of the following statements and "let your gut respond for you"...

- Does your partner insist that there is "nothing wrong" with the relationship despite your obvious unhappiness and dissatisfaction?
- Does your partner make your feel like you are the "real" problem with all your complaining, whining and expectations?
- Do you feel alone despite the fact that you are in a relationship?
- Do you feel like you are constantly walking on eggshells, censoring your thoughts, denying feelings, and monitoring your behaviour in order to maintain some level of peace in your relationship?
- Do you spend way more time focusing on what you can do to keep your partner happy than you ever spend thinking about your own well-being?
- Are you questioning your own worthiness and your right to have your own needs met in the marriage?
- Are you spending the majority of your free time thinking about your relationship, or alternatively, when thoughts arise you find yourself trying to push them away?

Reiner suggests that if one - or more - of the statements resonates with you, then your marriage may be in a "phase of instability". Are you investing more to maintain the status quo, than you are in growing, or nurturing, the relationship? "The extent to which these situations are occurring will have a direct impact on how happy, healthy, safe and loving you find your relationship. It will no doubt be impacting how you feel about yourself and mostly probably will have started to infiltrate other areas of your life," suggests Reiner.

The good news, however, is that you can actually "turn back the clock" and transform your relationship into a happy, healthy, safe and loving haven once again. Reiner proposes that through the simple act of "allowing yourself time to honestly appraise your relationship status you have opened yourself up to making bigger shifts".

Isiah McKimmie, in "*6 Relationship Habits All Really Happy Couples Have*," writes that "If we are going to form habits as a couple, why not form good ones?"

"The great thing about habits is that once they become habits, they don't feel like work anymore", says McKimmie, who suggests that you "start building habits that make your relationship amazing".

McKimmie lists six habits that she believes all really happy couples have:

1. They make time for each other.
2. They practice appreciation.
3. They make sex a habit.
4. They say sorry.
5. They reassess where the relationship is going.
6. They take time apart.

From one relationship with a significant other - from one pillar of society - to another...

You may be blessed to have a relationship with children of your own. You may, on the other hand, believe that you are blessed to *not* have children of your own... Either way, the majority of us continue to contribute to a family structure of some shape or form.

Whether you play the role of the parent, the child, or the sibling - you still have an integral role to play in the development of society. And society begins at home... Bhutan's Prime Minister Jigmi Thinley was quoted at a recent United Nations meeting as saying that "if mankind is to avoid its current unsustainable and self-destructive course, it needs to replace GDP with Gross Domestic Happiness".

We each grew up in the environment that was cultivated, or nurtured, by our parents or guardians. According to Freud, this environment moulds the child, and can either nurture, or hinder the development of the child into adulthood. Magali Peysha - Vice President and co-founder of Robbins-Madanes Training - is of the belief that "many relationship patterns (that) we live with are "ancestral". We inherit from our parents certain relationship patterns that they inherited from their (parents') patterns."[20]

Who ultimately determines what it is that you like? Think about it for a minute...

You like the food that you like because your parents put it in front of you from an early age. And their parents before them... And theirs before them... You would have to go back a long way to discover who is actually responsible for what it is that you do like. And your conditioning is not only inherited genetically, but environmentally - you are also a product of your surroundings...

Have you ever said something, and thought to yourself, "Wow, that sounded just like my dad?" or "I'm turning into my mom?" You've inherited their behavioural "patterns", or "traditions" - every family has them - be it a "tradition" of altruism, independence, self-sacrifice, introversion or even being short-tempered - to list but a few examples.

"These ancestral patterns affect family members at every level," proposes Peysha. Some families have traditions that place barriers between parents and their children - others develop traditions of competition which engender acrimonious rivalries between siblings. The patterns that we promote - or that we have "inherited" - are passed down through the generations.

In this relay race that we call life, we have a responsibility to ensure that the baton that we hand to our children is as opportunity-rich as it can possibly be. We have a duty of care to lay their foundation for success.

In Britain, however, this message seems to be getting "lost in translation"...

Far from being "successful", British children have been identified as the unhappiest of 21 nations across the developed world, with one child in ten suffering from a clinically-recognised mental health problem.[21]

In 2007, the UK had the worst problems with drugs, binge-drinking and under-age sex in Europe, and occupies "podium positions" in the international polls for anti-social behaviour, self-harm and eating disorders. In 2006, 24,000 youngsters in the UK tried to end their own lives - averaging an attempt every 22 minutes.[22]

What legacy are we leaving? What foundation are we laying for the hopes of our future generations? More importantly, what can we do to halt the slide into the yawning abyss? Consider also that "The children of today are the leaders of tomorrow…" *Nelson Mandela.*

Our hectic schedules have driven us towards ready meals and microwave dinners, whilst we perpetuate the "rat race", scurrying about haphazardly just to make ends meet - feeding the national economy, rather than nurturing our own families.

Whilst research suggests that eating together can boost achievement in children, lower the chance for eating disorders in girls, and lower depression rates in both girls and boys - we choose to eat hurriedly prepared meals of little or no nutritional value, whilst worshipping the gods of television and the internet.

Gone are the ancient traditions of communication, nutrition and health. Figures released in 2015, by *The English National Child Measurement Programme*, show that 19.1% of children aged 10-11 were obese, and 14.2% were overweight. A third of English children (aged 10-11 years) were either overweight or obese.[23]

---

21   UNICEF report on "Childhood well-being", June 2007

22   The Institute for Public Policy Research, 2006

23   Public Health England

We encourage the supervision of our children by the "digital babysitters" of television and the internet - admittedly, a poor substitute for *presence*. The "hamster-wheel" existence is born out of a perceived sense of necessity - rather than a willing choice over time well spent with family - something which I regretfully experienced first-hand.

A survey by *The National Consumer Council* revealed that children who watch too much television - and spend too much time on the internet - are "greedy and unhappy, and argue more with their families, have a lower opinion of their parents, and lower self-esteem than other children".

Professor Amy Cuddy (remember "Fake it 'til you make it"?) adds weight to the argument against the excessive reliance on small screens. In total contrast to the benefits of the "power pose" - when we focus on a small screen, our bodies are constricted and small. "Just working on a small device for five minutes seems to affect people's assertiveness levels", she claims. "I've talked to physiotherapists who are saying that they're seeing the sort of dowager's humps[24] they're used to seeing in older women in 16-year-old kids because they're spending so much time frozen over these tiny devices."

When we're too busy - or perhaps exhausted after *another* long day - to spend quality time with our children, their communication skills won't evolve as they should. Developing children need adults not only to provide a foundation of love, but to provide structured regularity, and to establish and maintain the boundaries for their behaviour.

A "good night's sleep" - including regular sleep patterns - is essential for good health. *The National Institute for Health* recommends that children aged between five and twelve years old should benefit from at least ten hours of sleep every night and recommend at least eight-and-a-half hours of sleep for children aged twelve to seventeen years.

We contribute to their lethargy, through unwittingly promoting nights of insomnia - most children now have a television set in their bedroom, or the added nocturnal distractions of a smartphone, tablet, computer or laptop. Research published by Digitaldetox suggests that artificial light from screens increases the brain's level of alertness and suppresses the release of the hormone melatonin by up to 22% - negatively affecting sleep, performance and mood.

Moreover, the wonderful British weather, coupled with the rise of the European Health and Safety nanny state, and the advent of popular, affordable, technology has sounded the death knell of the days of children playing together in an outside environment.

---

[24] A dowager's hump is a severe rounding of the upper back. In older women, it is a sign of advanced osteoporosis, the result of compression fractures of weakened vertebrae. These fractures can be painful, although in many cases there are no symptoms other than abnormal posture.

Developmental psychologists quote the need for children to play "in a relaxed, unstructured way, preferably outdoors with other children. It is through unsupervised play that they "learn how to make friends, resolve quarrels, work collaboratively and, indeed, avoid small enemies. They also learn how to take "safe risks" and make their own judgments, thus developing independence and self-reliance."

Through a classic series of papers, Alan Leslie - Professor of Psychology and Cognitive science at Rutgers University - argues that play is "one of the most important pathways to empathy - a key determinant of happiness and compassion".[25]

A 2007 report from *The American Academy of Paediatrics* documents that "play promotes not only behavioural development but brain growth as well". *The University of North Carolina's Abecedarian Early Child Intervention* programme determined that "children who received an enriched, play-oriented parenting and early childhood programme had significantly higher *IQ's* at age five, than did a comparable group of children who were not in the programme" (105 vs. 85 points).[26]

Several studies led by Kathy Hirsch-Pasek have compared the performance of children attending academic preschools with those attending play-oriented preschools. The results reflected "no advantage in reading and math achievement for children attending the academic preschools. But there was evidence that those children had higher levels of test anxiety, were less creative, and had more negative attitudes toward school than did the children attending the play preschools."[27]

Stuart Brown, MD, in researching his book - "*Play, How it shapes the brain, opens the imagination, and invigorates the soul*" - interviewed individuals prone to pathological violence. Interestingly, these individuals "had no experiences or memories of play as young kids. It was just absent from their lives."

Research published in *Psychology Today*, also shows that time spent outdoors - especially in nature - can "restore attention, lower stress, and reduce aggression. Time spent with electronics reduces exposure to natural mood enhancers."

Children also develop control and co-ordination through physical activities such as running, jumping, climbing, cycling, skipping - or even catching a ball. In the absence of physical play, a child's imagination and creativity is also likely to be stunted - in addition to their social skills.

---

25   The Greater Good Science Centre, University of California, Berkeley

26   The Greater Good Science Centre, University of California, Berkeley

27   The Greater Good Science Centre, University of California, Berkeley

How many times have you seen a parent hand over "the tablet" - or smartphone - in reaction to their beloved offspring's tantrums? How many children in buggies are being pushed around oblivious to the world around them? The environmental stimuli rejected for the "electronic babysitter" yet again. The tablet is the new digital dummy - or pacifier, as it's called in The States - and the distraction works a charm. Interestingly, "pacify" is defined as "quell the anger, agitation, or excitement of..."

Look up the definition of "tablet", and you will find a "wireless, portable personal computer with a touch screen interface", or "...typically a measured amount of a medicine or drug".

Coincidence?

There is a voice of opinion which suggests that educational games can improve a child's vocabulary and math skills, in a fun and enjoyable way. I couldn't agree more, but the problem with using technology to calm a tantrum, lies in the fact that the child is being stimulated, rather than being soothed, or calmed down.

They're being conditioned to believe that digital sensory overload is the solution to their difficult experiences – which is perhaps not ideal when they're tired or miserable, and sleep is most probably the best remedy. How are they being taught to calm themselves down, or how to interact with other children and to develop socially? I guess that's not a problem as long as the other child also has a tablet, or smartphone...

Spending hours on the tablet can promote a sedentary lifestyle that will most likely be carried through to adulthood. Studies suggest that too much screen time may have "a lasting effect on attention span, concentration, and even appetite control". Too much time on a tablet can also lead to poor posture, neck and lower back pain in children at a very early age, as referenced earlier by Professor Cuddy.

Moderation is the key. According to *Asian Mums Network*, "Spend some time interacting with your child while she (*sic*) plays games on the tablet and set a daily limit for tablet or phone use. As long as less than 2 hours a day is spent dedicated to screen time and your child's use is being closely monitored, allowing the use of a tablet should not carry any guilt."

When you go out to a restaurant for a meal, if you can tear yourself away from your own digital screen for a minute and survey your surroundings - how many other people are glued to their screens? Dinner used to be a time for families to connect - to reflect on the day and interact socially. These days, "there's an app for that..."[28]

---

28 Apple filed for a trademark application in December, 2009 for the company's now ubiquitous catchphrase, "There's an app for that".

Suzy Strutner - Associate Lifestyle Editor of *The Huffington Post* - reports on an American chain of restaurants, *Chick-fil-A*, which is attempting to encourage "family time" during dinner. "Food is for people, not phones", claims Strutner. "But all too often, we're caught staring at our screens during what is supposed to be a mindful, healthy meal," she adds.

A number of *Chick-fil-A* restaurants across America have launched the cell phone coop "family challenge". If a table can leave their silenced phones inside the box for their entire meal, then they are "rewarded" with free ice cream cones.

Research has shown that using your phone whilst eating not only means that you don't fully appreciate the meal, but that you're also more likely to eat more... It also affects your relationships and contributes to feelings of anxiety when you're "rejected" by your partner. (Remember it's all about the *meaning* that you give it.)

"*Chick-fil-A*'s challenge "has completely taken off", said Brad Williams, who pioneered the concept at his branch in Suwannee, Georgia. "We have families who aren't successful the first time and come back to try again. We even have people asking to take the boxes home with them! Our whole community is talking about it," says Williams. The concept has met with such support, that more than 150 *Chick-fil-A* franchises are now ordering and using the coops as an incentive to encourage patrons to enjoy the food and the company in front of them – rather than their screens.

We, as a society - (generalisation alert!) - have lost the art of communication - that "connection" - with our families because we know "everything" that is happening in their lives through their social media updates. There is no longer a need for the personal interaction, when we are already in possession of the minutiae. We have lost that element of deeper human connection.

How many times have you - or a member of your family, or a friend - looked up from a screen to realise that there is actually somebody else in the room? According to Digitaldetox, 50% of people prefer to communicate digitally than in person, and 61% of people admit to being addicted to the internet and their devices.

Sometimes we simply need to "disconnect to reconnect".

Victoria L. Dunckley M.D. - in her article "*Screentime is Making Kids Moody, Crazy and Lazy*", published in *Psychology Today* - agrees. "Time and again, I've realised that regardless of whether there exists any "true" underlying diagnoses, successfully treating a child with mood dysregulation today requires methodically eliminating all electronics use for several weeks - an "electronics fast" - to allow the nervous system to "reset".

Dunckley continues, "If done correctly, this intervention can produce deeper sleep, a brighter and more even mood, better focus and organisation, and an increase in physical activity. The ability to tolerate stress improves, so meltdowns diminish in both frequency and severity. The child begins to enjoy the things they used to, is more drawn to nature, and imaginary or creative play returns. In teens and young adults, an increase in self-directed behaviour is observed - the exact opposite of apathy and hopelessness."

"Children's brains are much more sensitive to electronics use than most of us realise", adds Dunckley. "Contrary to popular belief, it doesn't take much electronic stimulation to throw a sensitive and still-developing brain off track... Interactive screen time is more likely to cause sleep, mood, and cognitive issues, because it's more likely to cause hyperarousal and compulsive use," she warns.

Artificial light from electronic screens is registered as daylight by your subconscious mind. This slows the release of the "sleep hormone", melatonin.

"Minutes of screen stimulation can delay melatonin release by several hours and desynchronise the body clock," claims Dunckley. "Once the body clock is disrupted, all sorts of other unhealthy reactions occur, such as hormone imbalance and brain inflammation. Plus, high arousal doesn't permit deep sleep, and deep sleep is how we heal," she adds.

"Many children are "hooked" on electronics, and in fact gaming releases so much dopamine - the "feel-good" hormone - that on a brain scan it actually replicates the same results as cocaine use. But when reward pathways are overused, they become less sensitive, and more and more stimulation is needed to experience pleasure," she warns.

"Dopamine is also critical for focus and motivation, so needless to say, even small changes in dopamine sensitivity can wreak havoc on how well a child feels and functions." Artificial light from the use of electronics at night has been linked to depression and even suicide risk in numerous studies. Animal studies even show that exposure to screen-based light before or during sleep causes depression, even when the animal isn't looking at the screen.

Dunckley adds that "studies reveal that poor focus often leads to "explosive and aggressive behaviour". "When attention suffers, so does the ability to process one's internal and external environment, so little demands become big ones. By depleting mental energy with high visual and cognitive input, screen time contributes to low reserves. One way to temporarily "boost" depleted reserves is to become angry, so meltdowns actually become a coping mechanism."

John M. Grohol casts an interesting - alternative - perspective to Victoria Dunckley's article. In his article, *"Screentime Is NOT Making Kids Moody, Crazy & Lazy"*, Grohol, Psy.D. argues that "Most of the research support she (Dunckley) cites is specifically looking at people who have a significant problem with overuse or pathological use of technology - not ordinary teenagers using technology for socialising. You can't legitimately compare these two groups of people and say what applies to the pathological applies to all."

Our children spend countless hours of their day in a catatonic state in front of screens, exposed to aggressive marketing and advertising techniques - breeding a generation conditioned to equate contentment with materialism. "Safe" in their rooms, our youngsters are learning their valuable life lessons from media caricatures.

In a world of digital celebrity conformity, individuality of personality is the social outcast. *"Everybody is a genius. But if you judge a fish by its ability to climb a tree, it will live its whole life believing that it is stupid." Albert Einstein.*

Speaking of fish…

In the year 2000 - which coincides roughly with the beginning of the "mobile revolution" - the average human attention span was believed to be around twelve seconds. (In June 1999, Qualcomm released the "pdQ Smartphone", and in early 2000, Ericsson Mobile communications released the R380 - the first device marketed as a "smartphone".)

By the year 2013, a Canadian study revealed that the average human attention span had drastically reduced to a mere eight seconds - one second less than what is believed to be the attention span of the much-maligned goldfish! Coincidence? Or are our digital lifestyles altering our brain chemistry - is digital dependence "re-wiring" our brains - and irrevocably eroding our ever-diminishing levels of attention?

A recent survey of 30,000 pupils revealed that self-esteem of teenage girls - particularly 14–15-year-olds - has significantly dropped since the boom of social media and online communication. Figures show that many of today's teenagers struggle due to a variety of factors including schoolwork, looks, peer pressure and weight.[29]

---

29   Bev James, 5 Simple Ways For Teenage Girls To Boost Their Self-Esteem

You only have to browse through the list of the ten most *"Googled"* celebrities of 2015 - compiled by *Vogue* - to gain an insight into just who is setting the standards and values against which our younger society currently measures itself - the digital role models against which our future generations form their opinions of (relative) self-worth. I'll leave you to formulate your own opinions...

1. Lamar Odom
2. Caitlyn Jenner
3. Ronda Rousey
4. Donald Trump
5. Ruby Rose
6. Charlie Sheen
7. Brian Williams
8. Rachel Dolezal
9. Adele
10. Josh Duggar

And a few isolated examples of the sheer scope of social media... (At the time of writing.)

- Within four hours of joining Twitter, Caitlyn Jenner had amassed 1 million followers.
- Cristiano Ronaldo boasts some 110 million Facebook followers.
- Ronaldo, Taylor Swift and Justin Bieber are currently the three celebrities to reach 200 million combined followers (each) across Facebook, Twitter and Instagram.
- Ronaldo's posts on Facebook and Instagram result in an average of one million interactions each.

With reference to self-worth, the most important relationship that you are likely to experience is your relationship with *yourself*...

"If you have love for yourself, you will have plenty of love for those around you and you will only attract in your life people who have as much love for themselves as you do," proposes *purposefairy* Luminita Saviuc. The best way to be truly accepting of yourself, is to stop comparing yourself to others. It really is that simple! As Eleanor Roosevelt said, "comparison is the thief of joy".

The problem with comparing your *perception* of yourself to others, is that you have no idea of their "story". You formulate an opinion - embellished by your values and beliefs - and you make a subconscious judgement about them, when you haven't the faintest idea what their personal journey is all about.

You are basing your opinion on the visible tip of their personal iceberg and - remember - your opinion is subject to distortions, deletions, and generalisations. You can't possibly experience their version of reality from their perspective, so why even try?

"Don't compare yourself with anyone in this world… if you do so, you are insulting yourself." *Bill Gates.*

Your own self-esteem is usually a reflection of how you see yourself in comparison to others, which all too often only leads to a feeling of hopelessness, despair, or inadequacy. "Care about what other people think and you will always be their prisoner." *Lao Tzu.*

I admire the advice of JT Foxx - a self-declared polarising figure. "Haters don't really hate you. In fact they hate themselves because you are a reflection of what they wish to be."

Research shows that heavy internet users are 2.5 times more likely to suffer from depression, and that high social media usage can trigger an increase in loneliness, jealousy and fear.[30] Is it any coincidence that people in the United Kingdom are consuming more than four times as many antidepressants as they did two decades ago?

The UK now has the seventh highest prescribing rate for antidepressants in the Western world, with around four million Britons taking them each year - twice as many as a decade ago at a cost of more than £200 million a year for the 53 million prescriptions now written.[31]

We formulate our opinions of self - whether we think we are as intelligent, attractive, successful or even as confident as others. But to whom do we compare ourselves? The supermodels in the glossy coffee-table magazines? The "celebrities" which inundate the media frenzy that we have come to accept as everyday life? And at what detriment to family life? There's a shocking statistic which simply states that "33% of people admit to hiding from family and friends to check social media".[32]

In this technological age of social media, we all too often compare our "every day" with the highlights reels of our hundreds of *Facebook* "friends" - again, this is just the tip of the iceberg, you're only viewing their "highlights" - that they want you to see… By the way, how many of your Facebook "friends" do you actually personally know?

Take a look at the illustration on the following page - an excellent example of how perspective (and - more importantly - *context*) can influence the *meaning* that you attach to events. It's not what happens to you that shapes you, it's what you think about what happens to you - the *meaning* that you give it.

---

30 Digitaldetox

31 Dr Joanna Moncrieff, *University College*, London.

32 Digitaldetox

"If Facebook users experience envy of the activities and lifestyles of their friends on Facebook, they are much more likely to report feelings of depression," says Dr. Margaret Duffy - a University of Missouri journalism professor - following a study published in 2015. Reflect also on the thought that "no-one can make you feel inferior without your consent." *Eleanor Roosevelt.*

Social media could actually be creating barriers to personal, physical connections with other people. "I think it's the death of an actual civilised conversation," revealed Justine Harman, features editor at *Elle.com*, in an interview with *The Huffington Post* in 2014.

A report by Christina Sagioglou and Tobias Greitemeyer – Austrian behavioural scientists at The University of Innsbruck - proposes that "compared to browsing the Internet, Facebook is judged as less meaningful, less useful, and more of a waste of time, which then leads to a decrease in mood."[33]

How can you tell if you really love and accept yourself - warts and all? According to Gay Hendricks - contributor to *Hearts in Harmony* - there are two tell-tale signs to reflect that you don't truly accept yourself.

The first sign is that "you try to be everything to everyone" - you're very much a "yes" person, and you don't want to disappoint the people that depend on you. You try to be who you think others want you to be. You try to "fit in". You're always trying to prove yourself (or your worth) to someone – that you're a good partner, a good friend, or a good colleague.

The second sign, according to Gay, is that you constantly feel that you're "never enough". You don't feel that people love or respect you. Nothing that you do is ever enough for them, or – perhaps more importantly - for you. You never appreciate what you do - you don't give yourself any credit for the positive impact that you have on others.

---

[33] The Huffington Post

Another sign that you don't truly appreciate yourself is that you don't feel comfortable in offering your ideas, or opinions. You believe that other people's ideas are of greater value than your own. You possibly also don't value your own company or take pride in your physical appearance. You're not satisfied with your (internal) image of yourself.

Maxwell Maltz – a successful plastic surgeon, and author of *Psycho Cybernetics*, suggested that we have two images that we hold of ourselves – an internal and an external image. Maltz found that people were requesting surgery to improve their external image, in the belief that it would empower them to "feel" better about themselves (their inner image.)

Maltz discovered that even after successful procedures, certain clients still weren't satisfied with their image of themselves – their inner image. That's why it's important to live from the inside-out – no matter what you do on "the outside", ultimately it's what's "inside" that counts! Even plastic surgery won't necessarily change the way that you feel about yourself – you've also got to work on your internal self-image. That's crucial.

Self-doubt affects us all, but it all can be reversed when you learn how to tap into who you really are - who you're meant to be - and accept yourself fully, warts and all.

There is a theory that you detest in others the selfsame thing that you attempt to conceal within yourself. We bemoan others - or are acutely aware of their behavioural "triggers" - when they do the very things that we fear within ourselves.

"Why do you look at the speck of sawdust in your brother's eye and pay no attention to the plank in your own eye? How can you say to your brother, "Let me take the speck out of your eye", when all the time there is a plank in your own eye? You hypocrite, first take the plank out of your own eye, and then you will see clearly to remove the speck from your brother's eye."[34]

The belief will most probably be buried deep within your subconscious brain, which altruistically tries to protect you from it. Ironically, your brain will also try to seek a resolution to be able to put these negative thoughts to rest.

You will find yourself drawn into situations - or entering into relationships - where your subconscious fear can be addressed, in a warped attempt to raise your awareness of it.

---

34   Matthew 7:3-5 The Holy Bible, New International Version

The mind's intention is for you to face your fear, but their behaviour - which triggers the negative associations of your belief - will often cause you to be highly critical or judgemental, starting a wheel in motion - or perpetuating the cycle. Through being critical - and remember the recipient of your criticism doesn't necessarily share your "map" - you have the effect of pushing them further away, or them reacting defensively to what they perceive to be unfair criticism.

Their reaction will serve only to add "substantiating evidence" to the vicious circle of your belief. The correlation between their behaviour and your belief - or emotion - simultaneously serves to reinforce your self-fulfilling prophecy, and to accelerate the "snowball effect".

As we're on the topic of relationships, let's use the fear of rejection as an illustration. Meet the (fictional) characters of Tom and Geri - (*"the names have been changed to protect the innocent"*.) Tom is of the belief that nobody loves him, and he fears rejection - often rejecting himself. Maybe in childhood, he felt that he was "rejected" in some way, and he finds numerous examples to substantiate this belief. ("Seek and you will find". You will always find "evidence" to support, or substantiate, your beliefs.)

He doesn't believe that he's ever good enough, so he accepts the belief that he will continue to be rejected. This belief limits his interactions with others, and influences his attitude towards them, fueling his self-fulfilling prophecy - and adding credence to the paradigm that he's never good enough.

Say, for example, that Geri has to work late one evening. Tom genuinely believes that Geri would prefer to be at work, rather than in his company, because he projects the belief that she doesn't appreciate him, and - catastrophising[35] - he believes that ultimately she will reject him anyway.

When a tired and frustrated Geri does finally arrive home, Tom transfers his doubts and insecurities onto her. An exhausted Geri is on the receiving end of the "you don't love me, you'd rather spend time at work" emotional blackmail - to which she understandably responds with incredulous surprise - and possibly also a hint of frustration-induced anger.

Tom sees the anger as validation of his belief that nobody loves him, and that he will continue to be rejected, only serving to fuel Geri's frustration, which in turn feeds Tom's fires of insecurity.

You can see where this is heading…

---

[35]   Catastrophise - to view or present a situation as considerably worse than it actually is

"When you refuse - even subconsciously - to acknowledge your feelings, or to accept something about yourself, you'll never feel completely at peace with yourself, and will always find something to complain about. The people in your life will always be imperfect, because you think that you're less than perfect", suggests Hendricks.

As a quick aside, one nugget of advice for dealing with conflict – is to THINK about your choice of words and language. Ever heard of "*THINK* before you speak"?

T	-	Is it True?
H	-	Is it Helpful?
I	-	Is it Inspiring?
N	-	Is it necessary?
K	-	Is it Kind?

As Gay Hendricks writes in *Hearts In Harmony*, "when you learn to love yourself, all your relationships can be transformed. You'll no longer run yourself ragged, trying to please everyone and never feeling like you're enough at the end of the day," he says. "Relationships will energise you instead of draining you. You'll feel self-assured, relaxed and free, at last."

In *Psychology Today*, Deborah Khoshaba, writes that "self-love is a state of appreciation for oneself that grows from actions that support our physical, psychological and spiritual growth."

"Self-love is dynamic; it grows by actions that mature us", Khoshaba continues. "When we act in ways that expand self-love in us, we begin to accept much better our weaknesses as well as our strengths, have less need to explain away our shortcomings, have compassion for ourselves as human beings struggling to find personal meaning, are more centred in our life purpose and values, and expect living fulfillment through our own efforts."

"Allowing healing, growth and connection to become a natural part of your relationships, work and most importantly, allow it to become the way that you treat yourself" adds Magali Peysha. "Know that you always have a new way to see a problem, a different option that is possible, and deep love and understanding of yourself that keeps you focused on what matters most to you. When you approach your life and relationships from this place of knowing yourself and your purpose every day becomes exceptional," proposes Magali.

Through working with Bob Proctor, I have found that perhaps the key principle to influencing effective and lasting change is to look at the results that you are currently getting. If you're not happy with your results, then you need to change your paradigm - your internal collection of habits. Your model.

As Maxwell Maltz references in *"Psycho- Cybernetics"*, your internal "thermostat" will continue to deliver the same results, until it is "re-calibrated". If you're not happy with your results - with what's happening on "the outside" - then you must choose to change what's happening on "the inside".

Kerry Petsinger, on *Lifehack*, compiled a list of *"Fifty Small Things You Can Do To Really Love Yourself"*. Here are a few selected suggestions from Kerry's list:

- Connect with someone who is positive, inspiring, and encouraging.
- If you're dissatisfied, admit it to yourself, and create an action plan for change.
- You must accept that you're not perfect before you can love yourself.
- Get coaching - or therapy - if you're struggling. You're worth it!
- Practice an optimistic attitude and be mindful of your inner dialogue.
- Learn to say no.
- Have fun. Laugh every day. Get outside in nature.
- Compliment yourself.
- Seek an opportunity to grow in (at least) one of the challenges in your life.
- Discover your passion. Do something you love every day.
- Learn.
- Take a small step out of your comfort zone every day.
- Appreciate the amazing things you can do rather than focus on your "flaws"
- Nourish your body with healthy choices.
- Establish a routine for healthy sleep.
- Start a gratitude journal and list something you are thankful for every day.

With regards to "self-love", please take the time to read "*As I Began To Love Myself*" - a truly inspirational piece of literature, penned by none other than Charlie Chaplin, a man of many masks...[36]

"As I began to love myself I found that anguish and emotional suffering are only warning signs that I was living against my own truth. Today, I know, this is "AUTHENTICITY".

As I began to love myself I understood how much it can offend somebody if I try to force my desires on this person, even though I knew the time was not right and the person was not ready for it, and even though this person was me. Today I call it "RESPECT".

As I began to love myself I stopped craving for a different life, and I could see that everything that surrounded me was inviting me to grow. Today I call it "MATURITY".

---

[36] Charlie Chaplin "As I Began To Love Myself"

As I began to love myself I understood that at any circumstance, I am in the right place at the right time, and everything happens at the exactly right moment. So I could be calm. Today I call it "SELF-CONFIDENCE".

As I began to love myself I quit stealing my own time, and I stopped designing huge projects for the future. Today, I only do what brings me joy and happiness, things I love to do and that make my heart cheer, and I do them in my own way and in my own rhythm. Today I call it "SIMPLICITY".

As I began to love myself I freed myself of anything that is no good for my health - food, people, things, situations, and everything that drew me down and away from myself. At first I called this attitude a healthy egoism. Today I know it is "LOVE OF ONESELF".

As I began to love myself I quit trying to always be right, and ever since I was wrong less of the time. Today I discovered that is "MODESTY".

As I began to love myself I refused to go on living in the past and worrying about the future. Now, I only live for the moment, where everything is happening. Today I live each day, day by day, and I call it "FULFILLMENT".

As I began to love myself I recognised that my mind can disturb me and it can make me sick. But as I connected it to my heart, my mind became a valuable ally. Today I call this connection "WISDOM OF THE HEART".

We no longer need to fear arguments, confrontations or any kind of problems with ourselves or others. Even stars collide, and out of their crashing new worlds are born. Today I know "THAT IS LIFE"!

Perhaps better known for his silent acting, it may surprise you that Chaplin also delivered a rousing speech in a similar vein in *"The Great Dictator"*. Below I have included a few excerpts with the intention of raising your awareness around consolidating our relationships with each other… We can make a difference! Don't wait for "them" to make the first move…

"When "i" is replaced with "we" even illness becomes wellness." *Malcolm X*

"… I don't want to rule or conquer anyone. I should like to help everyone… We all want to help one another. Human beings are like that. We want to live by each other's happiness - not by each other's misery. We don't want to hate and despise one another. In this world there is room for everyone. And the good earth is rich and can provide for everyone. The way of life can be free and beautiful, but we have lost the way.

Greed has poisoned men's souls, has barricaded the world with hate, has goose-stepped us into misery and bloodshed. We have developed speed, but we have shut ourselves in. Machinery that gives abundance has left us in want. Our knowledge has made us cynical. Our cleverness, hard and unkind. We think too much and feel too little. More than machinery we need humanity. More than cleverness we need kindness and gentleness. Without these qualities, life will be violent and all will be lost…

The aeroplane and the radio have brought us closer together. The very nature of these inventions cries out for the goodness in men - cries out for universal brotherhood - for the unity of us all. Even now my voice is reaching millions throughout the world - millions of despairing men, women, and little children - victims of a system that makes men torture and imprison innocent people.

In the 17th Chapter of St Luke it is written: "the Kingdom of God is within man" - not one man nor a group of men, but in all men! In you! You, the people have the power - the power to create machines. The power to create happiness! You, the people, have the power to make this life free and beautiful, to make this life a wonderful adventure.

Now let us fight to fulfill that promise! Let us fight to free the world - to do away with national barriers - to do away with greed, with hate and intolerance. Let us fight for a world of reason, a world where science and progress will lead to all men's happiness… In the name of democracy, let us all unite!"[37]

---

[37] Charlie Chaplin "The Great Dictator"

Confidence, and Self-Esteem:

Self-confidence essentially means "to have faith in, or trust yourself". Confidence can be described as "the way that we project ourselves to others", and "a feeling of trust in your abilities, qualities and judgement".

Confidence can also be described as "a state of being certain either that a hypothesis or prediction is correct, or that a chosen course of action is the best or most effective".

Self-confidence is becoming increasingly more important in virtually every aspect of our "everyday" lives. Unfortunately, self-confidence is also becoming increasingly more elusive. Just as with Tom's debilitating self-belief, the pursuit of confidence can also be seen as a vicious circle.

Success breeds confidence, but, conversely, a lack of success often leads to a lack of self-confidence, resulting in perceived failure - "feedback"? - and a further drop in confidence. People with low self-confidence tend to be less resilient and may quite easily equate a lack of success with being a personal failure.

There is what is termed a "confidence-competence loop". Being good at something (competent) leads to increased confidence in that area. The better that we are – or become - at something, the more confident that we begin to feel in that particular regard. The problem lies in the fact that we rely on confidence as the motivation to take the initial action - which is necessary to develop the competence - and it's a sad truth that "it's the start that stops most people".

"The journey of a thousand miles begins with a single step" - face the fear and do it anyway! How are you ever going to master anything if you hide behind your fear of it? Can you remember how you learned to walk? Or how you learned to ride a bicycle, or perhaps drive a car? There are four stages of learning…

1. *Unconscious incompetence* – You don't know how to do it, and you don't know that you don't know it.
2. *Conscious incompetence* – You still don't know how to do it, but you now recognise the value of learning it.
3. *Conscious competence* – You now know how to do it, but to do it demands a certain degree of concentration.
4. *Unconscious competence* – You know how to do it so well, that you can do it easily, perhaps simultaneously with another task. Like a habit, it almost becomes "second nature".

"Our upbringing has an enormous impact on our self-esteem," says Sharon Wegscheider-Cruse - family therapist, co-founder of *The National Association of Children of Alcoholics* and best-selling author of *Learning to Love Yourself: Finding Your Self-Worth*.

Wegscheider-Cruse says one of the most important lessons that parents can impart to their children is to take unwavering action. "A lot happens before a child is 4 years old as to how we perceive the world", she says. Take the example above. When you started walking, you fell down. You dusted yourself off, and tried again... When you fell off your bicycle, you were committed to getting back "in the saddle".

It's important that you valued yourself enough to keep persevering. Wegscheider-Cruse suggests that you have to feel good enough about yourself to "allow failure". "It's in the picking up after failure that self-worth is supported and prospers", she proposes.

"What stagnates people is lack of action", claims Wegscheider-Cruse. "You can always make a second choice. You can always remedy a mistake that has been made. You can always go in another direction. But if you don't believe in yourself, then you procrastinate and you avoid, and that draws your self-worth down. Some decision", she adds, "is better than no decision at all".

There's a school of thought which proclaims that you attract what you look for. The "Law of Attraction" - "we become what we think about all day long". I'll give you a personal example. If you're of the belief that you're not intelligent, then you'll find the "irrefutable evidence" to substantiate your belief. You will distort or delete your conversations and will not hear other people telling you that you're intelligent, hearing only the minority telling you that you're "stupid". You may do something carelessly, and curse yourself for being stupid, and soon enough - you start to believe it - you're stupid!

"Psychologists have asserted for decades that there is a huge difference between having a negative thought and turning it into action. Yet this lesson never seems to sink in. Thoughts are just fleeting mental images. They have no consequences until you choose to make them important. Take the mental rock out of your shoe." *Deepak Chopra, "A Freer (Happier!) Way to Think"*.

Do yourself a favour - try a little exercise over the course of a week, or even one day! Give yourself permission to notice what you notice... In each of your interactions - in person, over the phone, at home - in your "everyday", take the time to pay attention to what is being said. Be aware of your tendency to distort and delete, and just pay attention. For this to work, you need to approach every interaction exactly as you usually would - remember your thoughts can "influence" the outcome to mirror your belief.

Look for the evidence to refute your belief.

So, if you believe that you're not attractive, for example, listen to your social circle telling you just how good you look. If you believe that you're inadequate, or simply not good enough, then listen to your friends telling you how great you really are... Now ask yourself, are you leading them into telling you? Or have they *always* been telling you, but you've not previously heard it because it conflicts with your subconscious belief?

If your subconscious believes that you're not attractive, it will not accept other people telling you that you are. Bypass your subconscious and pay attention to what people are saying - notice what you notice...

Pack a notepad, or record it on your phone. Notch up how many compliments you actually receive in a day. You don't need to record each one as it happens, just remember to record it at the end of each interaction. I'll bet that you'll be flabbergasted with the results. Amazing how powerful the subconscious mind is, isn't it?

So how about harnessing your subconscious to build positive affirmations, rather than to perpetuate your negative, limiting beliefs?

"Some people believe that self-confidence can be built with affirmations and positive thinking. It's just as important to build self-confidence by setting, and then achieving your *DO* – thereby building competence. Without this underlying competence, you don't have self-confidence: you have shallow over-confidence.

As Jim Rohn says, there are two ways to have the tallest building in town. "One is to tear down all the other buildings - the second is to build your building taller than everyone else's". In building your positive, "feel good" affirmations on the foundations of a physical sense of achievement - your confidence, your "building", will not only soar higher than everyone else's, but will also be resolutely steadfast against "the tall poppy brigade".

If you're seeking confidence for a particular event, or a *DO* - such as an interview, or exam, for example – here are a couple of tips. Prepare well. Learn as much as you can about the company, the role, or the subject. The more prepared and knowledgeable that you are, the more self-confident you will be. "He who fails to prepare is preparing to fail." *Winston Churchill.*

Think of something that you're proud of having achieved – even if it initially may *appear* to be totally unrelated to the forthcoming event... Remember how you felt when you started to do it for the first time - it's perfectly natural to feel nervous and stressed. Make a list of the things that you're proud of. Don't worry if you can't think of too many - we all find it easier to highlight our flaws and weaknesses than we do in recognising our own strengths. This list is evidence of your success - don't be afraid to revisit it whenever you feel that you may need a little boost.

Approach the event armed with the knowledge of your previous success, and carry the shield of positive, confident - "fake it 'til you make it" - body language. Walk tall, and take imperfect action towards your *DO* - if you wait for perfect conditions, you will never start anything. "He who observes the wind (and waits for all conditions to be favorable) will not sow, and he who regards the clouds will not reap." *Ecclesiastes 11:4*

If your *DO* is an interview, or an important presentation, for example, then remember to "dress for success". Research has shown that attractive people tend to be treated better - and seen in a more favourable light - by others, than less attractive people. Controversial, perhaps, but remember the old cliché, "beauty is in the eye of the beholder…"

"The evidence is pretty strong that people who improve their appearance tend to feel better about themselves, and while we can be critical about what that is saying about us as a society, we need to consider the individual. We all engage in a range of behaviours throughout the day to make ourselves feel better about ourselves," suggests David Sarwer, a Penn Associate Professor of Psychology in Psychiatry and Surgery - one of America's leading experts on physical appearance.

Remember, "fake it 'til you make it!" "When you look good, you feel good and you're more confident, too." *Nicole Munoz.*

"Self-confidence is a state of mind that can be achieved through intentional action. Allotting time to nurture your mind, body and spirit (preferably one hour a day) can be done in a variety of ways. If you're not taking time for yourself, then you're allowing someone or something to shape your view of the world." *Dustin Cucciarre.*

"Your self-confidence needs to be rooted in who you are… So find ways to get connected with yourself and grow. Perhaps volunteer, meditate, work out, read, hang out with friends. Whatever it takes for you to see your value…" *Darrah Brustein.*

An important facet of self-confidence is that of self-efficacy. Psychologist Albert Bandura defined self-efficacy as "one's belief in one's ability to succeed in specific situations or accomplish a task".

Bandura's *social cognitive theory* proposes that we develop self-efficacy when we master skills and achieve goals in certain skill areas - or through observing the successes of others similar to ourselves. In other words, self-efficacy is the belief that if we learn and work hard at a particular challenge, then we'll succeed. Remember, competence breeds confidence.

Think back to Professor Amy Cuddy... Remember the benefits of the power pose, and remember how your "mirror activities" made you feel? Try a different slant on the theme now - if you're feeling a little down, consciously straighten your back and raise your shoulders. If you're sitting down, pull yourself forward in your chair and sit up straight. Stand up and walk around for a minute if space and circumstances allow. Fresh air and a different perspective can work wonders! (*I'll be waiting right here when you get back...*)

Now, even if you're "faking" confidence, your "confidence" will inspire confidence in others - your family, your colleagues, your boss, or your friends. Through gaining the confidence of others, your own confidence will grow. If you truly believe in yourself, so will others. Isn't that a much more optimistic picture than that of the vicious circle?

You can begin with a small - yet effective - little "tweak" - how about being more mindful of your choice of language? When someone asks you how you are, rather than replying with "not bad", "can't complain" or "mustn't grumble", for example - how about "GREAT! Thank You!"? Notice the difference? Try it out for yourself - again maybe not too loud on the commute!

Make an effort to consciously eradicate negative words such as "not" or "mustn't", when you can reply in the positive. There's a reason it's "Have a great day", and not "Have a not too bad day".

Another simple step towards building your confidence may be something as simple as just saying "No!" Your confidence can be developed through standing up for what you believe in, rather than allowing others to walk all over you. Tony Robbins, in "*The Power of No*", suggests that when you say "no", you're not insulting someone, you're simply exercising your right to say "no".

So why the resistance to simply saying "no"? Robbins believes that it's our tendency to put others' objectives before our own. "Our inability to say "no" just to make someone else feel comfortable, is not only unfair to ourselves, but it can be unfair to the other person as well," suggests Robbins. "Just because it's easier to say "yes" doesn't mean that we should".

"What if "no" would result in a better outcome for both parties?" asks Tony. "Saying "no" doesn't have to mean you're being self-serving. Remember, it's your right to say no. It doesn't mean you're exercising some sort of immutable ego trip. It means you're saying "no" - and that's OK".

Self-worth, or self-esteem, describes the way that you feel about yourself - regardless of your looks, achievements, or other areas in which you may feel confident. Self-esteem is intertwined with your level of pride in yourself, and the amount of self-respect that you feel that you have.

Self-esteem also relates to the way in which we compare ourselves with others. This may include whether we think we are as intelligent, attractive, loveable, successful, or as worthy as others. Self-esteem relates to your self-worth and how you value yourself in the world. Nathaniel Branden, Ph.D - Psychotherapist and best-selling author of *The Six Pillars of Self-Esteem* - defines self-esteem as "the experience of being competent to cope with basic challenges of life and of being worthy of happiness".

Having low self-esteem can really affect your mood. Feeling that you are worth less than others may lead you to strive for perfection but never feel you have achieved enough. If you suffer with low self-worth or low self-esteem you may feel depressed or guilty, and you might try to prove your worth to others. You also may avoid situations that could cause anxiety or challenges you feel you cannot to cope with.

People with low self-esteem generally have an overall negative belief about themselves - tending to dwell on their perceived flaws and weaknesses. People with a higher level of self-esteem tend to recognise their strengths. "A stumbling block to the pessimist is a stepping stone to the optimist." *Eleanor Roosevelt.*

All too often, people with low levels of self-esteem are reluctant to view their strengths and positive attributes. Don't get drawn into the comparison trap - stop comparing yourself to others and start to focus on the things that you actually like about yourself. The more you can build on your own strengths and attributes, the more confident you will feel in your own skin. Live *your* life - "Be yourself; everyone else is already taken." *Oscar Wilde.*

Self-image can be seen as your personal recipe of self-esteem and confidence. It is the general perception that you have formed of yourself, incorporating looks, abilities, intelligence, worth, and more. It is the impression that you have of yourself. How you "feel" about yourself.

Free yourself of the weight of other people's expectations. What other people expect of you is irrelevant - they have no idea of your journey. Only you can ultimately know what it is that you are capable of - and even then, you have no idea of the untapped potential currently lying dormant within you! Take a moment to reflect on the thought that it might possibly be your *perception* of their expectation that is unrealistic… Live *your* life - let them live theirs!

Rather than living in the (self-imposed) material despair of what you desire - and what other people desire for you - try to be mindful, and appreciative, of what you already have. Not just in terms of your possessions, but in terms of your own quintessential endearing qualities. "If you can't enjoy what you have, you can't enjoy more of it." *Dr Richard Bandler.*

What do you have to be grateful for? Choose to find something positive - focus on what's working for you - what's going well in your life. "What you attract into your life is in harmony with your dominant thoughts." *Brian Tracy.*

Take the time to write a list of thirty things that you like about yourself. Go on, it's important - especially if you struggle with self-appreciation. If you can't scrape thirty, then start with fifteen, and then add one daily - no matter how trivial or insignificant you believe them to be - it can be absolutely anything...

See just how easy it is to break away from constantly beating yourself up? Make it a daily habit to list the things that you like about yourself. You'll thank yourself later!

If you're struggling with your own list, then why not "phone a friend"? It used to work on *"Who Wants To Be A Millionaire"*... It's pretty easy to believe the rhetoric of your subconscious negativity telling you that you're not good enough, and to believe that that is the way that the world sees you. "Phone a friend" - ask someone who knows you well, for their opinion. Listen to them point out your attributes and strengths, which you have a tendency to mask behind your "flaws and inadequacies".

Accept compliments - your subconscious will otherwise delete or distort them. Choose instead, to consciously - and graciously - acknowledge them, honour them, and - if you so wish - to return them. If not, a simple "thank you" will suffice. Learn to accept compliments with grace and humility. The person offering the compliments is not caught up in your "broken record" rhetoric.

Your sub-conscious deletes and distorts whatever isn't congruent with its beliefs, so seek out a second opinion. Sometimes you simply can't see the wood for the trees. The same principle applies also to criticism - seek to find the validity of the criticism, and the intention behind it. Learn from it, and move on - "there is no failure, only feedback".

"Nothing others do is because of you. What others say and do is a projection of their own reality, their own dream. When you are immune to the opinions and actions of others, you won't be the victim of needless suffering." *Don Miguel Ruiz.*

Kyle Hiller, on *Lifehack*, suggests that you *"Embrace Your Little Faults. They Are What Defines You"*. "How much of our lives have we dedicated to perfection?" asks Kyle. "The straight A's, the beach bodies, the perfect scores. Striving towards perfection and not achieving it can lead to depression, unhealthy mood swings, and self-deprecating doubt. These frustrations pile on, and eventually, a perfectionist may find themselves struggling to accept themselves."

"If a person can't accept who they are, they lose sight of their selves, and then, seek out ways to sculpt who they are supposed to be," says Hiller. "Faults and flaws are what make individuals different from each other."

"You will have to make mistakes along the way in order to learn what not to do," proposes Hiller. Your mistakes have simply informed you of what it was that you didn't know – your gaps – your areas of improvement. You've made mistakes, leaving you the opportunity to learn."

"By not being perfect, there is always room to grow," Hiller adds. "Striving and achieving perfection would infer that there is no more growth needed. You have peaked physically, mentally and spiritually. There is nothing else to satisfy. Nothing to learn. Nothing to do". And remember what Tony Robbins said, "If you're not growing, you're dying".

"Perfection sounds a little boring, doesn't it? Don't strive for perfection. Strive for balance. The reality is that what makes us strong can also make us weak". "Perfection is not attainable, but if we chase perfection we can catch excellence." *Vince Lombardi.*

"Accept that you could be better at something, but where you are now is where you're supposed to be", says Hiller. Trust yourself, believe in yourself, and allow yourself to be you.

"Forcing yourself to be something more can be disastrous for your personal and work life, and your health", he warns. "If someone was perfect, they'd be a robot", adds Hiller. "Ideas of perfection, whether they be of our intangible attributes or our bodies, are social constructs that dictate expectations and standards. Comparisons are often drawn to categorise people. That's what our minds do: organise the chaos. But if everyone was expected to look or behave a certain way, we'd all look and behave the same", he suggests.

"People come in all shapes, sizes and colours. They hold their own beliefs and morals, aspirations and fears. Their experiences are their own, and no one ever experiences precisely the same life as the other", says Hiller. "Everyone makes mistakes and has blemishes and faults. These elements cannot be manufactured. As a result, the standards dictated by social constructs are irrelevant. Everyone is different, and that is okay".

In *Psychology Today*, Amy Morin writes that "changing the way you think takes a lot of effort initially, but with practice, you'll notice big changes - not just in the way you think, but also in the way you feel and behave. You can make peace with the past, look at the present differently, and think about the future in a way that will support your chances of reaching your goals."

"The recognition of your beauty, intelligence and bravery can soon transform the beliefs you hold for yourself, making space for your inner light to shine.

When we get out of our own way by choosing self-empowerment instead of self-doubt, we fill ourselves with enough courage to get out there to be and do whatever we want. We open the door to a world of opportunity that's just waiting to be discovered, so what are you waiting for? It's your time to shine!" *Bev James* - bestselling author, and CEO of The Coaching Academy.

Choose to be your best self - identify your **DO**, and enjoy the journey!

In *"Feeling Good: The New Mood Therapy"*, David Burns suggests a few of - what he calls - our most common "thinking errors", which only serve to contribute to self-sabotage:

- Filtering Out the Positive - "We are "blinkered" to the good things that go on around us", David says. "If nine good things happen, and one bad, we are most likely to dwell on that single negative than to celebrate the positives."

- Mind-Reading - "We can never be sure what someone else is thinking - we don't share their "map" - nor do they share our "story", says Burns. "Thinking thoughts such as "She must have thought that I was really stupid at work today", generates unrealistic perceptions and further ingrains your own negative beliefs and destructive self-talk", he claims.

- Emotional Reasoning - We often assume that our emotions are rational. "If I feel inadequate, then I must *be* inadequate." Burns suggests that it's essential to recognise that emotions, like our thoughts, aren't necessarily based on fact. Remember, try to make a conscious effort to look for evidence to refute your belief.

- Labeling - Instead of thinking, "I made a mistake", you might be tempted to proclaim that you're "an idiot", says Burns. "Pigeonholing experiences and people - including yourself - places them into categories that are often based on isolated incidents. Make a conscious effort not to affix mental labels, or stereotypes", he adds.

- Personalisation - If, for example, Geri has to work late, Tom - catastrophising - may assume that "she doesn't love me". When you find yourself personalising situations, make an effort to weigh possible factors which may be influencing the circumstances - remembering also that you don't share their "map".

"Once you recognise your thinking errors, you can begin trying to challenge those thoughts. Look for exceptions to the rule and gather evidence that your thoughts aren't 100% true. The goal doesn't need to be to replace negative thoughts with overly idealistic or positive ones. Instead, replace them with realistic thoughts." *Amy Morin*

Recent research has revealed that optimists do better in most avenues of life - whether it's work, school, sports, or relationships. They get depressed less often than pessimists do, make more money, and tend to have happier marriages.

There's evidence to support the theory that optimists live longer, too. A Dutch study of cardiovascular health, found that - of the 900 subjects - pessimists die sooner of heart disease than optimists. Pessimism has also been found to increase your chances of developing dementia.

Fortunately, an optimistic outlook can be cultivated. Suzanne Segerstrom, PhD - an optimism researcher at *The University of Kentucky* and author of *Breaking Murphy's Law* - believes that "dispositional optimism"[38] can be achieved through a few small, gradual changes...

The key to learning optimism is strongly connected to changing the subconscious beliefs that you have about yourself and the world around you. American psychologist, Martin Seligman, suggests the process of *ABCDE*:

- *Adversity* - Identifying a particular difficulty in your life.
- *Belief* - Your ideas about the underlying cause for that difficulty.
- *Consequence* - Understanding the emotions that the belief will trigger.
- *Disputation* - Identifying what a better belief might look like.
- *Energisation* - Embedding and celebrating your "new" belief.

Your reaction to any given situation is determined by how your brain has been conditioned by your experiences - especially those learned in childhood, when your subconscious mind is more receptive and malleable. But you don't have to be bound by this conditioning. With a little time, effort, and a determined strategy, you can reprogramme it!" In fact, through The Proctor Gallagher Institute, we facilitate exactly that - a transformational mentorship programme - called "Thinking Into Results".

"To truly be happy, you have to stop trying... Engagement bypasses pessimism," says Suzanne Segerstrom. In one of her most referenced studies, researchers asked a group of people to listen to classical music to lift their spirits, whilst the other subjects were merely instructed to listen to the music. The music didn't help those who were focused on lifting their spirits, whereas the other group reported feeling more positive.

When you're totally engaged in an activity, that engagement diverts your attention from rumination - "the destructive pattern of obsessing endlessly over problems or concerns". And rumination often leads to catastrophising - imagining the absolute worst-case scenario.

---

38   Dispositional optimism is defined as a global expectation that more good (desirable) things than bad (undesirable) will happen in the future (Scheier and Carver, 1985)

If you find yourself catastrophising, Segerstrom suggests looking for a distraction to quell the negative thinking. Do something different to divert your attention. Try reading a book – (you're already one step ahead - you're reading this one!) Maybe something as simple as listening to some uplifting music?

The more that you allow your negative thoughts to carve that groove into your thinking, the more that your mindset will emulate the "broken record" and ingrain the thought processes as your self-fulfilling prophecy - your belief. Change the record. Change your mind - change your life.

Try amplifying *your* record. Rather than catastrophising, play around a little with your projected "consequences". Mentally run through your thoughts and imagine the scenario through the lenses and filters of your rich imagination. Go ahead, caricaturise it. Reduce it to the ridiculous. "The beauty of this… is that you feel a bit of power over your thoughts and the situation", says Karen Reivich, PhD, Penn Resiliency Project, University of Pennsylvania and co-author of *The Resilience Factor*. "That sense of control is the antidote to pessimism".

In maintaining the philosophy of "fake it 'til you make it", the simple act of smiling can help to promote confidence. Smiling - and making eye contact - will not only make others more comfortable around you, but it can make you feel better too - it tricks your mind into being happier.

Researchers at Wake Forest University asked a group of 50 students to act like extroverts for 15 minutes in a group discussion, even if they didn't feel like being extroverted. The more assertive and energetic the students acted, the happier they became. "What's best about this kind of cognitive behavioural change is that it doesn't even require much faith. You don't have to believe that an antibiotic is going to work for it to work." *Martin Seligman*.

Seligman's theory is supported by research conducted by Harvard University's Dr Henry Beecher, in which one hundred medical students were asked to participate in a study to test two new drugs - a "super stimulant" in a red capsule, and a "super tranquiliser" in a blue capsule.

The students were unaware that the contents of the capsules had actually been intentionally switched. What the students believed to be a stimulant, was actually a sedative - and vice versa.

Over half of the subjects returned results in keeping with their expectations of the drug - in direct contrast to the chemical reaction created by the drug itself. "Their *beliefs* overrode the chemical impact of the drug." *Tony Robbins*.

A drug's usefulness "is a direct result of not only the chemical properties of the drug, but also the patient's belief in the usefulness and effectiveness of the drug." *Dr Henry Beecher.*[39]

"Drugs are not always necessary, belief in recovery always is". *Orman Cousins.*

The same is true of reaping the benefits of adopting a positive mindset. View it as a placebo effect. A placebo is anything that appears to be a medical treatment, but actually isn't. It could be a pill, or some other type of "fake" treatment, free of any active health-affecting ingredient.

People develop reactions to a placebo - in some, their symptoms may improve; others may develop what appear to be side effects of the treatment. Your *expectation*, or *belief* in the drug - or in this case, *attitude* - is the sole determinant in the effectiveness of the course of action.

According to Seligman, there are three simple strategies, which, if adopted, can result in a marked improvement in "dispositional optimism" - in just one week.

- Use your strengths in a new way. "Researchers asked study participants to identify their top five attributes and instructed them to use one of these strengths in a new and different way - every day - for 1 week", says Seligman. "The subjects measurably increased their level of happiness for six months".

- Record the good things. "A group of adults was asked to write down each day, three things that had gone well and why they believed the events came about", adds Seligman. "The participants of the week-long study reported feeling happier for six months afterward."

- Pay a gratitude visit. "The subjects were given a week to write a letter of gratitude, and to deliver it in person to someone who had been kind to them, but whom they had never thanked properly" says Seligman. "The happiness boost from this experiment lasted about one month."

Another way to develop your confidence and self-esteem is to be pro-active. Initiate imperfect action - don't wait for "someday" to arrive, or for the perfect opportunity to present itself. Step out of your comfort zone and challenge your fears.

Life begins at the edge of your comfort zone.

---

[39] "Awaken The Giant Within," Tony Robbins

Ask yourself a (relatively challenging) question - how old would you *ideally* aspire to live to? What age would constitute "a good innings" for you? I'm not asking for a morbid, clinical prognosis, just pick a number that you would be happy to reach... 85? 90? 100? Obviously, we can't predict the exact time of our "departure", but that's not the point of the exercise. Just pick the first number that popped into your mind. Trust me, I know what I'm doing...

How many years are there between that number and your current age? If you're forty, for example, and you aspire to live to the ripe old age of say ninety, that's fifty years - or approximately 18,250 days (give or take the odd leap year).

Realising how finite life can be, can help to put a different perspective on your current list of priorities. As Bev James says, "Do it, or Ditch it" - if you're not willing to take action on it, then cast it aside. If you were to be told - God forbid - that you only had a month left to live, would you approach each day differently?

What are you waiting for?

"I have looked in the mirror every morning and asked myself: "If today were the last day of my life, would I want to do what I am about to do today?" And whenever the answer has been "No" for too many days in a row, I know I need to change something." *Steve Jobs*

If you desire different results, you need to commit to a different set of actions - if you do what you've always done, you'll get what you've always gotten.

Remember the important role that self-efficacy plays in terms of building your confidence - nothing builds confidence and self-esteem like an achievement, or a sense of accomplishment. Establish your **DO**, and take the first step of your journey.

"Opportunity does not knock, it presents itself when you beat down the door." *Kyle Chandler*. Go out and get it! "Feel the fear and do it anyway." *Susan Jeffers*.

"To perform like Linford, you have to think like Linford... PMA. Positive. Mental. Attitude..." So goes the 1996 *Persil* television advert. At the time of writing, Linford Christie was the only British man to have won gold medals in the 100 metres at the Olympic Games, the World Championships, the European Championships and the Commonwealth Games. He was also the first European man to break the 10-second barrier in the 100m event.

Possessing the courage, self-belief and PMA can be the "Turbo Boost"[40] that helps you to "perform like Linford", or to be invincible like Michael Knight's *K.I.T.T.* - for those of you of an age to remember the "hit" 1980's television series, "*Knight Rider*".

Tony Robbins says that "repetition is the mother of skill". If we repeatedly influence the way in which we think about ourselves, and how we perceive the world around us, we can form a natural habit, or develop a new skill.

Aristotle said that "we are what we repeatedly do". Through changing our perceptions, our newly-formed habits and positive mental attitude can effectively improve our levels of confidence, and our self-esteem.

---

40   The character of KITT (Knight Industries Two Thousand) in the original Knight Rider series was physically embodied as a modified 1982 Pontiac Trans Am with numerous special features such as Turbo Boost (which allowed quick bursts of speed or jumping over obstacles.)

~ PART 2 ~

"THE SCIENTIFIC BIT"...

Happiness, Optimism and Gratitude:

"Happiness does not depend on what you have or who you are; it solely relies on what you think." *Buddha.*

"Your joy is your sorrow unmasked. The deeper that sorrow carves into your being, the more joy you can contain… Your pain is the breaking of the shell that encloses your understanding. Even as the stone of the fruit must break, that its heart may stand in the sun, so must you know pain. Much of your pain is self-chosen." *Kahlil Gibran, "The Prophet".*

The physical and mental benefits of positive thinking have been illustrated by scores of independent studies. Positive thinking can "give you more confidence, improve your mood, and even reduce the likelihood of developing conditions such as hypertension, depression and other stress-related disorders".

Optimism can have profound effects on your physical health. The mere act of expecting positive outcomes and being hopeful can "boost your immune system, protect against harmful behaviours, prevent chronic disease, and help people cope following troubling news". Psychologically, "optimism may be one of the most important predictors of physical health".

In a study by Kohut, Cooper, Nickolaus, Russell, & Cunnick - elderly adults were vaccinated against the flu virus. Two weeks later, their response to the immunisation was measured. "Greater optimism predicted greater antibody production and better immune outcomes".

Studies have also investigated optimism and disease progression in people with HIV. Ironson and colleagues found that "people reflecting higher levels of optimism had the best suppression of viral load, and a greater number of helper T cells" - both important to limiting HIV. "An optimistic outlook appears not only to be strongly positively related to a healthy immune system but also to better outcomes for people with compromised immune systems."

Optimism has also been linked with improved recovery for people suffering from cancer. Research carried out by Carver *et al*, proposed that "optimistic people experience less distress when faced with potentially life-threatening cancer diagnoses". Furthermore, Schou and colleagues suggested that a superior "fighting spirit" found in optimists, predicted "substantially better quality of life one year after breast cancer surgery".

"Optimism also predicted less disruption of normal life, distress, and fatigue" in a study of women who were undergoing treatment for breast cancer.[41] In this study, optimism was also suggested to "protect against an urge to withdraw from social activities, which may be important for healing". People who tend to be more optimistic and more mindful, have also been shown to "have an increase in sleep quality".[42] (More on sleep, in the chapter on "Rest and Recuperation...)

Research conducted by Maruta, Colligan, Malinchoc, and Offord determined that "for every 10-point increase in the individual's score on their optimism scale, the risk of early death decreased by 19%". To put that into perspective, the difference between sudden death risk factors for smokers and non-smokers (for a middle-aged person of average health) is estimated at 5-10%

We all know the risks associated with smoking - why not the benefits of optimism?

"Optimists are also more likely to engage in problem solving when faced with difficulties, which is itself associated with increased psychological well-being. While pessimists tend to cope through denial and abandoning impeded goals, optimists rely on acceptance and the use of humour."

Winston Churchill once said that "a pessimist sees the difficulty in every opportunity; an optimist sees the opportunity in every difficulty". Or, as William James suggests, "Pessimism leads to weakness, optimism to power".

Countless studies support the same conclusion - that optimism really is GREAT for your health! Research shows that "optimists live longer, have better functioning immune systems, cope better with difficult circumstances, and even have healthier babies".

Great news for "natural optimists", but can "natural pessimists" learn to become more optimistic? Martin Seligman, author of *Learned Optimism* certainly thinks so. He began his career studying depression, stress, and anxiety, and discovered that "the optimistic explanatory style acted as a protective factor against the development of depression when faced with difficult circumstances".

In *"10 Troubling Habits of Chronically Unhappy People"*, Dr Travis Bradberry writes that "happiness has much less to do with life circumstances than you might think because much happiness is under your control - the product of your habits and your outlook on life. Psychologists from the University of California who study happiness found that genetics and life circumstances only account for about 50% of a person's happiness. The rest is up to you".

---

41   Carver, Lehman, & Antoni (2003)

42   Howell et al. 2008

Stanford psychologist Carol Dweck suggests that some people have a "fixed mindset" - that they believe that it is not possible to change their capabilities. Other people, however, have a "growth mindset", and believe that they can work towards improving themselves.

Remember, it's not what happens to you that moulds you, but rather it's what you think about what happens to you. It's the *meaning* that you give it, and - at the risk of inciting controversy - it's a choice… So, "**What DO You Think?**"

"Unhappiness can catch you by surprise. So much of your happiness is determined by your habits (in thought and in action) that you have to monitor them closely to make certain that they don't drag you down."

Some habits lead to unhappiness more than others. Dr Travis Bradberry has proposed a "top ten "Troubling Habits of Chronically Unhappy People".

1. Waiting for the future. "Telling yourself, "I'll be happy when…" is one of the easiest habits to fall into, because it puts too much emphasis on circumstances, and improved circumstances don't lead to happiness. Don't spend your time waiting for something that's proven to have no effect on your mood", says Dr Bradberry, suggesting to focus instead on being happy in the present.

2. Spending too much time and effort acquiring *things*. "People living in extreme poverty experience a significant increase in happiness when their financial circumstances improve," says Travis, but research indicates that – for Americans - it plateaus at around the $20 000 annual income mark. The suggestion – supported by UC Berkeley's Science of Happiness programme – is that material things don't make you happy.

   "When you make a habit of chasing things - beyond the disappointment you experience once you get them - you discover that you've gained them at the expense of the things that can make you happy, such as friends, family, and hobbies," suggests Dr Bradberry.

   The theory of *hedonic adaptation* suggests that the novelty associated with new acquisitions will soon wear off. That's not to say that we don't still enjoy them, it's just that the *initial* excitement soon deteriorates… We become accustomed to our new possessions, and then begin to desire more… and then more… It's a vicious cycle. As a society, we are on a constant quest for the next "shiny object".

3. Staying home. "When you feel unhappy, it's tempting to avoid other people," says Dr Bradberry. "This is a huge mistake as socialising - even when you don't enjoy it - is great for your mood. Get out there and mingle, and you'll notice the difference right away."

4. Seeing yourself as a victim. "Unhappy people tend to operate from the position that life is both hard, and out of their control," proposes Dr Bradberry. "This fosters a feeling of helplessness", he continues, and you're therefore unlikely to take action to improve things. "You have control over your future as long as you're willing to take action", claims Dr Bradberry.

5. Pessimism. "Nothing fuels unhappiness quite like pessimism", Travis says, warning that "a pessimistic attitude becomes a self-fulfilling prophecy. If you expect bad things, you're more likely to get bad things. Pessimistic thoughts are hard to shake off until you recognise how illogical they are. Force yourself to look at the *facts*, and you'll see that things are not nearly as bad as they seem", he suggests.

6. Complaining. "Complaining is a self-reinforcing behaviour. By constantly talking - and therefore thinking - about how bad things are, you reaffirm your negative beliefs", says Dr Bradberry. "While talking about what bothers you can actually help you feel better, there's a fine line between complaining being therapeutic and it fueling unhappiness." Besides fueling your misery, complaining also tends to push other people away.

7. Blowing things out of proportion. (*Catastrophising*). "Bad things happen to everybody," proposes Dr Bradberry. "Happy people see them for what they are, whereas unhappy people see anything negative as further evidence that life is out to get them."

8. Sweeping problems under the rug. "Happy people are accountable for their actions", he says. "When they make a mistake, they own it. Unhappy people find problems and mistakes to be threatening, so they try to hide them." The more that you ignore a problem, the more that you start to feel helpless, and then you revert to seeing yourself as a victim.

9. Not improving. "Because unhappy people are pessimists and feel a lack of control over their lives, they tend to sit back and wait for life to happen to them", he claims. "Instead of setting goals, learning, and improving themselves, they just keep plodding along, and then they wonder why things never change." Remember, "If you're not creating, you're disintegrating".

10. Trying to keep up with the Jones's. "Jealousy and envy are incompatible with happiness", says Dr Bradberry, "so if you're constantly comparing yourself with others, it's time to stop".

Gratitude is almost synonymous with optimism, and a number of studies have determined that grateful people are happier, receive more social support, are less stressed, and are less depressed. "Gratitude is not only the greatest of virtues, but the parent of all the others." *Cicero.*

"The feeling of gratitude is associated with less frequent negative emotions and more frequent positive emotions, such as feeling energised, alert, and enthusiastic."[43]

The simple act of giving thanks can have remarkable impact on a person's well-being.[44] "People who are generally grateful report being more agreeable and less narcissistic compared with less grateful people. People who are more grateful also report being happier".[45]

In 2008, Wood and colleagues' study suggested that "grateful people find themselves feeling a sense of belonging and a relative absence of stress and depression". Psychologists have repeatedly shown that *perceptions* are more important than objective reality, and Wood's study suggests that "grateful people possess benign interpretations of themselves, other people, and the world".

"Acts of gratitude require us to admire good characteristics of other people, thereby encouraging us to become closer to them. It has the added benefit of improving mood. In addition, the act of contemplating times in which another person had helped these participants resulted in the participants, themselves, expressing a desire for moral growth, and to help others."[46] "Grateful people have been shown to have greater levels of positive affect, a greater sense of belonging, and lower levels of depression and stress."

In his article, "*How to Be Happier than Anyone You Know*", Deepak Chopra - who I had the privilege of meeting in 2016 - claims that there is really only one true way in which to find what he terms "lasting happiness".

Chopra proposes that "The key lies within a teaching found in India and other wisdom traditions around the world, which says that a person must choose between the path of pleasure and the path of wisdom. The path of pleasure tries to achieve happiness by increasing pleasure and decreasing pain. In many ways, this path is inevitable for almost everyone, because since infancy we've been conditioned to follow it."

He continues, "The natural instinct to maximise pleasure and minimise pain isn't all that natural, however. Near the end of a marathon or a football game, muscles are painfully sore, but athletes are driven by other motivations, such as the desire to win."

43	McCullough, Emmons, & Tsang, 2002
44	Algoe and Haidt, 2009
45	Watkins, Woodward, Stone, & Kolts, 2003
46	Algoe & Haidt, 2009

"Soldiers endure pain out of patriotism; mothers endure the pain of childbirth because they want to have a baby. In a word, higher motivations exist in everyone, for better or for worse."

"A wife who stays with an abusive husband may be motivated by wanting security, feeling hopeless that she can exist on her own, or believing that she must be a loyal spouse", he continues. "In complex ways the simple maxim of being happy through maximising pleasure and minimising pain simply doesn't work."

And Chopra's proposal?

"The first step on the other path, the path of wisdom, is to reject the pointless project of pursuing pleasure, and for most people it's too big a step… We are overwhelmed by mass media, advertising, and pop culture. These combine to reinforce the myth that endless consumerism is the key to happiness, along with a belief that if you distract yourself with TV, movies, video games, restaurants, etc., you will wind up being happy."

"You can spend a lifetime floundering around in this welter of illusions, which is why the path of wisdom, although thousands of years old, remains rare. The path of wisdom seeks to untie the bonds that force us to identify with pleasure-pain. A new identity, based on a secure self, must emerge, and once that is accomplished, the foundation is laid for a higher self", says Chopra. "All of this happens "*in here*", as awareness expands, matures, and transcends old conditioning."

"The methods for walking the path of wisdom are well-known by now: meditation, mindfulness, contemplative practices, and so on", adds Chopra. "Practical things like taking downtime and "*in time*" every day are useful. So is avoiding and reducing stress, attending to symptoms of anxiety and depression, and working on personal issues embedded from past traumas and wounds."

"There's a lot to do that consumer culture ignores and minimises, because consumer culture, including the culture of corporate success, is totally external, relying on the illusion that if you change things "*out there*" (by getting more money, possessions, status, and power), everything "*in here*" will be taken care of. The path of wisdom teaches that the exact opposite is true. Taking care of things "*in here*" is the prerequisite for happiness", proposes Chopra. "The prospect of achieving lifelong happiness begins there, with one simple but profound realisation."

Heather Mcclees, in her article, "*How To Be Happy: 12 Things You Should Do Today*", has her own theory on why we fail to experience happiness. "We live in such a fast-paced world where nothing ever seems to be good enough, fast enough, affordable enough, or attractive enough," she claims.

"Money, jobs, people, flashy things, new tech items, and success take the reigns for what most of us look to at some point to find happiness."

"However, if you think back to the times you were the happiest because of no ulterior motives or external factors, you'd likely see that what truly brought joy to your heart was something much different than what it's now made out to be in the Western world. Happiness exists all the time within us, it's just taking the proper steps to actually find it again," Mcclees proposes.

She suggests that the most lasting habits are created – and the best way to teach yourself something valuable – is through a 12-step process. (She may have a point - our "Thinking Into Results" programme consists of 12 lessons…) Mcclees further divides her 12 steps into four distinct stages.

Mcclees recommends taking each stage - one at a time - on a weekly basis. "Within just one month, you'll find yourself in a place more able to receive and reach happiness, and it will likely come in ways you never expected," she claims.

Stage 1 (Week 1)

1. Heather recommends starting a daily journal, in which you write down (at least) 5 things that you're most grateful for every day - whether it be at the beginning of the day to inspire your day ahead, or at the end of each day to reflect on that day's successes.

   "Maybe it's as simple as a morning sunrise… Whatever it is, write it down. Don't forget the big things we often forget: a house over our head, a job to go to (whether it's your dream job or not), and food in the fridge", she suggests. "Write down at least five things that you're grateful for every single day - no matter how bad you felt your day was. This trains your brain towards gratitude and reverts it away from stress and worry."

2. She also recommends spending time outside - however you can. "Vitamin D is naturally found in the sun's rays and, therefore, natural sunlight is one of the most powerful tools we have that we can use to feel better quickly", she suggests. "It's been proven that those with depression or constant sadness have low Vitamin D levels in their body."

   Since we tend to work indoors all day, and given that there's not exactly an abundance of natural Vitamin D around the UK, try to boost your system with Vitamin D3 supplements – which are easier for the body to absorb than Vitamin D2.

3. Train yourself to think about what you eat - if you think about each individual meal, the bigger picture of healthy nutrition will naturally follow - think of each meal as a piece of the nutritional jigsaw puzzle. Mcclees suggests to "make it a goal to add more fresh foods into your meals, and skip the fast food, and junk foods with sugar".

"Sugar and processed foods, (along with fast foods high in harmful fats), force the body to work harder and also increase insulin levels that can lead to diabetes and imbalanced neurological function. It's been shown that those who eat these type of foods can often feel depressed or moody. Feed your body the right foods, and your brain will thank you in return", she says.

Consider also the fact that the more energy that your body requires to metabolise what you put into it, the less energy that is readily available in reserve for you… Remember this simple fact in your moments of lethargy and procrastination.

Mcclees suggests that you focus on these three tips for the first week - one day at a time. Remember, "how do you eat an elephant"?

"Attempt to be more mindful of these three areas the first week towards your goal to learn how to be happy more easily," says Mcclees. Then, starting the following week - Stage 2 - continue adding steps each week until you've reached all 12 of Mcclees' recommended steps.

Stage 2 (Week 2)

1. Add exercise into your day, at least three times per week. "Daily exercise is best for stimulating brain power and engaging neurotransmitters in the brain that help produce more seratonin and natural endorphins, but even a few times a week will make a difference," claims Mcclees.

2. Over and above your new healthy meals that you're now enjoying, Mcclees recommends adding probiotic-rich foods to your diet. "Probiotics help to repopulate the beneficial bacteria that the body uses to produce more feel-good hormones and to keep you healthy. The brain and gut are directly connected, and it's been shown that those who have a healthy gut feel less stressed and suffer less anxiety and depression," she adds.

3. "Sometimes, we just need to talk to someone who isn't at the office or that's not our parents. If you're not usually one to be social, then make it an attempt to meet with someone this week to chat," suggests Mcclees.

"It's nice to just have a conversation with someone you trust and care about even if you don't talk about anything heavy-hearted. Go for coffee, out to eat, or whatever else you enjoy. Or, ask a friend to join you for one of the workouts you're now doing," she recommends.

"You've taken six do-able steps already, so don't quit!" encourages Mcclees. Continue to build upon the foundation, and you'll find that it's a great way to balance your body and start training your brain to think differently. Remember - maintain the momentum!

Stage 3 (Week 3)

1. "Let go of what does not serve. You might have a so-called friend who puts you down all the time, a family member that doesn't treat you right, or maybe even a boss that takes advantage of you", she says. "Or, maybe none of those apply, and your diet or bad habits are just hurting you in more ways than one."

   "Think about things in your life that cause you pain and distress, even if those things may seem okay and manageable some days", she advises. "Whatever does not serve your future or road to happiness, learn to let it go. Write this down if you need to, and take action to learn to let go of these things."

   "This might mean telling a person who treats you poorly that you need to move on, it might mean changing jobs, and it might just mean overhauling your diet or stopping the late nights out drinking... Whatever it is, start to let go of what does not serve," she suggests.

   "This is one of the most important things you'll do when learning how to be happy for life. It's also a valuable tool you can use for the rest of your life that will help you stay accountable of your life and not engage in things that hurt you rather than help you."

2. Start to manage your finances. "Establishing a healthy relationship with money is important, and it will help alleviate at least one form of stress almost all of us suffer from", she suggests.

   "If you don't make enough money to cover your expenses, then evaluate your spending habits or consider finding additional work. Having a lot of money doesn't equal happiness, but having a manageable hold over your budget whether big or small, will make a huge difference in how you feel each day and will help you to feel less stressed."

   When you're "comfortable" in your relationship with money, your thoughts are unleashed to concentrate on more productive matters. If you are constantly worried about money, then you are simply not *creating...*

   According to a survey carried out by SunTrust Bank - finances are the leading cause of stress in a relationship. "35% of all respondents experiencing relationship stress said money was the primary cause of friction." Just Do It! Fix your finances!

3. "Re-think your relationship with alcohol. "If you have a drink occasionally, it's probably nothing to worry about," she says, "but if you use alcohol to take your mind off things, you're only hurting yourself in the long-run".

    Alcohol decreases mood-boosting hormones, and it's certainly no secret that alcohol also harms the liver.

    When your body works well, you feel so much better. "Start making it a goal to only have one drink per week, or a small glass of red wine with dinner," she suggests.

Stage 4

1. "You've already made it this far, so take joy in the daily things you do. Even if things aren't perfect and you're still trying to make a change from Stage 3, do whatever it takes to enjoy your current life right now", she suggests. "This is important for dealing with hard issues, and it can help make happiness come more easily over the long-term. Take actionable steps to really focus on enjoying your day-to-day life more as you continue making changes."

2. Mcclees also recommends "spending more time on your passions. We have a hard time seeing the possibilities of turning our passions into a career, but they're not always as far out of reach as we might imagine. Spend 30 minutes each day doing something you're passionate about", recommends Mcclees.

    "If you've always wanted to write a book, get up 30 minutes earlier and write. If you love playing music, spend 30 minutes each day playing at home or with friends. Doing something daily (or at least five times per week) that you truly love can lead to becoming better at your passion and possible avenues that could even lead you towards a career doing something you love," she says.

3. Write down 5 goals. (Desired Outcomes, or **DO**'s.)"… Having goals is incredibly important for finding long-term happiness", says Mcclees. "Maybe one goal is to spend more time with your loved ones, or maybe it's to travel to a city you've never been to, or maybe it's to change jobs. Write down 5 goals and start to work towards those goals until you achieve them. These will turn into the things you're grateful for in Stage 1, and you'll see a beautiful cycle start to take place that can lead to more happiness."

"Stage 4 is over! Congrats if you made it this far, but don't stop here… the road to happiness is a journey," Mcclees concludes.

Rather than advocating a four-stage plan, Benson Wong believes that there are certain things that "happy people frequently do to bring happiness into their lives". He lists them in "*11 Things To Do To Start Being Happy Today*", published on *Lifehack*.

i. Wong suggests to *decide* to be happy. "Happiness really is a choice that you have to make. We think that happiness is a byproduct of success, be it a high-paying job, a successful business, raising a family, or achieving a goal", he says. Ever heard of this old saying? "If I have the money, *then* I will do the things I want. Finally, I will be happy. Yet, dissatisfaction and sadness often keep us from doing the things we want," claims Benson, suggesting instead that you "challenge your thinking a bit, and turn it around. I will decide to be happy. Then I will do the things I want. Finally, I will get the money."

ii. Benson also recommends "Practicing gratitude daily". "When you start practicing gratitude, you re-frame your perception of the world", he suggests. "In the past, we tended to look at opportunities and resources as scarce. Practicing gratitude helps us to see limitless abundance. By being grateful for the here and the now - even in the absence of the very thing that you desire - you put yourself in harmony with the good that you desire."

Start moving towards what you want. You can't get to your desires and dreams from where you currently are. You have to come from the place of your dreams. You have to first believe in it in order to see it. One of Stephen Covey's "*7 Habits of Highly Effective People*" is "To begin with the end in mind". Or, as Walt Disney once said, "If you can imagine it, you can achieve it. "If you can dream it, you can do it."

iii. Practice affirmations daily. Affirmations are simply positive, pro-active statements that you say to yourself. Repitition is important when saying your affirmations. We learn through repetition - constant spaced repetition is how you have learned throughout the course of your formal education… "Be emotionally vested when you compose your own affirmations and recite them", says Wong. "They should make you happy, excited, passionate, appreciative, blissful, and in general, feel good. Hence, the name *AFFIRM*ations!"

iv. Meditate daily. "Meditation helps you to keep focus and to stay on track with your gratitude and affirmations", suggests Wong. "Meditation quiets your inner monologue and quells your negative mind-speak… Dismiss any random thoughts that enter your mind, without judgement or reservation. Develop a razor-sharp focus over time, develop the ability to manage the stressors in your life, develop the fortitude to respond to situations in a way of your choosing, and, ultimately, find inner peace," adds Wong.

v. Wong highly recommends harnessing the power of laughter. "Simply laugh more", he suggests. Find things to laugh at daily… "Consider laughing for the sake of laughing. Laugh and you will find yourself actually feeling better. Surround yourself with positive, upbeat people. Laughing also helps you look for the good in things", says Wong.

vi. Enjoy the Little Things. "The ability to express gratitude and joy for the little things is important to achieving more happiness your life," says Benson. "Finding joy in the little things opens your awareness to the abundance in the world. In this case, the abundance of things that bring you joy and bliss."

vii. Exercise Three Times a Week. "I won't tell you how good exercise is, for your mind and your body", teases Wong. "I won't tell you that exercising releases endorphins in your brain. I also won't tell you that exercise leaves you feeling positive, reduces stress, alleviates or staves off depression, and increases your quality of sleep."

"What I will tell you", says Wong, "is that exercise boosts your self-esteem, self-image, and confidence. You feel more energetic and develop a new vitality for life. You will develop a discipline that you can apply to other areas in your life. Safeguard your wealth and your relationships by ensuring that you will be healthy to enjoy them." If you don't look after your body, where else are you going to live?

viii. Spend Quality Time With Your Loved Ones. "Spend quality time with the people you care about", he says. "Life is about serving others and helping to bring value into their lives. We are all fundamentally the same and we all want the same things. When you realise this, you will eventually learn to stop judging others, and start developing your compassion," claims Wong.

ix. Make Time for Yourself. "While it's important to spend time with loved ones", Benson also suggests that "it's important to carve out time for yourself to rest, relax, and recharge your batteries. Do whatever it is that makes you happy. Master your craft. When you master something, your self-esteem and confidence grows. You learn more about yourself while you develop greater focus, intuition, will, reason, awareness, and perception," adds Wong.

x. Stop Blaming Other People. "Happy people learned a long time ago to be pro-active", suggests Benson. "Unhappy people tend to blame others. By being pro-active, you assume the mantle of responsibility for the direction in which your life is heading. Instead of saying to yourself, "I can't do this because of that person, thing, situation, condition, etc.", you start asking yourself, "What can I do?" You shift from looking for excuses why you can't, to reasons why you can."

"People are always blaming their circumstances for what they are. I don't believe in circumstances. The people who get on in this world are the people who get up and look for the circumstances they want, and if they can't find them, make them." *George Bernard Shaw.*

xi. Finally, Wong recommends the practice of starting a "Healing Journal". "A journal acts as your deepest confidant", Wong suggests.

"Verbalising in exact terms that which is frustrating you, and being specific in the role that it has in your life, starts the healing," he proposes. "It is difficult to heal when you only have a vague or general idea of what is troubling you. If you dwell on what you can't change (through a lack of clarity) - when we put all our energy on something negative - we only accelerate its growth. We get more of what we don't want". Remember, "Thoughts become things"...

Big changes come from minor tweaks. "The man who moves a mountain begins by carrying away small stones." *Confucius*. Take action - take the first step on the journey of one thousand miles and remember - maintain the momentum - into acceleration!

Esther Rivers, in her article, "*13 Important Life Lessons I Learnt In My 30s That I'd Like You To Know Earlier In Your 20s*", lists a few suggestions which I believe will help you towards your own happiness, and personal development.

- ✓ "Learn everything you can. As long as we are living we are learning!"
- ✓ "Don't sweat the small stuff".
- ✓ "Don't worry too much about the future. The future is happening regardless".
- ✓ "Do enjoy your youth, and being that age. Enjoy being exactly where you are".
- ✓ "Don't think you know everything. Never think this, no matter what your age".
- ✓ "Hold onto the things you care about. You get to choose what you treasure".
- ✓ "Do put your family first. They will be your greatest allies in life".

Similarly, Larry Alton, in "*7 Practical Tips to Achieve a Positive Mindset*", has a few suggestions towards cultivating a positive mindset.

- ✓ Focus on the good things, however small they may appear to be.
- ✓ Look for the humour in bad situations.
- ✓ Turn failures into lessons. Look for the learning.
- ✓ Transform negative self-talk into positive self-talk.
- ✓ Focus on the present. What in this *exact* moment is happening that is so bad?
- ✓ Find positive friends, mentors and co-workers.

"You need to eliminate the negativity in your life before it consumes you", suggests Alton. "Do what you can to improve others' positivity, and let their positivity affect you in the same way."

Dr Joseph Mercola, in "*9 Quick Tips You Can Do to Get Happy in the Next 30 Minutes*", suggests that "few things are more important than happiness. If you're living day to day simply by going through the motions, you're missing out on living - you're missing out on life."

"It's relatively easy to feel happier", says Dr Mercola. "It's a choice virtually everyone can make, and you can work toward it just like you would any other goal. The first step is making this choice…"

Dr Mercola suggests the following "simple happiness-boosting tips":

- ✓ Get up and get moving.
- ✓ Get outdoors.
- ✓ Reach out to others.
- ✓ Complete a task that you've been avoiding.
- ✓ Organise and de-clutter.
- ✓ Do a Good Deed.
- ✓ Donate Something. Register as an organ donor, donate blood or donate your time or skills where they're needed most.
- ✓ Smile.
- ✓ Learn Something New.

"Feeling happy isn't only a matter of emotional health", Dr Mercola continues. "Positive thoughts and attitudes prompt changes in your body that strengthen your immune system, decrease pain and chronic disease, and relieve stress. Happiness, optimism, life satisfaction, and other positive psychological attributes are associated with a lower risk of heart disease."

In a survey of 5,000 people by the charity *Action for Happiness*, people were asked to score themselves on a scale of 1 to 10, on 10 habits that were scientifically linked to happiness. While all 10 habits were strongly linked to overall life satisfaction, acceptance was the strongest predictor. The survey resulted in the following "*10 Keys to Happier Living*", which together form the acronym GREAT DREAM:

Giving: do things for others
Relating: connect with people
Exercising: take care of your body
Appreciating: notice the world around you
Trying out: keep learning new things

Direction: have goals to look forward to
Resilience: find ways to bounce back
Emotion: take a positive approach
Acceptance: be comfortable with who you are
Meaning: be part of something bigger

In "*10 Simple Steps to a Happier You*", Vanessa King elaborates on the concept of the "*GREAT DREAM*"…

- ✓ *Giving.* "Caring about others is fundamental to our happiness", suggests King. "Helping other people is not only good for them, but it also makes us happier and healthier. Giving also creates stronger connections between people and helps to build a happier society for everyone. So if you want to feel good, do good!" she says.

- ✓ *Relating.* "Relationships are the most important overall contributor to happiness", suggests Vanessa. "People with strong and broad social relationships are happier, healthier and live longer. Close relationships with family and friends provide love, meaning and support, and increase our feelings of self-worth. Broader networks bring a sense of belonging. Strengthening our relationships is essential for happiness".

- ✓ *Exercising.* Our body and our mind are inextricably connected. Being active boosts our happiness as well as our physical health. "It instantly improves our mood and can lift us out of a depression", says King. "We can all do more to be more active each day. We can also boost our well-being by unplugging from technology, getting outside and making sure we get enough sleep!" she says.

- ✓ *Appreciating.* "Ever felt that there must be more to life?" she asks. "There is! And it's right here in front of us. We just need to stop and take notice. Learning to be more mindful and aware can do wonders for our well-being in all areas of life", says King. "It helps us get in tune with our feelings and stops us dwelling on the past or worrying about the future, so we get more out of the day-to-day.

- ✓ *Trying Out.* "Learning affects our well-being in lots of positive ways. It exposes us to new ideas and helps us to stay curious and engaged", adds King. "It also gives us a sense of accomplishment and helps boost our self-confidence and resilience. There are many ways to learn new things", she suggests. "We can share a skill with friends, join a club, learn to sing, play a new sport and so much more."

- ✓ *Direction.* "Feeling good about the future is important for our happiness", Vanessa claims. "We all need goals (*DO's*) to motivate us, and these need to be challenging enough to excite us, but also achievable. If we try to attempt the impossible, it brings unnecessary stress. Choosing ambitious but realistic goals gives our lives direction and brings a sense of accomplishment and satisfaction when we achieve them," she says.

- ✓ *Resilience.* "We all have times of stress, loss, failure or trauma in our lives", says King. "How we respond to these has a big impact on our well-being. We often cannot choose what happens to us, but we can choose our attitude to what happens. In practice it's not always easy, but one of the most exciting findings from recent research is that resilience can be learned."

- *Emotion.* "Positive emotions - such as joy, gratitude, contentment, inspiration and pride - are not just great at the time", she says. "Research shows that regularly experiencing them creates an "upward spiral", helping to build our resources. Although we need to be realistic about life's ups and downs, it helps to focus on the good aspects of any situation - the glass half-full, rather than the glass half-empty", she suggests.

- *Acceptance.* "No one's perfect. But so often we compare our insides to other people's outsides. Dwelling on our flaws - what we're not rather than what we've got - makes it much harder to be happy", says Vanessa. "Learning to accept ourselves, warts and all, and being kinder to ourselves when things go wrong increases our enjoyment of life, our resilience and our well-being. It also helps us to accept others as they are", she adds.

- *Meaning.* "People who have meaning and purpose in their lives are happier, feel more in control and get more out of what they do", says King. "They experience less stress, anxiety and depression. Where do we find "meaning and purpose"? The answers vary for each of us, but they all involve being connected to something bigger than ourselves," concludes King.

Pursuit of Happiness lists the "*7 Habits of Happy People*" as relationships; caring; exercise; flow; spiritual engagement and meaning; strengths and virtues, and positive mindset.

1. Relationships: "People who have one or more close friendships appear to be happier. It doesn't seem to matter if we have a large network of close relationships or not. What seems to make a difference is if - and how often - we co-operate in activities and share our personal feelings, as well as provide support, to a friend or relative. It's not the quantity of our relationships, but the quality that matters".

    Ed Diener and Martin Seligman found that "the most salient characteristics shared by students who were very happy and showed the fewest signs of depression were "their strong ties to friends and family, and commitment to spending time with them".[47] In an independent study, people who were randomly asked about their mood were found to be happiest with their friends, followed by when they were with family members, and least happy if they were alone.

    A study conducted by Stillman *et al* revealed that "loneliness created lower levels of meaning and a greater increase in depression". According to statistics released by Age UK – the UK's largest charity for older people - loneliness can be as harmful for our health as smoking 15 cigarettes a day.[48]

---

47 "The New Science of Happiness," Claudia Wallis, Time Magazine, Jan. 09, 2005.

48 Age UK "Loneliness in Figures"

2. Caring. "People who care for others' well-being through acts of altruism, volunteering, or formation of communal relationships seem to be happier and less depressed. Most people who care for others in a selfless manner do so because of a genuine desire to help and improve the world around them."

"Psychological research has shown that caring has benefits for all involved; people who volunteer or care for others on a consistent basis tend to have better psychological well-being, including fewer depressive symptoms and higher life-satisfaction. Research also shows that individuals who receive social support (caring behaviour) are more protected from disease and even death".[49]

3. Exercise. "Lifestyle factors including exercise, nutrition and sleep are associated with improved mental well-being and lower incidence of depression and anxiety."

4. Flow. "If we are actively involved in trying to reach a goal, or an activity that is challenging but suited to our skills, we experience a joyful state called "flow" - a loss of self-consciousness when you are completely absorbed in an activity – intellectual, professional, or physical. People who regularly experience a lot of flow also develop other positive traits, such as increased concentration, self-esteem, and performance".

A study by Csikszentmihalyi & Csikszentmihalyi showed that "ultimately high-flow kids ended up having greater long-term happiness as well as success in school, social relationships and careers".

5. Spiritual Engagement and Meaning. "Studies demonstrate a close link between religious and spiritual engagement and happiness. Religious organisations provide strong social support from like-minded people, providing various opportunities for socialising, community service and making friends with individuals from a common network."

"Spirituality and prayer also provide people with an opportunity to engage in a meditative act, which has been shown to have a strong link with well-being because it calms the body, reduces stress and anxiety, and also supports positive thinking."

6. Strengths and Virtues. "The work of positive psychologists like Martin Seligman appears to show that the happiest people are those that have discovered their unique strengths (such as persistence and critical thinking) and virtues (such as humanity or justice) and use those strengths and virtues for a purpose that is greater than their own personal goals."

---

[49] Broadhead et al., 1983

"Research indicates that you are most likely to value a job, relationship, hobby or institution that aligns with your core signature strengths and allows you to regularly utilise them."

"One of the best ways to boost your long-term happiness is to use your strengths in new ways and situations, rather than focusing on your weaknesses."

This application of your own unique blend of strengths and virtues is very much aligned with the core principle of positive psychology; which is to focus on your positive attributes or scenarios, rather than the negative aspects of your life. Kristin Neff, a renowned psychologist and a researcher in the field of self-compassion, calls this "self-appreciation". "Whereas self-compassion generally refers to dealing with failures and setbacks, self-appreciation involves celebrating our best qualities", she explains.

"Many people are worried about feeling vain or narcissistic," adds Neff, "but you should appreciate your good qualities the same way you'd praise a friend's positive traits". You don't have to express this gratitude out loud (although you are more than welcome to do so - perhaps in front of the "*Wonder Woman* mirror" again?)

Simply thinking grateful thoughts about yourself should suffice. "When you give yourself that positive boost", she says, "it does help you move forward and helps you to do better in the future."

In "*15 Things You Should Give Up To Be Happy*", Luminita Saviuc - more popularly known as "purposefairy" - compiled a list which, she believes "if you give up on them, will make your life a lot easier and much, much happier".

"We hold on to so many things that cause us a great deal of pain, stress and suffering - and instead of letting them go, instead of allowing ourselves to be stress-free and happy - we cling on to them", claims Saviuc. "Nothing can drag you down if you're not holding on to it". *Tony Robbins.*

i. Give up your need to always be right. "So many of us can't stand the idea of being wrong - even at the risk of ending great relationships or causing a great deal of stress and pain - for us, and for others," says "purposefairy". "Whenever you feel the "urgent" need to jump into a fight over who is right and who is wrong, ask yourself, "Would I rather be right, or would I rather be kind?" *Wayne Dyer.*

ii. Give up your need for control. "Be willing to give up your need to always control everything that happens to you, and around you – like situations, events, or people", says Luminita. "Allow everything and everyone to be just as they are, and you will see how much better that will make you feel."

iii. Give up on blame. "Give up on your need to blame others for what you have or don't have, for what you feel or don't feel. Stop giving your powers away and start taking responsibility for your life," Suggests Saviuc.

iv. Give up your self-defeating self-talk. "Don't believe everything that your mind is telling you - especially if it's negative and self-defeating", she says.

"The mind is a superb instrument if used rightly. Used wrongly, it becomes very destructive". *Eckhart Tolle.*

v. Give up your limiting beliefs. "Give up your beliefs about what you can or can't do, about what is possible or impossible", suggests Luminita. "Nothing can stop the man with the right mental attitude from achieving his goal; nothing on earth can help the man with the wrong mental attitude". *Thomas Jefferson*

vi. Give up complaining. "Give up your constant need to complain about those many things - people, situations or events that make you unhappy, sad or depressed. Nobody can make you unhappy, no situation can make you sad or miserable unless you allow it to," she says.

vii. Give up the luxury of criticism. "Give up your need to criticise things, events or people that are different than you", says "purposefairy". "We are all different, yet we are all the same. We all want to be happy, we all want to love, and to be loved, and we all want to be understood. We all want something, and something is wished by us all".

viii. Give up your need to impress others. "Stop trying so hard to be something that you're not, just to make others like you", suggests Saviuc. "The moment you take off all your masks - the moment you accept and embrace the real you - you will find people will be drawn to (the real) you, effortlessly".

ix. Give up your resistance to change. "Change will help you move from A to B. Change will help you make improvements in your life and also the lives of those around you", she adds. "Change is inevitable. Personal growth is a choice". *Bob Proctor.*

x. Give up labels. "Stop labeling those things, people or events that you don't understand, as being weird or different,", she says. Minds - like parachutes - work best when open. "The highest form of ignorance is when you reject something you don't know anything about." *Dr Wayne Dyer.*

xi. Give up on your fears. "Fear is just an illusion, it doesn't exist - you created it. It's all in your mind", suggests Luminita.

If you look at the acronym for F.E.A.R. - *False Expectations Appearing Real* - it may help you to realise that fear is essentially just your reptilian brain projecting past experiences onto future events, in an attempt to preserve your comfort zone, or "thermostat". "The only thing we have to fear, is fear itself". *Franklin D. Roosevelt*

xii. Give up your excuses. "Send them packing, and - in true *"Apprentice"* style - tell them "they're fired". "We limit ourselves because of the many excuses we use", suggests Saviuc. "Instead of growing and improving ourselves, we get stuck, lying to ourselves, using all kind of excuses - that 99.9% of the time are not even real."

xiii. Give up the past. "The present moment is all that you have, and all you will ever have. The past that you are longing for - the past that you are dreaming about - was ignored by you when it was the present," proposes Luminita. "Stop deluding yourself. Be present in everything you do and enjoy life. Life is a journey not a destination. Have a clear vision for the future, prepare yourself, but always be present in the now."

xiv. Give up attachment. "The moment you detach yourself from all things, you become so peaceful, so tolerant, so kind, and so serene", she says. "(That doesn't mean that you give up your love for them - because love and attachment have nothing to do with one another. Attachment comes from a place of fear, while love… well, real love is pure, kind, and selfless. Where there is love there can not be fear, and because of that, attachment and love cannot co-exist.) You will get to a place where you will be able to understand all things without even trying."

xv. Give up living your life to other people's expectations. "Way too many people are living their lives according to what others think is best for them", says Luminita, adding that "they live their lives according to what their parents think is best for them, to what their friends, their enemies and their teachers, their government and the media think is best for them. They are so busy pleasing everybody, living up to other people's expectations, that they lose control over their own lives."

"They forget what makes them happy, what they want, what they need… And eventually they forget about themselves. You have one life - this one right now - you must live it, own it, and especially don't let other people's opinions distract you from your path," she concludes.

"If I want to be free, I've got to be me. Not the me I think you think I should be. Not the me I think she thinks I should be. Not the me I think they think I should be. If I want to be free, I've got to be me". *Bill Gove.*

So what is the missing piece with regards to happiness and optimism? Why not try practicing gratitude to complete the puzzle…

For example, in *"How to Foster Gratitude in Schools"*, published on *"Greater Good"* - the online magazine of *The Greater Good Science Centre* at The University of California, Berkeley - Giacomo Bono and Jeffrey Froh write that "... Teens who had high levels of gratitude when entering high school had less negative emotions and depression and more positive emotions, life satisfaction, and happiness four years later when they were finishing high school. They also had more hope and a stronger sense of meaning in life".

In *"Why Gratitude Is Good"* - another *Greater Good* publication - Robert Emmons, regarded as the world's leading scientific expert on gratitude, writes that "We've studied more than one thousand people, from ages eight to 80, and found that people who practice gratitude consistently report a host of benefits."

According to Emmons, these benefits include higher levels of positive emotions; being more alert, alive, and awake; more joy and pleasure; more optimism and happiness; stronger immune systems; lower blood pressure; better sleep patterns; being more helpful, generous, and compassionate; being more forgiving; being more outgoing, and feeling less lonely and isolated.

Emmons also proposes that "people are actually more successful at reaching their goals when they consciously practice gratitude".

"When we ask people to identify six personal goals on which they want to work over the next 10 weeks - academic, spiritual, social, or health-related goals, like losing weight - we find that study participants randomly assigned to keep a gratitude journal exert more effort toward those goals than participants who aren't made to practice gratitude. The grateful group makes 20% more progress toward their goals than the non-grateful group - but they don't stop there. They report still continuing to strive harder toward their goals."

Emmons chooses to highlight four reasons as to why he believes that gratitude is good:

i. "Gratitude allows us to celebrate the present: It magnifies positive emotions. Research on emotion shows that positive emotions wear off quickly. Our emotional systems like newness. They like novelty. We adapt to positive life circumstances so that before too long, the new car, the new spouse, the new house - they don't feel so new and exciting anymore," proposes Emmons.

"Gratitude makes us appreciate the value of something, and when we appreciate the value, we extract more benefits from it; we're less likely to take it for granted. Gratitude allows us to participate more in life. We notice the positives more, and that magnifies the pleasures you get. Instead of adapting to goodness, we celebrate it. We spend so much time watching things - movies, computer screens, sports - but with gratitude we become greater participants in our lives as opposed to spectators," suggests Emmons.

ii. "Gratitude blocks toxic, negative emotions, such as envy, resentment, regret - emotions that destroy our happiness", Robert adds. "You cannot feel envious and grateful at the same time. They're incompatible feelings. If you're grateful, you can't resent someone for having something that you don't. People who have high levels of gratitude have low levels of resentment and envy."

iii. "Grateful people are more stress resistant. A number of studies show that in the face of serious trauma, adversity, and suffering, if people have a grateful disposition, they'll recover more quickly. Gratitude gives people a perspective from which they can interpret negative life events and help them guard against post-traumatic stress and lasting anxiety," says Emmons.

iv. "Grateful people have a higher sense of self-worth. When you're grateful, you have the sense that someone else is looking out for you - you notice a network of relationships of people who are responsible for helping you to get to where you are right now. Once you start to recognise the contributions that other people have made to your life", adds Emmons, "once you realise that other people have seen the value in you - then you can transform the way that you see yourself".

Emmons, however, is also quick to point out that you will almost certainly encounter challenges to gratitude along the way… "Just because gratitude is good doesn't mean it's always easy. Practicing gratitude can be at odds with some deeply ingrained psychological tendencies", he warns.

"One is the "*self-serving bias*". When good things happen to us, we attribute them to something we did, but when bad things happen, we blame other people or circumstances. Gratitude really goes against the self-serving bias because when we're grateful, we give credit to other people for our success. Yes, we accomplished some of it ourselves, but we widen our range of attribution to also say, "Well, my parents gave me this opportunity". Or, "I had teachers. I had mentors. I had siblings, peers - other people assisted me along the way." That's very different from a self-serving bias".

Emmons continues, "Gratitude also goes against our need to feel in control of our environment. Sometimes with gratitude you just have to accept life as it is and be grateful for what you have."

"Finally, gratitude contradicts the hypothesis which suggests that we get what we deserve in life. Good things happen to good people, bad things happen to bad people. But it doesn't always work out that way. Bad things happen to good people and vice versa.

With gratitude comes the realisation that we sometimes get *more* than we deserve, which goes against a message we get a lot in our contemporary culture: that we deserve the good fortune that comes our way, that we're *entitled* to it. If you deserve everything, if you're entitled to everything, it makes it a lot harder to be grateful for anything", says Emmons.

Emmons concludes with a few suggestions about how to cultivate gratitude. "… Despite the fact that I've been studying gratitude for eleven years and know all about it, I still find that I have to put a lot of conscious effort into practicing gratitude", he admits. "In fact, my wife says, "How is it that you're supposed to be this huge expert on gratitude? You're the least grateful person I know!"

"It's easy to lapse into the negativity mindset, but these are some of the specific steps I like to recommend for overcoming the challenges to gratitude," says Emmons.

Emmons' first suggestion is to keep a gratitude journal. "This can mean listing just five things for which you're grateful every week. This practice works because it consciously, intentionally focuses our attention on developing more grateful thinking and on eliminating ungrateful thoughts."

"It helps guard against taking things for granted; instead, we see gifts in life as new and exciting. I do believe that people who live a life of pervasive thankfulness really do experience life differently than people who cheat themselves out of life by not feeling grateful."

"Practice counting your blessings on a regular basis, maybe first thing in the morning, or in the evening", suggests Emmons. "What are you grateful for today?" he asks. "You don't have to write them down on paper. You can also use concrete reminders to practice gratitude, which can be particularly effective in working with children, who aren't abstract thinkers like adults are."

Emmons also suggests that it's important to "think outside of the box when it comes to gratitude. Mother Theresa talked about how grateful she was to the people she was helping in the slums of Calcutta, because they enabled her to grow and deepen her spirituality. That's a very different way of thinking about gratitude - gratitude for what we can give as opposed to what we receive. But that can be a very powerful way, I think, of cultivating a sense of gratitude."

Jeremy Adam Smith - producer and editor of *The Greater Good Science Centre*'s website - in "*Six Habits of Highly Grateful People*" presents some practical advice regarding gratitude.

"Gratitude doesn't make problems and threats disappear", says Smith. "We can lose jobs, we can be attacked on the street, we can get sick. I've experienced all of those things. I remember those harrowing times at unexpected moments: My heart beats faster, my throat constricts. My body wants to hit something or run away, one or the other. But there's nothing to hit, nowhere to run. The threats are indeed real, but at that moment, they exist only in memory or imagination. I am the threat; it is me who is wearing myself out with worry," adds Smith.

"That's when I need to turn on the gratitude", Jeremy continues. "If I do that enough, the psychological research suggests that gratitude might just become a habit. What will that mean for me? It means that I increase my chances of psychologically surviving hard times, that I stand a chance to be happier in the good times. I'm not ignoring the threats; I'm appreciating the resources and people that might help me face those threats," he adds.

Smith provides some tips "for how you and I can become one of those fantastically grateful people," (in his words.)

- Once in a while, they think about death and loss. "Contemplating endings really does make you more grateful for the life you currently have. For example, when Araceli Friasa and colleagues asked people to visualise their own deaths, their gratitude measurably increased. Similarly, when Minkyung Koo and colleagues asked people to envision the sudden disappearance of their romantic partners from their lives, they became more grateful to their partners."

  When you find yourself taking a good thing for granted, try giving it up for a little while... Researchers Jordi Quoidbach and Elizabeth Dunn had 55 people eat a piece of chocolate -and then instructed some of those people to resist chocolate for a week, and others to binge on chocolate if they wanted. They left a third group to their own devices. The people who abstained from the chocolate were measured as the happiest, with the "chocolate bingers" the least happy

- They take the time to smell the roses. "And the coffee, the bread baking in the oven, the aroma of a new car - whatever gives them pleasure," adds Smith. "Loyola University psychologist Fred Bryant finds that savoring positive experiences makes them stickier in your brain, and increases their benefits to your psyche - and the key, he argues, is expressing gratitude for the experience. Appreciation and gratitude go hand-in-hand."

- They take the good things as gifts, not birthrights. "What's the opposite of gratitude?" asks Smith. *Entitlement.* "If we feel that that we are owed things from others, then we have no reason to feel thankful", writes Robert Emmons. "Counting blessings will be ineffective because grievances will always outnumber gifts".

"The antidote to entitlement", argues Emmons, "is to see that we did not create ourselves - we were created, if not by evolution, then by God; or if not by God, then by our parents. We are never truly self-sufficient. Humans need other people to grow our food and heal our injuries; we need love, and for that we need family, partners, friends, and pets. Seeing with grateful eyes requires that we see the web of interconnection in which we alternate between being givers and receivers", writes Emmons. "The humble person says that life is a gift to be grateful for, not a right to be claimed."

- They're grateful to people, not just things. "People will glow in gratitude", suggests Smith. "Saying "thank you" can strengthen social bonds - in part by deepening our understanding of how we're interconnected with other people."

- They mention the pancakes. "Grateful people are habitually specific", suggests Smith. "They don't say, "I love you because you're just so wonderful!" "Instead, the really skilled grateful person will say: "I love you for the pancakes you make when you see that I'm hungry, and the way you massage my feet after work even when you're really tired, and how you give me hugs when I'm sad so that I'll feel better!"

This makes the expression of gratitude feel more authentic. It demonstrates that the thanker isn't just going through the motions. "The richest "thank you's" will acknowledge intentions ("when you see I'm hungry"), costs ("...even when you're really tired"), and they'll describe the value of benefits received ("...so that I'll feel better".)

- They thank outside the box. "But let's get real: here's who the really tough-minded grateful person thanks: the boyfriend who dumped her, the homeless person who asked for change, the boss who laid him off," says Smith.

"No one *"feels"* grateful that he or she has lost a job or a home or good health or has taken a devastating hit on his or her retirement portfolio," adds Dr Emmons. "If we're willing and able to look," he argues, "we can find a reason to feel grateful, even to people who have harmed us. We can thank that boyfriend for being brave enough to end a relationship that wasn't working; the homeless person for reminding us of our advantages and vulnerability; the boss, for forcing us to face new challenges", he adds.

"Life is suffering. No amount of positive thinking exercises will change this truth", writes Emmons in his *Greater Good* article "*How Gratitude Can Help You Through Hard Times*". "So telling people simply to buck up, count their blessings, and remember how much they still have to be grateful for can certainly do much harm."

"Processing a life experience through a grateful lens does not mean denying negativity. Instead, it means realising the power you have to transform an obstacle into an opportunity. It means reframing a loss into a potential gain, recasting negativity into positive channels for gratitude", Emmons suggests.

Returning to "*How to Foster Gratitude in Schools*", Giacomo Bono and Jeffrey Froh write that "feeling grateful motivates adolescents to help others and use their strengths to contribute to society. We have solid scientific evidence that these practices boost students' moods, broaden their thinking, and energise greater learning."

"Perhaps most of all, gratitude is a social emotion - it brings people together. By promoting gratitude in schools, we'll foster these kinds of connections on a much wider scale, helping both students and schools to thrive."

From schools, students and teachers, to the workplace…

In "*5 Ways to Cultivate Gratitude at Work*", also published on *Greater Good*, Jeremy Adam Smith writes that "gratitude gives employees a tool to transform an obstacle into an opportunity".

Adam Smith suggests a series of questions to help people to recover from difficult experiences, which he has adapted for the workplace environment (but which I believe can be beneficial in almost all walks of life):

- What lessons did the experience teach us?
- Can we find ways to be thankful for what happened to us now, even though we were not at the time that it happened?
- What ability did the experience draw out of us that surprised us?
- Are there ways that we have become better because of it?
- Has the experience removed an obstacle that previously prevented us from feeling grateful?

There is *always* opportunity for learning in every day, as long as we are open to the concept. Choose to use today to learn to be more happy, optimistic and grateful…

Every day's a school day!

"If you want others to be happy, practice compassion. If you want to be happy, practice compassion." *The Dalai Lama.*

Mindfulness and Meditation:

"We are what we think.
All that we are arises with our thoughts.
With our thoughts we make our world." *Buddha.*

Mindfulness is defined as "a mental state achieved by focusing one's awareness on the present moment, while calmly acknowledging and accepting feelings, thoughts, and bodily sensations".

I believe that the easiest - and perhaps simplest - way to benefit from the essence of Mindfulness is through implementing the acronym *W.A.I.T.* (What Am I Thinking?) Wait, pause in the moment, and acknowledge the present - aware of your feelings, thoughts and sensations. What are you thinking? (And by logical extension, what are you feeling, and experiencing?) Accept and embrace them - "live in the now". "Every moment you live in the past is a moment you waste in the present." *Tony Robbins.*

All too often, we allow the regrets of our past to cloud our present. *Now* is all that we have - the past is gone, the future doesn't yet exist. The present is a gift - that's why it's called "*the present*". If we allow our regrets, and our projected (future) fears to rule our present, we will never fully live life, truly appreciative of what we have.

"It's being here now that's important. There's no past and there's no future. Time is a very misleading thing. All there is ever, is the now. We gain experience from the past, but we can't relive it; and we can hope for the future, but we don't know if there is one." *George Harrison.*

Again, it all distils down to comparison - "the thief of joy". The more that we want what we haven't got - the more that we are envious of others who have it, the less we appreciate all that we do have. The more that we dwell on what we *could* have done, what we *should* have done, what *might* happen tomorrow - the less we appreciate the moment in which we are - the here and now! Worry is essentially wasting today's time cluttering up tomorrow's opportunities with yesterday's troubles.

"I've had a lot of worries in my life, most of which never happened." *Mark Twain.*

An enhanced awareness of the present moment can help us to appreciate our environment, and to better understand ourselves, and our behaviour. We begin to savour experiences and things that we had previously simply taken for granted. "It is not happy people who are thankful. It is thankful people who are happy".

An important part of mindfulness is reconnecting with our bodies and the sensations they experience. This means waking up to the sights, sounds, smells and tastes of the present moment. That might be something as simple as the feel of a banister as we walk upstairs, or the sensation of the grass or the carpet under our feet.

Another important part of mindfulness is an awareness of our thoughts and feelings as they happen moment to moment. It's about allowing ourselves to see the present moment clearly. When we do that, it can positively change the way we see ourselves and our lives.

"Mindfulness allows us to become more aware of the stream of thoughts and feelings that we experience" - says Professor Mark Williams, former director of *The Oxford Mindfulness Centre* - "and to see how we can become entangled in that stream in ways that are not helpful".

"This lets us stand back from our thoughts and start to see their patterns. Gradually, we can train ourselves to notice when our thoughts are taking over and realise that thoughts are simply "mental events" that do not have to control us."

"Most of us have issues that we find hard to let go, and mindfulness can help us deal with them more productively. We can ask: "Is trying to solve this by brooding about it helpful, or am I just getting caught up in my thoughts?" he asks. "Awareness of this kind also helps us notice signs of stress or anxiety earlier and helps us deal with them better."

"Even as we go about our daily lives, we can notice the sensations of things, the food we eat, the air moving past the body as we walk," says Professor Williams. "This may sound very small, but it has huge power to interrupt the "autopilot" mode we often engage day to day, and to give us new perspectives on life. Trying new things, such as sitting in a different seat in meetings or going somewhere new for lunch, can also help you notice the world in a new way."

"Some people find it very difficult to practice mindfulness. As soon as they stop what they're doing, lots of thoughts and worries crowd in," says Professor Williams. "It might be useful to remember that mindfulness isn't about making these thoughts go away, but rather about seeing them as mental events."

"Imagine standing at a bus station and seeing "thought buses" coming and going without having to get on them and be taken away", suggests Williams. "This can be very hard at first, but with gentle persistence it is possible. Some people find that it is easier to cope with an over-busy mind if they are doing gentle yoga or walking."

Mindfulness advocates how to change the negative thought patterns and emotions that accompany stress, and how to recognise reactions to stress. Mindfulness demonstrates more effective ways to respond to stressful situations, and illustrates how to tap into your own inner resources to discover a sense of greater health and well-being.

Mindfulness is also recommended by the National Institute for Health and Care Excellence (*NICE*) as a way to prevent depression in people who have suffered from three or more bouts of depression.

Furthermore, an ICM (a market research agency) survey of General Practitioners in the UK found that...

- ✓ 72% of GPs think that it would be "helpful for their patients with mental health problems to learn Mindfulness skills".
- ✓ 66% of GPs say that they would "support a public information campaign to promote the potential health benefits of Mindfulness meditation".
- ✓ 64% of GPs think that it would be "helpful to receive training in Mindfulness skills themselves".

Still not convinced?

Participants in the 2013 *Penn Medicine Programme for Mindfulness* foundation courses reported the following significant changes after completing the (8-week) Mindfulness foundation course:

- ✓ A 29% Reduction in Confusion
- ✓ A 34% Reduction in Anxiety
- ✓ A 39% Reduction in Depression
- ✓ A 39% Reduction in Anger
- ✓ A 30% Increase in Energy
- ✓ A 40% Decrease in Fatigue

"A whole new branch of psychology is dedicated to mindfulness, but it boils down to this: Negative thoughts and insecurities pop up like pimples. And, like pimples, picking at them - even if you mean to discredit and burst that negative bubble - ultimately makes it worse. So, mindfulness practice teaches you to treat thoughts as tools. Use and strengthen the ones you need; discard the ones you don't". *Manpreet Singh*.

"I always find that confidence starts with mindfulness. A confidence issue is usually a symptom of an underlying fear. This fear is often not a conscious fear, but something lurking beneath the surface. If you can get to a point where you welcome failure as much as you welcome success, both being essential elements of life, then it's hard not to have confidence." Bob Buch, CEO of *Socialwire*.

Do you currently incorporate a meditation or other mindfulness practice in your day? Tony Robbins channels his energy with a ten minute priming exercise every morning. Others, like Brendon Burchard, for example, use breathing and movement practices to centre, reflect and strengthen - to "win the morning". In fact, most of these practices have been around for millennia. "They improve overall health, combat depression, lower blood pressure, help with pain management and reduce anxiety."

"So what exactly makes them so powerful? And how can you use these practices in today's world? To put it another way, what if you want to discover and change the patterns of behaviour that drive you, not just be content with where you are right now?"

Jill Suttie, in "*My Trouble With Mindfulness*", relates the example of an experimental study led by Paul Condon of Northeastern University, in which participants - following an eight-week mindfulness meditation course - were tested on their likelihood to assist someone in need. While seated in a full waiting room (with no empty seats), the participants observed a woman - who was actually collaborating with the researchers - on crutches and in obvious pain, enter the room and lean against a wall.

The researchers wanted to see whether "the participants trained in mindfulness would be more likely to get up and offer her their seat, even though two other people seated in the room (also collaborating) ignored her. What they found was that participants who'd attended the meditation class got up five times more often than those who hadn't. The meditation course made them more likely to take compassionate action," suggests Suttie.[50]

"Mindfulness training may also help people to cope better with typical barriers to compassionate action, such as experiencing strong emotions - like fear, sadness, or anger - when confronted with the suffering of others, or stressed", says Rick Hanson - neuropsychologist and best-selling author of "*Buddha's Brain*".

"Literally hundreds of studies have found that mindfulness meditation training - such as *Mindfulness-Based Stress Reduction*, the programme pioneered by Jon Kabat-Zinn - helps to reduce stress and improve distress-tolerance", adds Hanson.

One of the most notable benefits of mindfulness is that it improves focus. According to Daniel Goleman's book, "*Focus*", "these attention skills are important for excelling at work, because focus is useful for sticking with problems, navigating relationships with colleagues, understanding your own motivations, avoiding emotional reactivity, and fostering innovation".

---

[50] "My Trouble With Mindfulness," by Jill Suttie

In a study conducted by researchers at the University of Washington, HR professionals were trained in either mindfulness meditation or relaxation skills over an eight-week period and then tested on their ability to handle complex multitasking. The mindfulness training participants "remained more on task, with less task-switching, and reported better moods, than those who underwent relaxation training or were on a waiting list to receive training". This suggests that mindfulness enhances your ability to focus more effectively on a task.

A study conducted by Erik Dane and Bradley Brummel measured service workers in the restaurant business, with regards to their "mindfulness levels, engagement at work, and their commitment to staying at their present job, with their job performance independently assessed by managers".

The study showed "a positive correlation between workplace mindfulness and job performance that held true even when accounting for worker engagement, meaning that even among workers who all seemed engaged in their jobs, the mindful ones performed better. They also found evidence linking mindfulness to a worker's lower intent to leave the job, although this was not independent of how engaged that worker was in his or her job."[51]

The University of Wisconsin trained non-meditators in mindful attention meditation over a five-week period. Their brain activity patterns were recorded using an EEG.[52] "Mindful meditators who practiced on average five to 16 minutes a day saw significant, positive changes in their brain patterns - suggesting a greater orientation toward positive emotions and connections with others - as compared to those on a waiting list for the training."

In an independent study, participants were taught mindful breathing techniques for a mere 20 minutes over a three-day period. They were then tested to evaluate "how reactive they were to mild and stronger" electrical shocks. After the mindfulness training, the participants "experienced significantly less anxiety, less suffering from pain, and less reactivity to the pain relative to where they were beforehand".

"Mindfulness has been studied to see if it helps with pain, immune response function, over-eating, drug addiction, pregnancy, depression, obsessive-compulsive disorder. You name it, mindfulness has been tried, either to augment standard treatments or to replace them".

---

51   "My Trouble With Mindfulness," by Jill Suttie

52   An electroencephalogram (EEG) is a recording of brain activity

"Whether it's astronauts or professional athletes, more and more elite performers are appreciating the power of mindfulness and meditation training," says neuropsychologist Rick Hanson, who adds that mindfulness teachings have also "infiltrated settings as diverse as prisons, marine boot camps, and Fortune 500 companies".[53]

Pick a practice that suits you - maybe a body scan practice if you have trouble connecting with your body, a loving-kindness meditation if you are suffering from a lot of negative thoughts, or a simple breath meditation if you are looking for calming stillness or a greater understanding of how your mind works. Begin with a practice that meets your needs, and you'll be more inclined to do more of it, and thereby benefit more from it.

In *"Which Kind of Mindfulness Meditation is Right for You?"*, Hooria Jazaieri asks, "There are many different forms of meditation. Which one is best for you?"

"A study published in *Mindfulness,* observed 141 undergraduates over the span of three weeks - separating them into three groups that each engaged in one of these forms of mindfulness meditation:

1. The sitting meditation, which involves sitting in a relaxed but erect posture and cultivating awareness of each breath you take.
2. The body scan, which entails methodically paying attention to each part of your body, from top to bottom.
3. Mindful yoga, the practice of deliberate, intentional movement.

The participants were asked to answer a series of questions – before and after the three-week period - measuring depression, anxiety, stress, emotion regulation, rumination, mindfulness (observing, describing, non-judging, non-reactivity, and acting with awareness), well-being, and self-compassion.

"In all three groups, the participants reported reduced rumination, as well as greater self-compassion and well-being. These results echo decades of research showing that mindfulness practices improve physical and mental health."

Then the researchers looked at each of the three groups individually and compared those results to the other two groups. They observed the following differences:

- ✓ The yoga practice improved well-being more than the sitting meditation and body scan, which the authors argue may be linked to "longstanding evidence that physical exercise promotes psychological health" and well-being, rather than specifically mindfulness."

---

[53] "My Trouble With Mindfulness," by Jill Suttie

- ✓ The yoga and sitting meditation improved emotion regulation more so than in the body scan group. The authors note that sitting meditation "involves explicit instructions to observe strong emotions without holding on or trying to get rid of them, simply allowing them to be as they are."

- ✓ Members of the sitting meditation group were significantly less judgmental towards their own feelings and experiences than the other two groups, which was attributed to the sitting meditation's "more explicit instructions against judging one's experiences".

So which mindfulness practice would be best for you?

"If you find yourself overwhelmed by anger against yourself or others, sitting meditation sounds like the one for you. If you frequently feel tired or sick, yoga is worth a try. While the body scan did not seem to yield as many benefits as the other two practices, it's possible that body scan paired with sitting meditation or yoga could be helpful."

So now that you've settled on the best form of mindfulness for yourself, why not include children into your routine? Or find the practice that would work best for them? They don't have to be yours, but children can definitely also benefit from the practice of mindfulness...

In *"Mindful Kids, Peaceful Schools"*, Jill Suttie discusses the merits of mindfulness in schools, and the impact that mindfulness is having on "the youth of today"...

Steve Reidman, a fourth grade teacher at Toluca Lake Elementary School in Los Angeles, had been "experiencing problems with classroom management", writes Suttie. "Conflicts on the playground were escalating and affecting his students' ability to settle down and concentrate in class." When he shared his problems with a personal friend, Susan Kaiser – a mindfulness educator - she offered to teach them mindfulness, which she had previously taught to children as a volunteer at a local club.

"I noticed a difference right away," says Reidman. "There was less conflict on the playground, less test anxiety - just the way the kids walked into the classroom was different. Our state test scores also went up that year"

Kaiser's curriculum was inspired by the work of Jon Kabat-Zinn, founder of *The University of Massachusetts Medical School's Centre for Mindfulness*. Kabat-Zinn was one of the first scientists to recognise that mindfulness meditation might have healing benefits for adult patients suffering from chronic pain. He developed what he termed Mindfulness-Based Stress Reduction (*MBSR*).

"Kabat-Zinn's programme has been found to reduce not only chronic pain but also high blood pressure and cholesterol levels. Evidence also suggests *MBSR* can help improve one's ability to handle stress and alleviate depression, anxiety, post-traumatic stress, and eating disorders."

At *The University of British Columbia*, psychologist Kimberly Schonert-Reichl and graduate student, Molly Stewart Lawlor, conducted a study in six Vancouver schools, where the students were "instructed in mindful awareness techniques and positive thinking skills, then tested for behavioural changes, social and emotional competence, moral development, and mood".

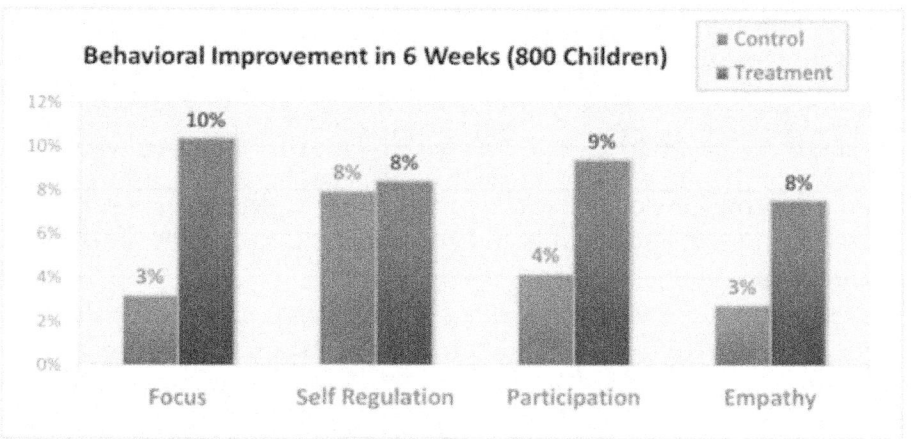

Courtesy of Mindful Schools (www.mindfulschools.org)

"In one classroom, the children went from having the most behavioural problems in the school - measured by the number of visits to the principal's office - to having zero behavioural problems, after only two to three weeks of instruction," says Schonert-Reichl. "These children were less aggressive, less oppositional toward teachers, and more attentive in class".

"Those who received the mindfulness training also reported feeling more positive emotion and optimism, and seemed more introspective than children who were on a waiting list for the training. "It's important to do research like this because kids need something to cope with all the pressures at school," says Schonert-Reichl. "If we don't find something to help them, there are going to be tremendous health costs for these kids down the road."

"Similar research was carried out by Susan Smalley, a geneticist and the director of the new *Mindful Awareness Research Centre* at the University of California, Los Angeles. Smalley suggests that "a modified version of MBSR can help teenagers with Attention Deficit Hyperactivity Disorder (ADHD) by reducing their anxiety and increasing their ability to focus".

A survey of mindfulness programmes by *The Garrison Institute* in New York showed that many schools are adopting mindfulness training because the techniques are easy to learn and can help children become "more responsive and less reactive, more focused and less distracted, (and) more calm and less stressed". The Garrison report also found that mindfulness "can create a more positive learning environment", where children are "primed to pay attention".

As actress Goldie Hawn says, "Mindfulness gives kids a tool for understanding how their brain works, for having more self-control. If we know it also has the potential to decrease stress, decrease depression, and increase health and happiness - wouldn't it be selfish to withhold it from children?"

"Meditation brings wisdom; lack of meditation leaves ignorance. Know well what leads you forward and what holds you back and choose the path that leads to wisdom." *Buddha*

"Suppose you read about a pill that you could take once a day to reduce anxiety and increase your contentment. Would you take it? Suppose further that the pill has a great variety of side effects, all of them good: increased self-esteem, empathy, and trust; it even improves memory. Suppose, finally, that the pill is all natural and costs nothing. Now would you take it? The pill exists. It's called meditation". *Jonathan Haidt, "The Happiness Hypothesis"*.

"Meditation allows you to de-clutter your mind of distracting thoughts and negative emotions." Imagine a pool of water. You throw some pebbles into the pool and the water becomes murky. The ripples collide and overlap and you strain to distinguish what lies beneath. These are the thoughts in your mind. "Muddying the water and consuming your thought processes so frequently that you never make time to let the water be still, to be calm."

"If the mind is muddy like the murky pool, the only way for us to really think clearly is to be quiet long enough to let the silt fall. To meditate. One of the beautiful things about meditation is that there is no one, single way to achieve a meditative state. Exploring Meditation simply means to go within."

Meditation has been shown to decrease stress, increase levels of happiness, improve your quality of life, and increase the levels of grey matter in the brain. Meditation has also been credited with making people more compassionate, lowering blood pressure, and increasing memory skills.

Research conducted by Sara Lazar, PhD - of *The Massachusetts General Hospital Psychiatric Neuro-Imaging Research Programme* - suggests that "people are not just feeling better because they are spending time relaxing. Although the practice of meditation is associated with a sense of peacefulness and physical relaxation, practitioners have long claimed that meditation also provides cognitive and psychological benefits that persist throughout the day."

"One of the most significant changes to our brains when we meditate, is that meditation allows the brain to stop processing the otherwise incessant barrage of external sensory stimuli." (Remember the 50,000 – 70,000 each and every day?)

For the study, *MRI*[54] images were taken of the brain structure of 16 research participants two weeks before - and after - they took part in the 8-week Mindfulness-Based Stress Reduction (*MBSR*) Programme at *The University of Massachusetts Centre for Mindfulness*. MRI brain images were also taken of a control group, over a similar period of time.

Beta waves generally indicate a processing of information - when beta waves decrease, we can observe a decrease in the volume of information that is being processed. Using *MRI* images, we can see how and where beta waves are decreasing the most. This is reflected in the image below, reproduced courtesy of Massachusetts General Hospital.

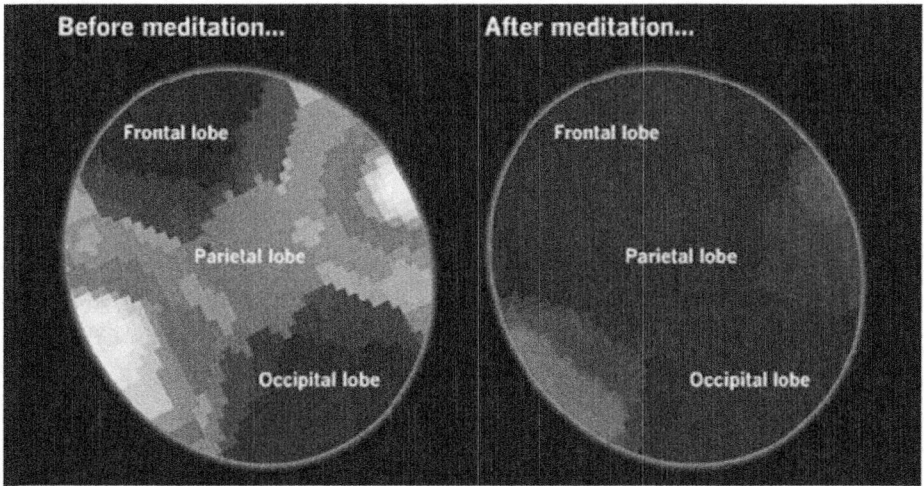

- The Frontal lobe - contains most of the dopamine-sensitive neurons in the cerebral cortex. Is associated with reward, attention, short-term memory tasks, planning, self-conscious awareness, emotions, and motivation.

- The Parietal lobe - integrates sensory information (touch, temperature and pain), and also includes spatial sense, and navigation.

- The Occipital lobe - the visual processing centre of the brain.

The *MRI* scans of the mindfulness-meditation candidates "reflected an increase in the grey matter concentration within the left hippocampus, the posterior cingulate cortex, the temporo-parietal junction, and the cerebellum - the cerebral regions associated with learning and memory, and the regulation of emotions."

Britta Hölzel - lead author on the paper, and a research fellow at Massachusetts General Hospital, and Giessen University in Germany - says, "It is fascinating to see the brain's plasticity and that, by practicing meditation, we can play an active role in changing the brain and can increase our well-being and quality of life."

Researchers at the Universities of Washington and Arizona found that "eight weeks of Mindfulness Meditation training enabled managers to multi-task without feeling as much stress or fatigue. The subjects also claimed a better memory for detail, and were less likely to stop and start tasks, focusing their attention on a particular task, through to completion."

"Studies at *UCLA* showed that people who meditate have more "folding" of the brain's cortex, which is believed to promote and enhance neural processing. And the more you meditate, the more the brain develops. The research suggested that meditation was also likely to help with better judgement, emotional control, self-regulation and even increasing pain thresholds. The study also revealed that meditation can help to increase your levels of compassion."

A study at *The Maharishi University of Management* showed that people who had heart disease were "48% less likely to suffer a heart attack, or stroke, if they practiced Transcendental Meditation. Compared to the control group - which was merely given information about exercise and diet - those who meditated also returned an average 4.9 *mmHg* drop in blood pressure."

Bob Proctor is also one to "sing the praises" of the benefits of meditation. "Most people sleepwalk through their lives", suggests Bob. "They get up and go to work every day, raise their family, reminisce about the past and worry about the future. But through all that activity, they are never truly awake."

"Their life would be much different if they were aware of their oneness with the spiritual power that is constantly flowing into their mind. Then, instead of walking around in a state of unconsciousness, they would be able to create incredible mental power and focus," he adds.

"The great thinkers share an ability to access this powerful mental state naturally. They can shut out all distractions and become totally connected with the inspiration and imagination that's always inside them. One of the best ways to cultivate that ability - and to live a more awakened life - is through meditation," suggests Proctor.

Proctor continues, "...Meditation means awareness. Whenever you do something with awareness, it is meditation. That may be sitting with your eyes closed while watching your breath. It can also be listening to birds sing or a waterfall. As long as these activities are free from any other distraction, it is effective meditation. When you think of it that way, meditation becomes less of a technique and more of a way of life. It leads us to a state of stillness or a state of consciousness when the mind is free of scattered thoughts."

"When Albert Einstein developed the theory of relativity, he was operating from that still, focused state of consciousness", suggests Bob. "Thomas Edison was operating from that same state when he invented the lightbulb. When Steve Jobs came up with Apple's sleek designs, he was operating from a state of stillness too."

"Meditation allows us to experience that state more often. It clears out the clutter - so distractions don't steal our attention away from the power that is always flowing to and through us. It provides fertile soil in which we can use our higher faculties - the will, imagination, intuition, memory, perception and reason - to originate, nourish and grow big ideas", says Bob.

"Being in and operating from this state gives you access to the vast haven that provides every creative solution and every breakthrough idea that you need and desire", concludes Bob.

Why not try meditation for yourself - maybe for ten minutes a day, for ten days? It might not be your cup of tea (*matcha, anyone?*) - but "don't knock it until you've tried it". Meditation has been proven to:

- ✓ Improve your sleep, energy and mood
- ✓ Increase your focus, memory and concentration
- ✓ Reduce your stress and anxiety

Again, meditation is not a "one size fits all" exercise, but rather a personal experiment for you to explore through experience. "All life is an experiment, the more experiments you make the better." *Ralph Waldo Emerson.*

To give yourself the best possible opportunity to benefit from the "experiment", try and choose a quiet and peaceful environment - free from distractions - within which to start meditating. Sit comfortably - but steady and supported. Be mindful of your posture - sit up straight, keep your back straight, and try to relax your neck and shoulder muscles. It may help - definitely when first starting out - to keep your eyes closed.

You may also benefit from setting a timer so that you do not find yourself distracted by how long you think you have been meditating for - or how much of your ten minutes remain? (If you choose to follow a guided meditation - and again, this may be particularly beneficial to those just starting out - then you will have no need to time the meditation.) Guided meditations are freely available across the internet…

Just be present in the moment. If you find yourself unable to control your thoughts - again, a common dilemma for beginners - try asking yourself, "what am I going to think of next?" which normally helps to re-align the wandering mind. It may also help to initially focus on the rhythm of your breathing, as you start to transcend into deeper awareness.

Mark Robert Waldman - considered one of the world's leading authorities on spirituality and the brain, according to *Time*, *Newsweek*, and *The Washington Post* – suggests not to quiet your mind, but rather to listen to it.

"You don't have to quiet your mind at all", says Waldman. "When you choose to meditate, or when you slip into that peaceful state of daydreaming, just observe - without judgment - how your thoughts and feelings continually float in and out of consciousness. The more you just sit and watch them, the more you will feel a growing sense of inner peace. What's important is developing your ability to observe all the subtle feelings, thoughts and sensations that you are constantly experiencing. They're just the ramblings of a creative brain", he suggests.

Rebecca Beris, in *"Science Says Silence Is Much More Important To Our Brains Than We Think"*, writes that "As the world around becomes increasingly loud and cluttered you may find yourself seeking out the reprieve that silent places and silence have to offer. This may be a wise move as studies are showing that silence is much more important to your brains than you might think."

The journal *Brain, Structure and Function*, published a study in 2013, measuring the effect that sound and silence had on mice. When the mice were exposed to two hours of silence per day – which was originally intended to serve as the control - they developed new cells in the hippocampus, a region of the brain associated with memory, emotion and learning.

Researcher Imke Kirste reported that "silence is really helping the new generated cells to differentiate into neurons and integrate into the system". Silence can quite literally grow your brain.

An unrelated study reported that even when the brain was "resting" it was "perpetually actively internalising and evaluating information. During these periods of silence, your brain has the freedom it needs to discover its place in your internal and external world. The default mode helps you think about profound things in an imaginative way." As Herman Melville once wrote, "All profound things and emotions of things are preceded and attended by silence."

Conversely, it has been shown that noise can have an effect on our brains, resulting in elevated levels of stress hormones. Studies have shown that your body reacts to sound waves even while you are sleeping. The amygdalae - associated with memory formation and emotion - is activated, and this causes a release of stress hormones. "If you live in a consistently noisy environment then you are likely to experience chronically elevated levels of stress hormones."

A study published in *Psychological Science* (Vol. 13, No. 9) examined the effects that the relocation of Munich's airport had on children's health and cognition. Gary W. Evans, a professor of human ecology at *Cornell University* noted that "this study is among the strongest, probably the most definitive proof that noise - even at levels that do not produce any hearing damage - causes stress and is harmful to humans".

Studies have also concluded that "children exposed to households or classrooms near airplane flight paths, railways or highways have lower reading scores and are slower in their development of cognitive and language skills".

In *"How to Trick Your Brain for Happiness"*, neuropsychologist Rick Hanson, Ph.D. writes, "More activation in the left prefrontal cortex is associated with more positive emotions. So as there is greater activation in the left, front portion of your brain relative to the right, there is also greater well-being. The left prefrontal cortex is a major part of the brain for controlling negative emotion. So if you put the brakes on the negative, you get more of the positive," claims Hanson.

"On the other hand, people who routinely experience chronic stress - particularly acute, even traumatic stress - release the hormone cortisol, which literally eats away, almost like an acid bath, at the hippocampus, which is a part of the brain that's very engaged in visual-spatial memory as well as memory for context and setting. For example, adults who have had that history of stress and have lost up to 25% of the volume of this critically important part of the brain are less able to form new memories", adds Hanson.

There is good news, though. Hanson suggests that "as the mind changes, the brain changes". Hanson refers to a study of London taxi drivers. "To get a taxi license, you've got to memorise the spaghetti-like streets of London. At the end of the drivers' training, the hippocampus of their brain - involved in visual-spatial memory - is measurably thicker. Neurons that fire together wire together, even to the point of being observably thicker", reveals Hanson.

Hanson adds, "This has also been found among meditators: People who maintain regular meditative practice actually have measurably thicker brains in certain key regions, such as the insula and the frontal regions of the prefrontal cortex. The insula is involved in "interoception" - tuning into your body, as well as your deep feelings, whilst the prefrontal cortex is primarily associated with controlling attention.

"Research has also shown that it's possible to slow the loss of our brain cells", says Hanson. "We lose about 10,000 brain cells each day. We were born with 1.1 trillion, and also have several thousand *born* each day, mainly in the hippocampus", so "losing 10,000 a day isn't that big a deal", reassures Hanson. "A typical 80-year-old will have lost about 4% of his or her brain mass - it's called "cortical thinning with ageing".

"In one study, researchers compared meditators and non-meditators of the same age. The non-meditators experienced normal cortical thinning in those two brain regions, along with a third, the somatosensory cortex. However, the people who routinely meditated and "worked" their brain did not experience cortical thinning in those regions," adds Hanson.

He goes on to add scientific weight to what we already know – that "we become what we think about all day long". Hanson proposes that "You can use the mind to change the brain to change the mind for the better. This is known as "self-directed neuroplasticity," he says.

"Neuroplasticity refers to the malleable nature of the brain, and it's constant, ongoing. Self-directed neuroplasticity means doing it with clarity and skillfulness and intention. The key is a controlled use of attention. Attention is like a spotlight, shining on things within our awareness. But it's also like a vacuum cleaner, sucking whatever it rests upon into the brain, for better or worse."

Hanson continues, "For example, if we rest our attention routinely on what we resent or regret then we're going to build out the neural substrates of those thoughts and feelings. On the other hand," Hanson suggests, "if we rest our attention on the things for which we're grateful, the blessings in our life - the wholesome qualities in ourselves and the world around us; the things we get done, most of which are fairly small yet they're accomplishments nonetheless - then we build up very different neural substrates."

"And today we are constantly bombarded with stimuli that the brain has not evolved to handle. So gaining more control over attention one way or another is really crucial, whether it's through the practice of mindfulness, for instance, or through gratitude practices, where we count our blessings", he suggests. "Those are great ways to gain control over your attention because there you are, for 30 seconds or 30 minutes, coming back to focus on an object of awareness."

"Just having positive experiences is not enough to promote lasting well-being", Hanson concludes. "If a person feels grateful for a few seconds, that's nice. That's better than feeling resentful or bitter for a few seconds. But in order to really suck that experience into the brain, we need to stay with those experiences for a longer duration of time - we need to take steps, consciously, to keep that spotlight of attention on the positive."

"All negativity is caused by an accumulation of psychological time and denial of the present. Unease, anxiety, tension, stress, worry - all forms of fear - are caused by too much future and not enough presence. Guilt, regret, resentment, grievances, sadness, bitterness, and all forms of nonforgiveness *(sic)* are caused by too much past, and not enough presence." *Eckhart Tolle.*

Motivation:

Napoleon Hill writes that "whatever the mind can conceive and believe, it can achieve". Bob Proctor has personally shown me that "if you can hold it in your mind, then you will hold it in your hand". Buddha proffered that "the mind is everything. What you think, you become".

Motivation is the driving force behind all of our actions. It is the feeling of wanting to do something, and the force that keeps us going even when that initial desire goes away. When you begin a challenge, you will need a certain degree of motivation to reach your *DO* - to win the battle of "mind over mattress".

Feeling demotivated in day-to-day life can have a profound effect on your happiness, the quality of your relationships, the likelihood of you succeeding and most importantly - your enjoyment of life. Be honest...

- ✗ Do you find it a struggle to get out of bed?
- ✗ Do you feel stuck in a rut at work, or perhaps in your personal life?
- ✗ Do you give up easily when you feel challenged?
- ✗ Do you often feel bored?

Did your answers surprise you? You don't know what you don't know, until you know that you don't know it... Think about that for a second.

Boredom is also a sign that you are lacking motivation. There will always be *something* out there for you to do - or something new to learn. Seek it out. Find the opportunity for learning in every day. Every day's a school day!

It is not uncommon for people to tolerate mediocrity at work, because it's "easy". Most people are content with "average" - after all isn't that in itself the very definition of "average"? A lot of people don't desire change, or seek out a challenge - they are more than satisfied to perpetuate their own definition of their "comfortable" existence. They settle for mediocrity because it feels "safe" and reassuring... This book is not for them! (And the fact that you've read this far would suggest that perhaps you're not one of them.)

It is *so* easy to give up when times get tough. Sometimes we get so close to achieving something but give up when we feel ourselves weakening slightly. Napoleon Hill, in *"Think and Grow Rich"*, tells the story - "Three Feet From Gold" - of a man (named only as "an uncle of R. U. Darby") who left his home in Williamsburg, Maryland to follow the gold rush in Colorado.

After initially striking gold, he borrowed the funds required to purchase machinery to extract yet more of the precious ore. But, to his horror, the rich vein of gold that he had discovered "disappeared". Try as he might, he was unable to find more gold. Finally, he decided to quit - he sold the machinery to a "junk" man for a few hundred dollars and returned home - demoralised and dejected.

The "junk" man, however, called in a mining engineer, who calculated - with his knowledge of "fault lines" - that a rich vein of gold would be found "just three feet from where the Darbys had stopped drilling! That is exactly where it was found! The "junk" man took millions of dollars in ore from the mine, because he knew enough to seek expert counsel before giving up."[55]

"One of the most common causes of failure is the habit of quitting when one is overtaken by *temporary defeat*. Every person is guilty of this mistake at one time or another."[56]

It is of essential importance to find the motivation - whatever it takes! Find the motivation to break through that "temporary defeat" - what we at The Proctor Gallagher Institute call "The Terror Barrier" - and to keep pushing through to your promised land beyond.

It has been suggested that there are two main types of motivation:

1. *Intrinsic* motivation - from within yourself. Intrinsic motivation tends to originate from a genuine enjoyment of an activity. The phrase, "life is a journey, not a destination" perfectly encapsulates the mind-set of an intrinsically motivated person, who derives their satisfaction from the experience, rather than the reward.

2. *Extrinsic* motivation - from outside the self. Extrinsic motivation is rooted in the desire for external reward, such as money, fame or success. An extrinsically motivated person will work hard whether they enjoy something or not - as long as they receive recognition, or reward, after the event.

Which of the two motivational types do you believe that you are? What drives, or motivates, you? The experience? Or the reward? How you are driven will determine how successfully you are likely to be motivated - with particular reference to intensity and persistence.

If you are intrinsically motivated, you are more likely to be motivated by incentives offering enjoyment or a sense of personal satisfaction. If you are extrinsically motivated, you would probably prefer the motivation of recognition or reward.

---

55 "Think and Grow Rich", Napoleon Hill

56 "Think and Grow Rich", Napoleon Hill

It is believed that there are three distinct elements to motivation - activation, intensity and persistence. Remember, you are unique - you may find that some elements come naturally to you, whilst others take a little longer for you to develop and nurture.

People with low activation levels rarely feel the desire to do or achieve anything. These people tend to live lives avoiding challenge and generally "playing it safe" within their relative comfort zones. There could be any number of reasons why a person may have low activation levels, including:

- The fear of failure
- Being unaware of their true potential
- A lack of self-confidence or low self-esteem
- Suffering from mental health problems such as depression and anxiety
- Feeling "*comfortable*" living a risk-free existence

Having a low activation level is perfectly fine if you feel happy and fulfilled. However, it soon becomes a problem if you wish that you could build more motivation, but find that you simply can't.

Both intrinsically motivated and extrinsically motivated people can achieve high activation levels if the relevant incentives are put into place. Having the desire to start something is awesome, but activation is only the beginning - the tip of the proverbial iceberg...

People with high activation levels often find themselves constantly setting goals and writing lists of things that they want to do. Goal setting is only the first stage of motivation, and people with high activation levels can set millions of goals but never move towards any of them. Failure to achieve your goals, however, can make you feel inadequate and demotivated. Remember also the confidence-competence loop? *How do you eat an elephant?*

Motivation is more than just the desire to do something. Just because you *want* to do something doesn't mean that you *will* do it. Wanting something is only the beginning. And this is where intensity comes into play. How much do you *really* want to achieve your **DO**? What happens when you want to lose weight, for example, but you also crave that slice of chocolate cake? (And that's where the "knowing-doing gap" raises its ugly head again.) Remember also, the concept of "loss aversion" - your brain's stubborn reluctance to work towards losing anything...

How much do you want it? Are you willing to make sacrifices? Are you *interested*? Or *committed*? Some people may reach their ideal weight by sacrificing their favourite foods, whilst others get to the top of Everest, for example, because they trained extensively for years, and then literally risked their lives to get there.

It doesn't matter where your motivation comes from - to realise your dream - your **DO** - you *really* have to want it.

People with high intensity levels really want to achieve their goals. Although they may be extremely enthusiastic, they can also be reckless and disorganised. People with these traits often fail to achieve their dreams simply because they lack the persistence to stay on track. They quit "three feet from gold".

"Persistence is about determination, structure, will-power and most importantly, patience. It's persistence that you will need when you "hit the wall" - the point at which your whole being screams out for you to stop and give up".

If you are intrinsically motivated, persisting when times get tough can be difficult - what's the point in the sacrifice, if the process offers no enjoyment? Persistence tends to come a lot easier to extrinsically motivated people because they're better able to focus on what happens after the goal has been achieved.

"Activation, intensity and persistence are all vital components of motivation. Without all three, you stand little chance of ever reaching your goal. Without activation, you will never feel the impulse to start something. Without intensity, you will eventually lack the desire to keep going. Without persistence, you will never have the drive to overcome the obstacles separating you from your goal."

It can be difficult, though, to muster the will or the courage to just go out and do it. It is so easy to become demotivated when we don't enjoy everyday life, or when our hard work goes unnoticed and we just don't feel appreciated. Sometimes it's important to be *reminded* that we can succeed. Remember, "if you can hold it in your mind, then you will hold it in your hand". We can get whatever we desire. We have the strength and the will to push through obstacles and to overcome any challenges along the journey.

"The will to win, the desire to succeed, the urge to reach your full potential; these are the keys that will unlock the door to personal excellence." *Confucius*. "There is nothing you can't achieve with time, attention and effort." *James Shelton*.

Tony Robbins suggests that there are two master lessons in life. One is the science of achievement. "How do you take the invisible and make it visible?" How do you make your dreams happen?" asks Tony. "The other lesson that is rarely mastered is the art of fulfillment". The reason that it is rarely mastered, proposes Tony, is that "it's about appreciation and contribution. You can only feel so much by yourself".

Tony proposes that there are six "basic, universal needs that make us tick and drive all human behaviour. Every single person in this world has these same six needs, but each of us values these needs in different ways, and each of us have varied beliefs about what it means to satisfy those needs", he says.

"This is what becomes the driving force behind everything we do and determines the direction of our lives." Robbins introduced these six human needs in Monterey, California, in 2006. His *TED* talk - "*Why We Do The Things We Do*" - was one of the first ever delivered, and – to date - is the sixth most viewed *TED* talk of all time.

1. Certainty. "Everyone needs certainty that they can avoid pain and at least be comfortable", says Tony. "While we go for certainty differently, if we get total certainty, we get what? You know what will happen, when and how it will happen, what would you feel?" asks Tony. "Bored out of your minds".

2. "So, God, in Her infinite wisdom, gave us a second human need, which is uncertainty", adds Robbins. "We need variety. We need surprise. You like the surprises you want. The ones you don't want, you call problems, but you need them. So, variety is important".

3. Significance. "We all need to feel important, special, unique. You can get it by making more money or being more spiritual. The fastest way to do this, if you have no background, no culture, no belief and resources or resourcefulness, is violence. If I put a gun to your head, instantly I'm significant," Tony suggests.

   "How certain am I that you're going to respond to me? How much uncertainty?" asks Robbins. "Who knows what's going to happen next? Kind of exciting. Total variety and uncertainty. And it's significant, isn't it? So you want to risk your life for it. That's why violence has always been around and will be around unless we have a consciousness change as a species. You can get significance a million ways, but to be significant, you've got to be unique and different."

4. Connection and love. "We all want it", says Tony. "Most settle for connection, love's too scary. Here's what's true: we need it. We can do it through intimacy, friendship, prayer, through walking in nature", suggests Robbins

   "These first four needs, every human finds a way to meet. I call the first four needs the needs of the personality. The last two are the needs of the spirit. And this is where fulfillment comes. You won't get it from the first four", says Robbins.

5. Growth. "If a relationship or business is not growing, if you're not growing, doesn't matter how much money or friends you have, how many love you, you feel like hell. I believe that we grow is so we have something to give of value", says Robbins.

6. "The sixth need is to contribute beyond ourselves. Because we all know, the secret to living is giving", claims Robbins. "We all know that life is not about me, it's about we".

"So, here's what's different about people", proffers Tony. "We have the same needs. But are you a certainty freak, or uncertainty? Are you driven by significance or love? We all need all six, but what your lead system is tilts you in a different direction. And as you move in a direction, you have a destination or destiny".

"The second piece is the map. The operating system tells you how to get there. For some people it's, "I'm going to save lives even if I die for other people", and they're a fireman. Somebody else says, "I'm going to kill people to do it". They're trying to meet the same needs of significance", Tony suggests. "They want to honour God or honour their family. But they have a different map. One of the parts of the map is like time. Some people's idea of a long time is 100 years. Somebody else's is three seconds".

"The last thing is emotion" claims Robbins. "There are 6,000 emotions that we have words for in the English language, which is just a linguistic representation that changes by language. If I have 20,000 people and I have them write down all the emotions that they experience in an average week, and I give them as long as they need, and on one side they write empowering emotions - the other disempowering - guess how many emotions they experience? Less than 12..."

If you're still struggling with "mind over mattress", and – unlike Brendon – you just can't seem to "win the mornings", Rida Sadiq, in *"7 Ways To Wake Up Motivated When You're Definitely Not A Morning Person"*, suggests seven (elephant?) bite-sized tips to kick-start your morning…

1. Hygiene - "Brushing your teeth will make you feel fresh, take away that bad breath and have you feeling like a new person. Also try washing your face or scrubbing it with an exfoliator. Not only will washing your face help you wake up, it will also get rid of all those dead skin cells that form while you sleep," suggests Sadiq.

2. Breakfast - "Eating a decent-sized breakfast can do wonders", adds Sadiq. "It gives you energy and allows you to actually get up and start your day. "Try to eat with someone", she suggests. "This allows you to start your day with conversation."

3. Outfit - "Whether it's for your job, a day at class or a visit to grandma, having an amazing outfit for the day will help you take it on with strength and confidence", she suggests. "Look good, feel good".

4. Exercise - "Having a great workout will motivate you to take on the day", recommends Rida. "Working out releases dopamine, which makes you feel happy and energised. Its release can give you a kick-start for the day ahead."

5. Conversations - "Conversations can actually get you in the mood to do things", says Sadiq. "Conversations can sometimes help solve problems, and they release unwanted stress or anxiety."

6. Music - "Putting on music can actually make a person feel very energised and happy", she says. "Music makes you want express yourself, and it also helps you feel open. Music makes you want to conquer the day."

7. Confidence - "Never doubt yourself", says Sadiq. "The more confident you are, the more energised and positive you will feel. The right mindset is everything..."

Transforming from sluggish, bored, unhappy and unsatisfied to enlivened, enthusiastic, happy and highly motivated, is not something that can happen overnight. It takes time, dedication and practice.

Remember, the journey of a thousand miles begins with a single step - start to take your first step and build on the momentum - every accomplishment starts with the decision to try.

Time to put those wheels into motion. Time to focus your momentum into direction.

Resilience:

"Out of the night that covers me,
  Black as the pit from pole to pole,
I thank whatever gods may be
  For my unconquerable soul.

In the fell clutch of circumstance
  I have not winced nor cried aloud.
Under the bludgeonings of chance
  My head is bloody, but unbowed.

Beyond this place of wrath and tears
  Looms but the Horror of the shade,
And yet the menace of the years
  Finds and shall find me unafraid.

It matters not how strait the gate,
  How charged with punishments the scroll,
I am the master of my fate,
  I am the captain of my soul."

"*Invictus*" by William Ernest Henley

"The difference between a successful person and others is not a lack of strength, not a lack of knowledge, but rather in a lack of will." *Vince Lombardi.* The Cambridge Dictionary defines will as "the mental power used to control and direct your thoughts and actions, or a determination to do something, despite any difficulties or opposition."

Rebecca Beris, on *Lifehack*, writes that, "Often when we try to focus on a task or avoid temptation, we try to use all our willpower. We invest all our energy into concentrating on one thing or not thinking about the temptation. However, a study has shown that when we do this, we deplete our willpower. The harder we try, the more we end up fatigued and out of strength."

Price Pritchett tells a powerful story of a fly trying to escape through a window in his (highly recommended) book, "*You²*". The fly is embroiled in a life and death struggle in an attempt to escape through the window. Fatigued, the fly will ultimately breathe its last breath in a vain attempt to escape, whilst all the time – merely feet away – there is an open door...

Roy Baumeister, of the Case Western Reserve University, conducted a study in which he engaged 67 participants in a food challenge intended to evaluate their will power. They were led into a room with the smell of freshly baked chocolate biscuits. The biscuits and other assorted chocolate confectionery were then brought into the room. Some of the participants were allowed to consume the chocolate, whilst the control group were instructed to eat radishes.

Following the cookies and radishes, Baumeister and his team gave the participants another seemingly unrelated test, requiring the participants to solve a puzzle intended to challenge their persistence. The participants were led to believe that they were undertaking an intelligence test, but the intention was to determine how long the students would persist before giving up.

"The participants who had been allowed to eat the chocolate treats worked on the puzzle for an average of 20 minutes. The radish eaters didn't last nearly this long. On average they gave up after only 8 minutes. Those people who had to resist the confectionery could not engage in a second demanding task. Their willpower was already drained and they were too tired."

Baumeister's study suggested that "self-control is a general strength that's used across different sorts of tasks - and it could be depleted. It's like using a muscle: After exercising it, it loses its strength, gets fatigued, and becomes ineffectual, at least in the short-term." Willpower, like a muscle, gets tired through use.

The good news is that like muscles, willpower can also be strengthened with practice. Colin Robertson writes that "when you focus on one goal at a time, you actually strengthen your willpower. If we try to do too much, like, for example go on a diet and try to focus intensely on our work we end up depleting our willpower."

"We are like the radish eaters", says Robertson, "we take too much on, and end up getting fatigued". It's like going to the gym and trying to bench press an enormous weight, or attempting to transform into Arnold Schwarzenegger overnight - you will end up disillusioned and demotivated.

If, however, you start with a smaller weight, which you then gradually increase, then you can build up muscle strength – over time. Be wary of any "short cuts" or "quick fixes". Don't commit too much too soon in the quest for the ultimate snake oil.[57] Don't be the fly in You^2.

Amy Morin, in "*What Mentally Strong People Don't Do*", proposes that "most of us understand how we can build physical strength, but there's a lot more confusion over the steps to take to develop mental strength." She lists three "secrets to build your mental strength":

---

[57] Snake oil - a substance with no real medicinal value sold as a remedy for all diseases.

1. Talk to yourself like a trusted friend. "Your thoughts greatly influence how you feel and behave", says Morin. "Your inner monologue has a tendency to become a self-fulfilling prophecy". "Whatever we consistently focus on becomes our idea of reality". *Tony Robbins.*

   Try to consciously replace your negative self-talk. It doesn't always have to be positive, just realistic. Amy suggests that you ask yourself, "What would I say to a friend who said this about himself or herself?" And then, offer those kind and gentle words to yourself".

2. Take charge of your emotions. "Allowing your emotions to control your life will deplete your mental strength", says Amy. "There's nothing wrong with being in a bad mood sometimes, but staying stuck in a negative rut can be a slippery slope: Sadness can lead to self-pity, anger can turn to bitterness, and mild anxiety can become paralysing fear."

   "A lot of problems stem from our desire to avoid discomfort. For example, people who fear failure often avoid new challenges in an effort to keep anxiety at bay. Avoiding emotional discomfort, however, is usually a short-term solution that leads to long-term problems. Decide that you're going to be in control of your emotions so that they don't control you. (Living from the inside-out.) "The more you practice tolerating discomfort, the more confidence you'll gain in your ability to accept new challenges," she proposes.

3. Make productive choices. "It's impossible to feel mentally strong when you're engaging in self-destructive behaviours that sabotage your best efforts", suggests Morin. "Yet, most people have a few unproductive habits that they indulge in, on a regular basis. Many of these bad habits seem minor - complaining about your boss, hosting your own pity party, or trying to please everyone - but they can wreak havoc on your mental state. You only have a finite amount of time and energy in life", she concludes.

In *"11 Signs You Have the Grit You Need to Succeed"*, Dr Travis Bradberry - author of *"Emotional Intelligence 2.0"* - relates the example of Angela Lee Duckworth, a teacher who realised that her "highest performing students weren't those who had the most natural talent; they were the students who had that *"extra something"* that motivated them to work harder than everyone else." She quit her teaching job so that she could study the concept while obtaining a graduate degree in psychology at The University of Pennsylvania.

Angela Duckworth has "analysed a bevy of people to whom success is important: students, military personnel, salespeople, and spelling bee contestants, to name a few. Over time, she has come to the conclusion that the majority of successful people all share one critical thing – grit."

"Grit is that *extra something* that separates the most successful people from the rest. It's the passion, perseverance, and stamina that we must channel in order to stick with our dreams until they become a reality. Developing grit is all about habitually doing the things that no one else is willing to do", says Dr Bradberry.

Dr Bradberry writes, "There are quite a few signs that you have grit, and if you aren't doing the following on a regular basis, (then) you should be. You have to make mistakes, look like an idiot, and try again, without even flinching."

"In a recent study at *The College of William and Mary*, over 800 entrepreneurs were interviewed, and the most successful among them were found to have two things in common: They were "terrible at imagining failure" and they tended "not to care what other people thought of them". The most successful entrepreneurs put no time or energy into stressing about their failures as they see failure as a small and necessary step in the process of reaching their goals."

"You have to fight when you already feel defeated. A reporter once asked Muhammad Ali how many sit-ups he does every day. He responded, "I don't count my sit-ups, I only start counting when it starts hurting, when I feel pain, cause that's when it really matters.""

You have two choices when "the going gets tough". You can overcome the barrier, and grow in the process, or let it beat you. As creatures of habit, if we quit when things get tough, it becomes that much easier to quit the next time. Conversely, if you push through that *terror barrier*, then "the grit begins to grow in you". As Nelson Mandela once said, "I never lose. I either win, or I learn."

Dr Bradberry suggests that "Sometimes we have to do things we don't want to do because we know they're for the best in the long-run. It's easy to let the looming challenge paralyse you, but the most successful people know that in these moments, the best thing they can do is to get started right away. Every moment spent dreading the task subtracts time and energy from actually getting it done." Just "*Eat That Frog*"...

"You have to keep your emotions in check. Negative emotions will challenge your grit every step of the way."

"While it's impossible not to feel your emotions, it's completely under your power to manage them effectively and to keep yourself in a position of control. When you let your emotions overtake your ability to think clearly, it's easy to lose your resolve. A bad mood can make you lash out, or stray from your chosen direction just as easily as a good mood can make you overconfident and impulsive," says Dr Bradberry.

"You have to give more than you get in return", proffers Dr Bradberry, relating a famous Stanford experiment where an administrator leaves a child in a room with a marshmallow. Each child was told that they could eat the marshmallow, but if they could delay eating it until the experimenter's return 15 minutes later, they would be rewarded with a second marshmallow.

The children that were able to wait returned experienced better outcomes in life, including better test results, greater career success, and even lower body mass indexes. "Delay of gratification and patience are essential to success. People with grit know that real results only materialise when you put in the time and forego instant gratification", suggests Dr Bradberry.

"You have to lead when no one else follows. It's easy to set a direction and believe in yourself when you have support, but the true test of grit is how well you maintain your resolve when nobody else believes in what you're doing", maintains Bradberry. "People with grit believe in themselves no matter what, and they stay the course until they win people over to their way of thinking."

"You have to meet deadlines that are unreasonable and deliver results that exceed expectations. Successful people find a way to say yes and still honour their existing commitments. They know the best way to stand out from everyone else is to outwork them. For this reason, they have a tendency to over deliver, even when they over promise," claims Travis.

"You have to focus on the details even when it makes your mind numb. Nothing tests your grit like mind-numbing details, especially when you're tired. The more that people with grit are challenged, the more they dig in and welcome that challenge," he says.

Dr Bradberry concludes that "Grit is as rare as it is important. The good news is any of us can get grittier with a little extra focus and effort."

Jim Rohn, in *Seven Traits of the Most Resilient People*, suggests that "Resilience is the ability to return to the original form after being bent, stretched or compressed. It's the ability to readily recover from illness, depression or adversity."

"What would it take for you to pull yourself up and start all over again? How resilient are you? Could you learn from your disappointments and start all over again? What would it take?" he asks.

"First, it would take a lot of self-discipline. It would take a lot of positive self-talk to muster up the energy to begin again. It would take a lot of concentration to block out the noise and the clutter of all the negative voices trying to get through, as well as the negative voices of others around you. It would take a lot of discipline to balance the fear and anxiety with the knowing that, if you did it once, you can do it all over again," suggests Rohn.

Rohn continues, "Whether your losses had anything to do with you or not, your future success has everything to do with you. It would take a lot of self-reliance to avoid blame. What's happened has happened. You need to get on with your life and begin again."

"If you lost everything tomorrow and were gathering the courage to try again, it would take a lot of self-appreciation", Rohn suggests. "You need to know in your heart and mind that you have the skills, the talent and the strength to do it one more time. Cultivating a resilient character turns failure into success. A resilient person won't give up. A resilient person will, in spite of all obstacles and setbacks, keep doing it until…"

Jim Rohn also wrote an article titled *"How to Bounce Back From Failure"*, in which he suggests two ways to keep yourself encouraged…

1. Take responsibility for the missed opportunity. "This lost opportunity just set you up to take advantage of the next one", says Rohn. "You can make the necessary alterations next time. Make the changes that will make the difference. Study your mistakes and learn from them. Instead of dwelling on the mistakes, simply acknowledge them and learn from them."

2. Remind yourself that you're bound to get better. "It's the next opportunity that matters, not the previous one", he proffers. "The previous one matters only in that you must learn from your mistakes. The next one gives you the opportunity to show that you have learned. You can do it better next time. Don't beat yourself up for messing up. Pat yourself on the back for figuring it out. You can't wait and hope that someone else will come along and cheer you up, make you feel better; to tell you that you'll do better next time. You have to rely on yourself. You have to encourage yourself with future successes," he says.

    "Sometimes defeat is the best beginning… If you're at the bottom, there's only one way to go. More importantly, if you're flat on your back, mentally and financially, you'll usually become sufficiently disgusted to reach way deep down inside yourself and pull out miracles and talents and abilities and desire and determination," Rohn adds.

    "In the face of adversity is when things begin to change, when you begin to change", Rohn suggests. With enough disgust, desire and determination to change your life, you'll start saying, "I've had it. Enough of this. No more. Never again! These words and these thoughts really rattle the power of time, fate and circumstances."

"A lot of people don't change themselves. They wait for change. They accept their defeats and wallow in their self-pity. They refuse to take control of the situation. If you're disgusted and in need of change, then your present failure is a temporary condition. You will rebound from failure, just as surely as you gravitated into failure."

"This too shall pass", says Rohn. "I firmly believe that you're only given as much as you can handle, as much negativity, as much failure, as much disappointment. Grasp for a new beginning. You need to pull yourself up and move back into the world with a plan," he suggests. "Your current limitations or failures are the building blocks from which to create greatness."

"You can go where you want to go. You can do what you want to do. You can become what you want to become. You can do it all, starting now, right where you are", says Rohn. "Make your failures give birth to great opportunity, not prolonged agony. Make your disgust lead to inspiration, not depression," he suggests. "The doors will open once you decide to get back on your feet and make your mark. Keep your eyes firmly set on achievement. Don't settle for mere existence and self-pity. Make a commitment to excellence," suggests Rohn.

In *"The Resilient Self"*, authors Steven and Sybil Wolin propose that "The more obstacles you face and overcome, the more times you falter and get back on track, the more difficulties you struggle with and conquer, the more resiliency you will naturally develop. If you are resilient, there is nothing that can hold you back."

Maria Konnikova, writing for *newyorker.com*, believes that *perception* is key to resilience. In *"The Secret Formula For Resilience"*, she asks, "Do you conceptualise an event as traumatic, or as a chance to learn and grow?"

Emmy Werner – a developmental psychologist – dedicated 32 years to answering that question. In 1989, Werner published the results of her longitudinal project, which had followed 698 children, in Kauai, Hawaii, from before birth through to their thirties.

"She monitored them for any exposure to stress: maternal stress *in utero*, poverty, problems in the family, and so on. Two-thirds of the children came from backgrounds that were, essentially, stable, successful, and happy; the other third were deemed as "at risk". She soon discovered that not all of the "at risk" children reacted to stress in the same way."

Two-thirds of the subjects "developed serious learning or behaviour problems by the age of ten, or had delinquency records, mental health problems, or teen-age pregnancies by the age of eighteen". But the remaining third developed into "competent, confident, and caring young adults." They had attained academic, domestic, and social success - and they were always ready to capitalise on new opportunities that arose," reported Werner.

"What was it that set the resilient children apart? After thirty years of research, Werner found that several elements predicted resilience. Some elements had to do with luck: a resilient child might have a strong bond with a supportive caregiver, parent, teacher, or other mentor-like figure. But another, quite large set of elements was psychological, and had to do with how the children *responded* to the environment."

"From a young age, resilient children tended to "meet the world on their own terms". They were autonomous and independent, would seek out new experiences, and had a "positive social orientation", reports Werner.

The resilient children had what psychologists call an "internal locus of control". They believed that they - and not their circumstances - affected their outcomes. The resilient children saw themselves as the orchestrators of their own fates. Measuring locus of control, they scored more than two standard deviations away from the standardisation group."

George Bonanno - a clinical psychologist at *Columbia University's Teachers College* – has been studying resilience for nearly twenty-five years. "All of us possess the same fundamental stress-response system, so when it comes to resilience, why do some people use their system so much more frequently or effectively than others?" asks Bonanno.

According to Bonanno, "One of the central elements of resilience is perception. Events are not traumatic until we experience them as traumatic," he suggests. "To call something a "traumatic event" belies that fact." He argues that the terminology of *PTE* - or potentially traumatic event - is more accurate. "Every frightening event, no matter how negative it might seem from the sidelines, has the potential to be traumatic or not - to the person experiencing it."

According to Bonanno, the "stressful" or "traumatic" events themselves don't carry much predictive power when it comes to life outcomes. "The data shows that exposure to potentially traumatic events does not predict later functioning", he said. "What matters is whether that adversity becomes traumatising," says Bonanno.

Martin Seligman - the University of Pennsylvania psychologist who pioneered much of the field of positive psychology – suggests that "training people to change their explanatory styles from internal to external ("bad events aren't my fault"), from global to specific ("this is one narrow thing rather than a massive indication that something is wrong with my life"), and from permanent to impermanent ("I can change the situation, rather than assuming it's fixed") made them more psychologically successful and less prone to depression."

"The same goes for locus of control: not only is a more internal locus tied to perceiving less stress and performing better, but changing your locus from external to internal leads to positive changes in both psychological well-being and objective work performance. The cognitive skills that underpin resilience can indeed be learned, creating resilience where there was none."

"Unfortunately, the opposite may also be true. "We can become less resilient, or less likely to be resilient," says Bonanno. "We can create or exaggerate stressors very easily in our own minds. Human beings are capable of worry and rumination: we can take a minor thing, blow it up in our heads, run through it over and over, and drive ourselves crazy until we feel like that minor thing is the biggest thing that ever happened." (Remember catastrophising?)

"In a sense, it's a self-fulfilling prophecy. Frame adversity as a challenge, and you become more flexible and able to deal with it, move on, learn from it, and grow. Focus on it, frame it as a threat, and a potentially traumatic event becomes an enduring problem; you become more inflexible, and more likely to be negatively affected," he says.

In *"The Three Traits of Great Entrepreneurs"*, Tony Robbins suggests that "Successful people share three powerful capabilities that place them above those who try and fail..."

He lists them as hunger, drive and dedication...

1. Hunger. "As any ambitious person knows, there isn't any more painful word in any human human language than "no". The hard truth is that there is no success without rejection and it's the quality of hunger that gets you from where you are now, as a dreamer, to where you want to be, as an achiever", claims Tony.

    The best entrepreneurs on earth never lose that hunger" says Tony. "They are hungry to grow, hungry to give, hungry to contribute. It's more important than intelligence. Nothing that will stop a person who is hungry enough. Failure doesn't stop them".

2. Drive. "Setting goals is the first step in turning the invisible into the visible", says Tony. "Develop a purpose and a vision that's greater than yourself, then create a map to get you there."

3. Dedication. "Anticipation is power. The key competence successful leaders have over followers is applied dedication," he proposes.

"It's not what we get, but who we become and what we contribute that gives meaning to our lives." *Tony Robbins.*

In *"Six Ways to Keep Your Attitude Up When Life Tries to Bring You Down"*, Chris Widener suggests adopting an optimistic outlook, proposing "Instead of spending your time thinking about how bad things are, think about how good they will be."

Chris advocates that "A positive attitude is key to a successful life, so what happens when things go wrong? We have a tendency to let our attitudes take a dive along with our state of affairs. But life is going to deal setbacks, both minor and major, on a regular basis, and if we are going to be successful, we need to know how to keep our attitudes intact. We need practical tools to help us understand how we can keep our attitudes up when the circumstances are down." He suggests the following six tips…

1. Take some time away. "The next time life turns against you, take some time to just step back from the problem and think", he says. "This will enable you to rationally deal with the issue at hand, instead of emotionally reacting. It will allow you to put your state of mind back in its proper place" - living from the inside-out. "You have power over your mind – not outside events. Realise this, and you will find strength". *Marcus Aurelius.*

2. Keep your eye on the goal. "One of the biggest problems with trouble is that it takes your focus off where it should be", suggests Widener. If you find yourself getting down about circumstances, sit down and write out what your goal is, and give some thought to how you can achieve it. Make sure that you're keeping the important things important. We should be focused on the goal and moving forward".

3. Focus on solutions, not problems. "The squeaky wheel gets the grease. Negative circumstances scream for our attention", says Chris. "When we face difficult circumstances, we tend to dwell on them. Instead of talking about problems, talk about solutions."

4. Get some positive input. "When we begin to go in one direction, it can be a slippery slope. We must get our thoughts back on track with positive ideas", he suggests. "When circumstances have you against the emotional wall, meet with a friend who can encourage you. Pick up a good book and read. Get a coach. Whatever external influence you can get to put your attitude back on the positive side of the tracks - do it!"

5. Tell yourself the good. "One of the greatest internal powers we have is the power to control our thoughts", says Widener. "Spend time dwelling on the good things instead of the problems. Think about the positive things - things that you enjoy and that give you a sense of happiness and peace. Let your positive attitude develop from within, as well as from without."

6. Remember that circumstances are not forever. "Sometimes it seems like we are going to be up to our eyeballs in the situation forever, when in reality, "this too shall pass".

   Circumstances will change and you will be on the mountain instead of in the valley. This will give you a sense of hope as you live and work that will change your attitude, make you feel better and put you on the fast track for growth," suggests Widener.

Let me ask you a question... If you had £86,400 in your bank account and somebody stole £10 from you, would you become angry, and forget about the remaining £86,390 in the hope of exacting revenge on the person who stole the £10?

Or move on…?

We each have 86,400 seconds in every day, so why do you choose to allow somebody else's "10 seconds" of negativity to ruin the remaining 86,390 seconds in your day? Don't sweat the small stuff. "He is a wise man who does not grieve for the things which he has not, but rejoices for those which he has." *Epictetus*

"Even the darkest night will end, and the sun will rise." *Victor Hugo, "Les Misérables"*

"Life isn't about waiting for the storm to pass; it's about learning to dance in the rain." *Tony Robbins*

"Where there is no struggle, there is no strength." *Oprah*

"It's not that I am so smart, it's just that I stay with my problems longer." *Albert Einstein*

"I will love the light for it shows me the way, yet I will endure the darkness for it shows me the stars." *Og Mandino*

"The gem cannot be polished without friction, nor man perfected without trials." *Chinese Proverb*

"Everything can be taken from a man but one thing, the last of the human freedoms - to choose one's attitude in any given set of circumstances, to choose one's own way." Viktor Frankl, *"Man's Search For Meaning"*, published in 1946 after four years in a Nazi concentration camp as Auschwitz prisoner 119104.

"Each one has to find his peace from within. And peace to be real must be unaffected by outside circumstances." *Mahatma Gandhi*

"Success":

"Success consists of going from failure to failure without loss of enthusiasm." *Winston Churchill*. Success can mean many different things to many different people. My preferred definition is that of Earl Nightingale's, "Success is the progressive realisation of a worthy ideal."

Jim Rohn, in *"A Good Life Contains These 6 Essentials"*, suggests that "The ultimate expression of life is not a paycheck. The ultimate expression of life is not a Mercedes. The ultimate expression of life is not a million dollars, or a bank account, or a home. The ultimate expression of life is living a good life." Rohn suggests a short list of what he believes would constitute a good life.

1. Productivity. "You won't be happy if you don't produce. The game of life is not rest", claims Rohn. "Yes, we must rest, but only long enough to gather strength to get back to productivity."

2. Good friends. "Friendship is probably the greatest support system in the world, so don't deny yourself the time to develop it", suggests Rohn. "Nothing can match it. It's extraordinary in its benefit."

3. Culture. "Language, music, ceremonies, traditions, dress. All of that is so vitally important that you must keep it alive. The uniqueness of all of us, when blended together, brings vitality, energy, power, influence, and rightness to the world," he adds.

4. Spirituality. "It helps to form the foundation of the family that builds the nation. And make sure you study, practice and teach - don't be careless about the spiritual part of your nature - it's what makes us who we are, different from dogs, cats, birds and mice."

5. Don't miss anything. "My parents taught me not to miss anything", says Rohn. "Go to everything you possibly can. Buy a ticket to everything you can. Go see everything and experience all you can. Live a vital life. If you live well, you will earn well. If you live well, it will show in your face; it will show in the texture of your voice. There will be something unique and magical about you. It will infuse not only your personal life but also your business life. And it will give you a vitality that nothing else can give."

6. Your family and the inner circle. "Invest in them, and they'll invest in you. Inspire them, and they'll inspire you. If a husband walks out of the house and he can still feel the imprint of his wife's arms around his body, he's invincible all day. It's the special stuff with your inner circle that makes you strong and powerful and influential. So don't miss that opportunity", pleads Rohn.

"There is no greater value than love, so make sure in your busy day to remember the true purpose and the reasons you do what you do. May you truly live the kind of life that will bring the fruit and rewards that you desire."

Ask yourself, "What, for me, would represent a good life?"

Ayodeji Awosika, writing for *The Huffington Post*, poses an interesting question. "If money and fame weren't part of the equation, how would you define success?" In *"8 Clear Signs of a Successful Life That Have Nothing to do With Money or Fame"*, Awisoka suggests that there are "clear cut signs of success that have nothing to do with money or fame".

1. You Quit. "Success happens when you quit living your life to please everyone around you. When you quit listening to the noise of the world and focus on what's important to you", says Awosika. "When you quit thinking reality is anything but what you want it to be. Quit viewing the world with the preconceived notions you were taught growing up. Quit being *"realistic"*. Quit worrying and start living," he says.

2. You Try Things With Uncertain Outcomes. "All of the world's most successful people had to try something with an uncertain outcome. Even if things don't go your way you learn a valuable lesson - it's not the end of the world". "You can try again and again. Success and failure are intertwined with one another. Find someone who's achieved success and you'll discover a string of failures along the way. "It doesn't matter how many times you've failed, you only have to be right once." *Mark Cuban*

3. You're Polite. "One of the most successful self-help books of all time, *"How to Win Friends And Influence People"*, proposes "smile; be polite; praise others for their good work; and don't argue with other people" as a recipe for success. "Every person you encounter is the most important person in the world in their own eyes - successful people know to treat them as such," says Awosika.

4. You Have Many Moments Where You Lose Yourself. "A life well lived has many moments in a state of flow, described as *"being in the zone"*. The value of engagement trumps the value of money. Search for work you get completely lost in," says Awosika.

5. Someone Has Thanked You For What You've Done. "Has anyone ever gone out of their way to thank you for your work? That's success. No matter how badly you want success for yourself you'll never get it until you find a way to provide value to other people.

    Your business isn't about you - it's about your customer. Your creative work isn't about you - it's about touching others," advises Awosika.

6. You P**sed Someone Off. "Because you believed in something. Because you have a (well-informed) opinion that others may disagree with. Because you had the audacity to say what we're all afraid to say. Successful people don't seek to maintain the status quo", suggests Awosika. "When they see that the system's broken, they look for ways to change it and find like-minded people to help them."

7. You Do Things That Excite You. "The opposite of love is indifference, and the opposite of happiness is boredom", *Tim Ferriss.* "You're successful if you trade comfort for excitement, a job with decent pay for a vocation, a monotonous existence for a life rich with experiences. Successful people collect memories, not dollar bills."

8. You Lived A Life That Met Your Expectations. "That's happiness in a nutshell", says Awosika. "The only thing you have do to to be successful is to live up to your own standards. Not the standards of society. Not the standards of your friends or family".

"We all deserve to be fully present - to live in a way that's satisfying more often than not. Money and status are great, but they're usually by-products of working towards something with meaning and doing it well. Define what success means to you and do what ever it takes to become it," concludes Awosika.

Brian Tracy, in "*Six Qualities of Wildly Successful People*"- adapted from his "*Success Mastery Academy*" - is of the opinion that the most successful people think in certain ways, and adopt certain habits. He believes that there are six characteristics of what he calls a "master achiever".

1. They are ambitious. "They see themselves as capable of being the best. They see themselves with the capacity of being really good at what they do. When I saw people who were doing better than I was, I naturally assumed that they were better than I was. Then I must be worse than them. They were superior and I was inferior".

   "That's a big problem in our society - we have feelings of inferiority, and these feelings are often translated into feelings of undeservedness", suggests Tracy. "The word "deserve" comes from two Latin words meaning "from service". You deserve 100% of everything you make and enjoy, as long as you get it from serving other people. If you serve better and serve more and serve at a higher level and serve more enthusiastically and serve a higher quality, then you'll have a wonderful income - and you'll deserve every penny of it. You just must see yourself capable of being the best", says Tracy.

2. They are courageous. "Successful people work to confront the fears that hold most people back. The two biggest enemies to our success are fear and doubt", he proposes.

"Make a habit throughout your life of doing the things that scare you. If you do the thing you fear, the death of fear is certain. The ability to confront your fear is the mark of the superior person. If you have high ambition and you decide to be at the top, and you can confront your fears and do the things that are holding you back, those two things alone will make you a great success," he says.

3. They are committed. "The top people in every field are completely committed. They believe in themselves; they believe in their companies; they believe in their products and services; they believe in their customers. They have an intense belief", suggests Tracy. "We know that there is a one-to-one relationship between the depth of your belief and what happens in your reality. And if you absolutely believe in the rightness and the goodness of what you're doing, you become like a catalyst," he adds.

    "People who are not committed to what they do lead very empty lives. Caring is a critical element in life - all men and women who enjoy great lives care about what they do. They have passion about what they do. They love what they do," adds Tracy.

4. They are prepared. "Successful people review every detail in advance. They do things that the average person is not willing to do", suggests Tracy. "They make sacrifices the average person is not willing to make. The difference it makes is extraordinary".

    "Before you go into a meeting, do your homework. Before you give a speech, research the information and practice your talking points. Dive in deep to review every detail of every situation before you take it on. Successful people are more concerned about pleasing results than they are about pleasing methods. There is nothing more complimentary to your team, your client, your audience, than the feeling that you have thoughtfully prepared."

5. They are continuous learners. "High achievers recognise that if they're not continually getting better, they're getting worse. They read, they listen to CDs and they take additional training. The professional never stops learning". "The day you stop learning is the day you start dying", *Robert Kiyosaki*, author of *"Rich Dad, Poor Dad"*.

6. They are responsible. "The top people in our society have an attitude of self-employment. 100% of us are self-employed - we are presidents of our own personal services corporation", he suggests. "You work for yourself, and the biggest mistake we can ever make is to think that we work for anyone else.

    The person who signs our paycheck may change, our jobs may change, but we are always the same. We are the one constant. This is not optional - it is mandatory".

"You're the president of your own career, your own life, your own finances, your own body, your own family, your own health. You are totally responsible. We have to be responsible. No one will ever do it for us. It's the most liberating and exhilarating thought of all, to think - to realise - that you are the president of your own life."

Writing for *success.com*, Caren Merrick's "*10 Daily Habits Holding You Back From Success*", suggests that "Highly successful people regularly assess their habits and strive for continuous improvement." Merrick proposes that "if you want more success in your work and life, start by changing your day. Losing a bad habit and creating a new one is the first step to propel you forward to greater success, impact and fulfillment."

Merrick suggests the following destructive habits which may be "holding you back from success"...

1. Your morning routine is non-existent. "When you have so much on your plate and everything is urgent, your precious morning moments are spent in a rush just doing whatever it takes to get out the door. But you're missing one of the most important opportunities within your control to ensure success," she suggests.

    "You can design a morning routine unique to your life, that will prime you physically and mentally for better performance. If you allowed even 10-15 more minutes to develop a routine that energised you and brought greater focus, you would have more confidence and be more effective through the day - instead of beginning it with a sense of overwhelm," claims Merrick.

2. You forget your strengths when hard things emerge. "Often, when we encounter unexpected setbacks, we flounder, or are paralysed like a deer in the headlights", she says. "Remind yourself every day of your strengths, it will jump-start your path to a solution better and faster than jumping into the spin cycle of self-doubt."

3. You let energy vampires consume your time. "These "vampires" can be time-wasting tasks like checking your email too often, or they can be people who have latched onto you in conversation because they are avoiding their own work," she suggests.

4. You major in the minors… "instead of prioritising the most important things that need to be accomplished."

    "You will be more productive and happier if you make incremental changes in how you manage your time", suggests Merrick. "Decide each morning the top three things that must be done each day, or set a timer to focus on just one thing for 60 minutes without interruptions." ("*Eat That Frog*"…)

5. You work on tasks that could be delegated to someone else. "You think that you can do a better job, so you just do it yourself", proposes Caren. "Or, you constantly correct or micromanage your team, which drains their motivation and distracts you from doing what you do best."

6. You spend too much time recovering from a stumble or setback. "Instead of quickly assessing a situation and determining a plan, you get sucked into a cycle that drains your energy and focus. You may have forgotten that every person you admire has had many failures and setbacks - some of them are legendary. You can develop habits and a mindset to find the many benefits of a setback," encourages Merrick.

7. You procrastinate. "A lot of what our perfectionism is ties back to procrastination. Procrastination can mask a lack of confidence, or a fear of being wrong or being criticised", she suggests. "Perfectionism makes us slow to start on a new initiative, or to begin the next stage of an existing one, because we want to be sure that the strategy or plan will be flawless. Just recognising when perfectionism is creeping into your thinking and time management is a big step forward," she adds.

8. You avoid difficult conversations. "Over time, I've realised that difficult conversations can be pivotal opportunities to gain clarity, to listen and learn, and to end the conversation having enriched the relationship", says Caren. "And I've learned that avoiding a difficult conversation means that we're not identifying, facing or solving problems that, if unaddressed, will fester and get worse."

9. You don't say thank you. "You won't succeed alone. Every day, there are many people on your team who deserve to be thanked - from colleagues up and down the career ladder, to the *Uber* driver and even the barista at your coffeehouse. And smile more, too! Research shows that it positively benefits you and those around you," she adds.

10. You forget that your inner life determines your outer success. "The good life sometimes has little to do with outside circumstances. We are happy and fulfilled mostly by who we are on the inside." *Dr. Henry Cloud.* "And our internal lives largely contribute to producing many of our external circumstances".

We are conditioned to react to external stimuli - "living from the outside-in". Once we are able to shift our paradigms and start to live from the "inside-out," we can determine our own results. We can literally turn our thinking, into results. "It forms the basis, too, for learned optimism. Anyone can learn to be more optimistic. As Winston Churchill said, "A pessimist sees the difficulty in every opportunity; an optimist sees the opportunity in every difficulty."

Tony Robbins - discussing "The mindset of a champion" - proposes that "where your focus goes, energy flows. If you focus on your negativity and fears, those thoughts and beliefs will consume you and suck all of your energy."

"Beliefs – a feeling of certainty about something - create the maps that guide us toward our goals and give us the power to take action. But in the same way that they can drive us forward to the lives we want to live, they can also create obstacles in our path and cause us to miss out on the things we want most. By focusing the power of your beliefs, you can turn your dreams into reality", says Robbins.

"Our beliefs come from five places: our environment or circumstances, powerful life events, our knowledge, past results and future vision. Free yourself from the beliefs that limit positive action and prevent you from reaching your potential. Learn how to turn your negatives into positives with these empowering beliefs," suggests Robbins.

"Once you've learned how to break your negative state and adopt empowering beliefs, the challenge is to maintain that state. What is your definition of a beautiful state? Is it grateful, playful, loving? Once you identify which power emotions give you the most joy, cultivate them and keep them alive", says Tony. "Where your limiting beliefs end, your extraordinary potential begins".

"Success leaves clues. People that are the most successful in the world over and over again are not lucky", proffers Robbins. "They have found what works, and doing that consistently leads to consistent success. The rich life is living, not just winning. And living requires fulfillment, not simply achievement," he advises.

"An extraordinary life depends on the science of achievement and the art of fulfillment. Striving without ever being satisfied makes successes hollow, not enriching. There's always a way to make more money, but what makes you happy? What brings you joy? Finding what's going to fulfill you is critical for happiness and a life of fulfillment. In other words", advises Tony, "trade expectation for appreciation".

John Addison, in *"Three Daily Habits of Very Successful People"*, writes that "Your habits and patterns determine the direction of your life, so it should come as no surprise that successful people have successful habits." Addison advocates three particular habits which - he believes - play a major role in achieving success.

1. Winners get out of bed early. "While you're in bed sleeping, someone else is out working. And, the fact is, most CEOs get up early and attack the day. Remember the saying "the early bird gets the worm?" Addison claims that the people who are up early are the people who seize the opportunities first. "Put in the extra time and effort it takes to chase success. It's not going to wait around for you," he adds.

Robin Sharma, author of *"The Monk Who Sold His Ferrari"*, is an advocate of *"The 5am Club"*, and Laura Vanderkam devoted a book to *"What The Most Successful People Do Before Breakfast"*. Brendon Burchard also proposes that a large proportion of his High Performance is attributed to "winning the mornings".

2. Be a daily goal setter and a daily goal hitter. "There is nothing wrong with having long-range goals and dreams (*DO*'s), but what you do today greatly affects whether or not you will achieve them. Intentionally design each and every day in a way that leads to getting things done that will maximise your results", recommends Addison. "That does not mean being busy every minute of the day just for the sake of being busy," he warns. "That means knowing what is important and focusing on those things".

3. "Every night, or in those early morning hours you are using to prepare for the day ahead, set your daily goals. Don't make goals for the entire week, just the upcoming day. Ask yourself what you must get done each day that will produce the most results and only work on those things. And make setting those goals a daily habit". *"Eat That Frog!"*

4. Focus, focus, focus. "Even if you set the goals, if you aren't focused - and by that I mean working on what's important now - you won't be successful. Successful people always know what is important in the moment", he suggests. "They are relentless in getting it done, and they don't get distracted by unimportant stuff. They have the ability to stay focused when other people are unfocused, which is no easy feat when everyone wants your attention," he adds.

"It's doing the same successful thing over and over again", suggests Addison. "Establishing repetitive habits that lead to effective performance is the key to winning results - and results are what matters."

Jim Rohn is also of the belief that success is the direct result of effective habits. In *"Four Straightforward Steps to Success"*, Rohn writes that "Success is nothing more than a few simple disciplines practiced every day. Success is neither magical nor mysterious. Success is the natural consequence of consistently applying basic fundamentals."

1. Collect good ideas. "My mentor taught me to keep a journal", says Rohn. "It's the best place for all of the ideas and information that comes your way. And that inspiration will be passed on to my children and my grandchildren. If you hear a good idea, capture it, write it down. Dive back into the ideas that changed your life, the ideas that saved your marriage, the ideas that bailed you out of hard times, the ideas that helped you become successful," Rohn suggests.

"So be a collector of good ideas, of experiences, for your business, for your relationships, for your future. It is challenging to be a student of your own life, your own future, your own destiny."

2. Have good plans. "Building a life, building anything, is like building a house", Rohn suggests. "You need to have a plan. What if you just started laying bricks and somebody asked you what you were building, Rohn supposes. "You put down the brick and say, "I have no idea." When should you start building the house? As soon as you have it finished. It's simple time management. Don't start the day until it is pretty well finished - at least the outline of it. Leave some room to improvise, leave some room for extra strategies, but finish it before you start it."

"Lay it out, structure it, put it to work. The same goes for the month ahead - don't start it until you have a plan in place. And, the big one, don't start the year until it is finished on paper," proposes Rohn. "The reason why most people face the future with apprehension instead of anticipation is because they don't have it well designed."

3. Give yourself time. "It takes time to build a career. It takes time to make changes. It takes time to learn, grow, change, develop and produce", suggests Rohn. "It takes time to refine philosophy and activity. So give yourself time to learn, time to start some momentum, time to finally achieve. Life is not just the passing of time. Life is the collection of experiences and their intensity."

4. Change yourself. Rohn suggests that you learn to solve problems - business, family, financial, or emotional problems. "What's the best way to treat a challenge?" he asks. "An opportunity to grow. Change if you have to, modify if you must, discard an old philosophy that wasn't working well for a new one. The best phrase my mentor ever gave me: "If you will change, everything will change for you." "The more I improved, the more everything improved for me," says Rohn.

"You cannot change your destination overnight, but you can change your direction overnight."

Brendon Burchard - whose philosophy of "Live. Love. Matter." serves as a daily inspiration – says, "I've been blessed to work with Olympians, billionaires, media moguls, celebrities, and every day people from all walks of life seeking a better life. Those who succeed and those who perpetually struggle THINK *soooo* differently."

"When it's easy to stop momentum by making the excuse, "I don't know how to do that," successful people say, "It's my mission to go learn how," adds Brendon. "They make a to-do item on their agenda to go learn the area they have a deficiency in."

"When unsuccessful people quit by saying, "I don't have that...(enough resources, assets, followers, etc)," successful people say, "Then it's my time to go build that". They immediately start building the reality they desire. Not talking. Not waiting. Building," says Brendon.

"When it's easy to say, "Well, I'm not like them... so talented, so natural, so skilled, so lucky," then that's the time they say, "It's my time to grow into my best self, to become the person who would deserve to succeed like that," suggests Burchard. "They focus on personal development not excuses. They create a learning plan, they forge new habits, they get to work on their character and discipline."

Brendon goes on to say that "At some point, we must elevate and say, I must change and take charge in order to advance toward my dreams:

- ✓ I can't wait for circumstances to change.
- ✓ I don't need permission.
- ✓ It's time I challenge myself and bend reality to my will.

"Successful people do what unsuccessful people are not willing to do. Don't wish it were easier; wish you were better." *Jim Rohn.*

"Success is not final, failure is not fatal. It is the courage to continue that counts." *Winston Churchill*

Emotional Intelligence (EQ):

The concept of emotional intelligence dates back to the early 1990's, when Yale psychologists John D. Mayer and Peter Salovey presented the concept to the academic world. Also referred to as *"EI"* or *"EQ"*, *Psychology Today* describes Emotional Intelligence as:

- The ability to accurately identify your own emotions, as well as those of others.
- The ability to utilise emotions and apply them to tasks, like thinking and problem-solving
- The ability to manage emotions, including controlling your own, as well as the ability to cheer up, or calm down, another person

In Rhett Power's *"Seven Qualities of People with High Emotional Intelligence"*, Daniel Goleman Ph.D proposes that "If your emotional abilities aren't in hand, if you don't have self-awareness, if you are not able to manage your distressing emotions, if you can't have empathy and have effective relationships, then no matter how smart you are, you are not going to get very far."

Goleman - author of *"Emotional Intelligence: Why It Can Matter More Than IQ"*, adds that "what makes people successful, comes down to their emotional intelligence. That's what drives a person to excellence." Goleman proposes that there are seven definite characteristics of emotionally intelligent people:

1. "They're change agents". People with high *EI* aren't afraid of change. They understand that it's a necessary part of life - and they adapt," says Goleman.

2. They're self-aware. "They know what they're good at and what they still have to learn - weaknesses don't hold them back", suggests Goleman. "They know what environments are optimal for their work style".

3. They're empathetic. "The ability to relate to others - makes them essential in the workplace", proposes Goleman. "With an innate ability to understand what co-workers or clients are going through, they can navigate difficult times "stress-free".

4. They're not perfectionists. "While extremely motivated, people with *EI* know that perfection is impossible" says Goleman. "They roll with the punches and learn from mistakes".

5. They're balanced. "Their self-awareness means that they naturally know the importance of - and how to maintain - a healthy professional-personal balance in their lives. They eat well, get plenty of sleep and have interests outside of work," he adds.

6. They're curious. "An inborn sense of wonder and curiosity makes them delightful to be around", suggests Goleman. "They don't judge; they explore the possibilities. They ask questions and are open to new solutions".

7. They're gracious. "Every day brings something to be thankful for", he suggests. "They feel good about their lives and don't let critics or toxic people affect that".

In *"Habits of Highly Emotionally Intelligent People"*, Dr Travis Bradberry - co-author of *"Emotional Intelligence 2.0"*, proposes that "Emotional intelligence served as the missing link" as to why "people with average *IQs* outperform those with the highest *IQs* 70% of the time. Decades of research now point to emotional intelligence as the critical factor that sets star performers apart from the rest of the pack," suggests Dr Bradberry.

Dr Bradberry adds, "Of all the people we've studied at work, we've found that 90% of top performers have high *EQs*. You can be a top performer without emotional intelligence, but the chances are slim," he adds. "Emotional intelligence is the "something" in each of us that is a bit intangible. It affects how we manage behaviour, navigate social complexities, and make personal decisions that achieve positive results."

Dr Bradberry proposes that "Emotional intelligence is made up of four core skills that pair up under two primary competencies: personal competence and social competence."

- *Personal competence.* "Your self-awareness and self-management skills, which focus more on you individually than on your interactions with other people. Personal competence is your ability to stay aware of your emotions and manage your behaviour and tendencies", says Dr Bradberry.

    i. "Self-Awareness - your ability to accurately perceive your emotions and stay aware of them as they happen."
    ii. "Self-Management - your ability to use awareness of your emotions to stay flexible and positively direct your behaviour."

- *Social competence.* "Your social awareness and relationship management skills. Social competence is your ability to understand other people's moods, behaviour, and motives, in order to respond effectively and improve the quality of your relationships."

    i. "Social Awareness - your ability to accurately pick up on emotions in other people and understand what is really going on."
    ii. "Relationship Management - your ability to use awareness of your emotions and others' emotions to manage interactions successfully."

"Despite the significance of emotional intelligence, its intangible nature makes it very difficult to know which behaviours you should emulate," says Bradberry. Through analysing *TalentSmart* data of over one million people tested, Dr Bradberry, however, believes that he has been able to "identify the habits that set high-EQ people apart".

- ✓ "They're relentlessly positive. "They don't get caught up in things they can't control. They focus their energy on directing the two things that are completely within their power - their attention and their effort. Optimists are physically and psychologically healthier than pessimists, and also perform better at work", claims Dr Bradberry.

- ✓ "They have a robust emotional vocabulary. "All people experience emotions, but it is a select few who can accurately identify them as they occur. Our research shows that only 36% of people can do this, which is problematic because unlabeled emotions often go misunderstood, which leads to irrational choices and counterproductive actions" proposes Dr Bradberry.

"People with high *EQs* master their emotions because they understand them, and they use an extensive vocabulary of feelings to do so", he continues. "While many people might describe themselves as simply feeling "bad", emotionally intelligent people can pinpoint whether they feel "irritable", "frustrated", "downtrodden", or "anxious". The more specific your word choice, the better insight you have into exactly how you are feeling, what caused it, and what you should do about it," suggests Dr Bradberry.

- ✓ "They're assertive. "People with high *EQs* balance good manners, empathy, and kindness with the ability to assert themselves and to establish boundaries", proposes Dr Bradberry. "This tactful combination is ideal for handling conflict. When most people are crossed, they default to passive or aggressive behaviour. Emotionally intelligent people remain balanced and assertive by steering themselves away from unfiltered emotional reactions. This enables them to neutralise difficult and toxic people without creating enemies."

- ✓ "They're curious about other people. It doesn't matter if they're introverted or extroverted, emotionally intelligent people are curious about everyone around them", says Travis. "This curiosity is the product of empathy, one of the most significant gateways to a high *EQ*. The more you care about other people and what they're going through, the more curiosity you're going to have about them," he suggests.

- ✓ "They forgive, but they don't forget. Emotionally intelligent people live by the motto "Fool me once, shame on you; fool me twice, shame on me". They forgive in order to prevent a grudge, but they never forget", adds Dr Bradberry.

"The negative emotions that come with holding on to a grudge are actually a stress response. Holding on to that stress can have devastating health consequences, and emotionally intelligent people know to avoid this at all costs. However, offering forgiveness doesn't mean they'll give a wrongdoer another chance. Emotionally intelligent people let things go quickly, and are assertive in protecting themselves from future harm."

- ✓ "They won't let anyone limit their joy. When your sense of pleasure and satisfaction are derived from comparing yourself to others, you are no longer the master of your own happiness. When emotionally intelligent people feel good about something that they've done, they won't let anyone's opinions or accomplishments take that away from them", he says. "While it's impossible to turn off your reactions to what others think of you, you don't have to compare yourself to others, and you can always take people's opinions with a grain of salt. That way, no matter what other people are thinking or doing, your self-worth comes from within", says Bradberry.

- ✓ "They make things fun. Emotionally intelligent people know exactly what makes them happy, and they constantly work to bring this happiness into everything they do." Dr Bradberry proposes that "they turn monotonous work into games, go the extra mile to make people they care about happy, and take breaks to enjoy the things they love, no matter how busy they are. They know that injecting this fun into their lives fights off stress and builds lasting resilience", he adds.

- ✓ "They are difficult to offend. If you have a firm grasp of whom you are, it's difficult for someone to say or do something that gets your goat", he says. "Emotionally intelligent people are self-confident and open-minded, which creates a pretty thick skin."

- ✓ "They quash negative self-talk. The more you ruminate on negative thoughts, the more power you give them. Most of our negative thoughts are just that - thoughts, not facts. You can stop the negative and pessimistic things your inner voice says by writing them down" he suggests.

"Once you've taken a moment to slow down the negative momentum of your thoughts, you will be more rational and clear-headed in evaluating their veracity. You can bet that your statements aren't true any time you use words such as "never", "worst", and "ever". If your statements still look like facts once they're on paper, take them to a friend and see if they agree with you. Then the truth will surely come out," he advises.

In summary, Dr Bradberry goes on to say that "Unlike your *IQ*, your *EQ* is highly malleable. As you train your brain by repeatedly practicing new emotionally intelligent behaviours, your brain builds the pathways needed to make them into habits."

"Before long, you will begin responding to your surroundings with emotional intelligence without even having to think about it. And as your brain reinforces the use of new behaviours, the connections supporting old, destructive behaviours will die off."

Paul Grossinger, on *inc.com* proposes that there are "*Ten characteristics of people with high Emotional Intelligence*". "What is it about how certain people behave and interact, how they are "wired" that drives them to greater success than their peers?" asks Grossinger. "More often than not, it is their emotional intelligence (*EQ*), or, in other words, their ability to identify and manage the emotions of themselves and others."

Grossinger believes that there are "critical ways that high achievers with strong emotional intelligence handle their lives, which you can learn from..."

1. Embrace Work-Life Balance. "People who work too hard without rest or focusing equally on personal relationships usually burn out before they can reach their potential. Those who don't work particularly hard tend to simply underachieve," claims Grossinger.

2. Empower Your Partner. "Finding the right partner is a critical part of achieving emotional balance" proposes Grossinger. "That person should stabilise, compliment, and empower you - and they can only do that if you empower them in turn. Successful partner EQ support relationships are symbiotic - and it starts with you," he suggests.

3. Focus. Grossinger says that he tries "to draw a key distinction between multitasking and multifocusing. Although I may be doing three tasks at once, at any given moment, I keep my overall goals very focused and don't change them until those goals are achieved, or I need to pivot them," he adds.

4. Be Creative. "Boredom hampers creativity, which in turn hampers emotional welfare. Individuals who are genuinely and positively curious about others tend to form powerful and enduring relationships," suggests Grossinger.

5. Listen First. "Listening is often empowered by emotional creativity mixed with discipline. It is a sign of great emotional intelligence - and not one that all of us have any easy time with - to be genuinely curious about people and disciplined enough to remove the focus from oneself and listen to them 75% of the time," he proffers.

6. Embrace Dynamism and Positive Volatility. "Too much safety leads to boredom, which over time stunts intellectual stimulation and often leads to insecurity, which typically hampers emotional intelligence.
Change, especially when embraced as a positive, can be a powerful catalyst," proposes Grossinger.

7. Don't Be a Perfectionist. Perfectionism, according to Grossinger, "leads to intense frustration and emotional distress. It also leads to placing blame on others for failing to live up to unacceptable standards, which is a major drag on *EQ*, and on your relationships with others."

8. Don't Accept the First Answer. "Use curiosity and listening to gently probe for many solutions to different problems. *EQ* is one of the best ways to identify multi-layered solutions, and to incorporate the ideas of multiple participants seamlessly," proposes Grossinger.

9. Move Past Mistakes. "Dwelling on the past, and on the mistakes of either yourself or others, causes distress, anger, and misplaced blame," he adds.

10. Channel Anger. "Anger is not a negative emotion in itself - it is the most powerful catalyst in the human arsenal", suggests Grossinger. "But it must be controlled and channeled into the appropriate action - and away from people. *EQ* helps people use anger the right way," he concludes.

Physiology and Energy:

"The difference between peak performance and poor performance is not intelligence or ability; most often it's the state that your mind and body is in." *Tony Robbins.*

"Emotion is created by motion", proposes Tony Robbins. "Emotions are linked to movement in our bodies. Observe your posture when you are happy, as opposed to when you are sad - or what you look like when you are angry, versus when you are elated. There's a difference".

"It is not only in your physical appearance but also in your brain. If you have a poor posture, it only lends itself to poor emotions, or a negative state", claims Robbins. "Good posture and alertness produces a more positive state. We all get in a lousy psychological and emotional states at times, but when you find yourself in that place, change your body and get in state." Remember Professor Amy Cuddy's studies, which show that "small changes in body language change your body chemistry".

David De Las Morenas suggests something as simple as taking a cold shower to change your state. "Cold showers have been clinically proven to have anti-depressive effects. By immersing ourselves in cold water, we release key hormones and neurotransmitters that make us feel happier", he suggests.

"Cold showers also cause us to breathe deeply (this is the first thing your body will do when you step in) and feel more awake and energised", De Las Morenas suggests. "This combination of feeling happier, breathing deeply, and being energised is a killer combination when it comes to assuming a confident state of mind. If you're lethargic, sad, and tired it's going to be very tough to feel confident and project this confidence to the world around you," he proposes.

What is your understanding of the term "*energy*?" By definition, energy is a power - a force that fuels life, actions, strength and vitality. Energy is the force behind motions and reactions; it moves the Earth, it keeps our feet on the ground, it heats our homes, lights up our cities and it even powers our bodies. Energy powers us on every level - not just physically, but mentally, emotionally and spiritually too.

When you learn how to suppress your negative energies, and how to channel your positive energies, "you could be in a better position to reach your full potential in all aspects of life - from your performance at work, to the quality of your love life and friendships."

What gives you your energy? What makes you feel energised? What leaves you feeling alive, or invigorated? On the other hand, what leaves you feeling tired and demotivated? What (or who) drains you?

Are there people that you find it physically exhausting to be around? Are there certain aspects of your life that particularly drain you? Try to focus your energies away from them, and towards the things that make you happy.

What makes you feel good? What puts the spring in your step? What gives you the motivation to get out there and do things? There are lots of different things that give people energy, from doing certain things, to being with certain people.

Here are some of the most common energy boosts:

- Food. The energy in our body comes from the food that we eat. Our bodies are essentially walking, talking energy generators - they take in nutrients from food and then convert those nutrients into energy. How else would you be sitting here, reading these words? Right now, your nervous system is generating energy from food molecules to process what you see in front of you.

  There's plenty of scientific evidence to suggest that different foods have different effects on how we feel and function in everyday life. You will know from your personal experience that some foods will leave you feeling drained and groggy, while others will provide you with an invigorating boost.

- Exercise. Exercise might initially drain your physical energy, but scientific research shows that in the long run (*no pun intended*), regular exercise can boost general energy levels. Scientists from the University of Georgia, claim that it can help energise people suffering from fatigue-associated conditions such as cancer and heart disease, for example. Tim Puetz, PhD, suggests that "people in today's society are too keen to reach for their coffee or energy bars when really they should be reaching for their trainers".

- Environment. "Where you live is just as important as how you live. "*Feng Shui*" - a Chinese belief based on the idea that there are energy pathways (*chi*) flowing through everything in the world – proposes that the way that you position your home and possessions can affect the quality of your energy.

  Clutter and disorder only serve to block chi pathways, resulting in unhappiness and ill health. Throw away the old things that you don't really need anymore and have a thorough clean. Your living environment can boost your creative energy, as well as help to relax you. If you're constantly misplacing things, like your keys for example, a "spring clean" could do wonders for your stress and energy levels. An unexpected bonus is that a recent survey determined that "the average home in the UK has around £4,000 worth of unused items" just sapping your energy.[58] Why not revitalise your energy, and your bank balance at the same time?

How do you channel your energy? If you exhibit any of the following behaviours, then chances are that you are channeling your energy negatively…

- ✗ Anger
- ✗ Jealousy
- ✗ Guilt
- ✗ Competitiveness

If you haven't yet learned to direct your energy constructively, you're probably directing it destructively. "If you're not creating, you're disintegrating". Destructive energy can lead to frustration, unhappiness and dis-ease. It could also lead to destructive activities, such as binge drinking, smoking, gambling and drug abuse, for example.

If, however, you benefit from the following behavioural characteristics, then you are most probably channeling your energy in a positive manner…

- ✓ Creativity
- ✓ Physical activity or exercise
- ✓ Leadership
- ✓ Compassion or empathy
- ✓ Ambition (Not to be confused with Competitiveness)

Deepak Chopra - who I had the honour of meeting in person in 2017 - wrote "*The Secret of Lifelong Energy*", which was published on LinkedIn. Deepak suggests that "One of the most positive trends in modern society is a belief that a person's entire lifespan should be healthy and valuable. We expect to be engaged and involved into our seventies and eighties, a far cry from the automatic decline that prior generations identified with ageing," he claims.

"But the ageing process undermines many people, who find that they lose energy as the years go by. I don't mean just diminished physical energy, because mind and body are linked. Consider the entire person who is thinking, feeling, hoping, and wishing every day," says Deepak.

Deepak asks, "Where do you get enough energy to keep going on all fronts? Physics offers a simple but profound answer. In every physical system, the law of entropy dictates that energy will dissipate over time, which is why ice cubes melt and stars burn out. But a counter force, evolution, allows energy to be stored and increased," Chopra proposes.

"Life is the prime example of negative entropy - as this energy storage is called - because living things use food, air, and sunlight to extract more energy than they give off," suggests Chopra.

"A human being is too complex to reduce to simple physics, but it's still true that we must favour evolution over entropy if we want to have energy for a lifetime. In us there is energy loss on the physical, emotional, and spiritual plane if we fail to counter it", warns Chopra.

"Physical entropy is linked to ageing in most people's minds, but in reality, we are worn down by overwork, stress, the inability to take downtime, bad sleep, and a frenetic pace that the body can adapt to for only so long", suggests Chopra. "Emotional entropy can't be separated from the physical, since factors like bad sleep, overwork, and stress have emotional consequences - we lose enthusiasm and interest in what we're doing. Emotional entropy is also caused by psychological issues like depression, anxiety, bad relationships, abusive behaviour, and low self-esteem."

"Spiritual entropy comes about when we lose our sense of purpose and meaning", suggests Chopra. "This is a prevalent danger for millions of people when they retire or see their children leave home. But there's also spiritual depletion through grief, abuse, lack of productive work, and any occasion of personal defeat", Deepak proffers.

Deepak continues, "entropy is a powerful force that can invade any part of our lives, and if we had to counter it one piece at a time, we could only hope for partial success. In a society where mass media equates happiness with youth, beauty, a toned body, sex, and riches, the reality of life is being hidden from sight, because none of these things, desirable as they are, will prevent the gradual inroads made by entropy as it inexorably works its way year after year," adds Chopra.

"Which isn't to say that the situation is grim. In modern times there have been major victories against entropy, most of them physical", adds Chopra. "We can cure diseases that have sapped the life out of people for centuries. We know how prevention works."

"We can have clean air and water, along with natural, whole foods, by exerting some effort. Recovery from debilitating strokes and heart attacks is better than ever. These are all positive signs of evolution or progress," Deepak adds.

"But the subtle aspects of entropy, the psychological and spiritual setbacks that drain us, need to be countered, too, and that requires expanded awareness", claims Deepak. "The evolution of the inner person holds the key to energising the entire system, including the body. Research into meditation, for example, indicates that its benefits are holistic. Yet many people have negative associations with the whole project of consciousness raising, self-awareness, and the alien Eastern ethos surrounding yoga and meditation."

"The rap against these things is that with meditation one becomes calm and passive at the expense of achievement. Yoga has been tagged as belonging to women rather than to everyone..."

"Self-awareness is suspicious because it supposedly forces you to think about all the conflicts and problems hidden beneath the surface of one's inner existence. Better not to stir sleeping dogs and just get on with life," Deepak laments.

"All of these attitudes are mistaken, and more importantly, they are entropic. If you ignore the emotional and spiritual issues that drain away enthusiasm, self-confidence, curiosity, inspiration, and self-worth, you have pushed away the possibility of evolving and growing. When that possibility lies fallow, entropy finds a way to win, no matter how smart, good-looking, physically fit, and rich you are."

"The reason we are here as living creatures is entirely due to the force of evolution. For billions of years evolution operated as an external, physical agent of growth. Now the frame has shifted, and as conscious beings we must go inward to activate our evolution. The evolution of consciousness sounds pretentious, overly ambitious, and selfish to those who haven't experienced it. But if you want to have energy that lasts a lifetime, here is the key", proposes Deepak.

If you can learn to think positively, you can ultimately change your behaviour and, in turn, improve the direction and quality of your life. Your thoughts determine your energy, which in turn influences your behaviour, actions, and – ultimately - your results.

Remember, "thoughts become things".

Diet and Nutrition:

- The number of overweight and obese adults in the developing world has almost quadrupled to approximately one billion, since 1980.
- One in three people worldwide is overweight.
- 64% of adults in the UK are classed as being overweight or obese.
- A report from *The Overseas Development Institute* predicts a "huge increase" in heart attacks, strokes and diabetes.
- Globally, the percentage of overweight or obese adults - having a body mass index (*BMI*) greater than 25 - grew from 23% in 1980, to 34% in 2008.
- A total of 904 million people in developing countries are now classed as overweight or above - spiralling from 250 million in 1980.

The Overseas Development Institute's Future Diets report claims that this is "due to changing diets and a shift from eating cereals and grains to the consumption of more fats, sugar, oils and animal products".

Do you need a better reason to review your diet? Recent studies suggest that "nutrition plays an important role in our mental acuity and well-being and that poor nutrition can negatively affect mental health".

Here in the United Kingdom, the ubiquitous recommendation - in an attempt to improve our diets and nutrition - is that of *"5 a day"*, a campaign based on advice from the World Health Organisation. Their recommendation is to eat a minimum of 400g of fruit and vegetables a day, to lower the risk of serious health problems, such as heart disease, strokes, obesity, and Type 2 Diabetes.

Why *"5 a day"*?

- Fruit and vegetables are a good source of vitamins and minerals, including folate, vitamin C and potassium.
- Fruit and vegetables are an excellent source of dietary fibre, which helps to maintain a healthy gut and prevent constipation and digestion problems. A diet rich in fibre can also reduce your risk of bowel cancer, lung cancer, and diverticular disease.
- Fruit and vegetables are generally low in fat and calories (provided they're not fried or roasted in lots of oil).
- People who eat more fruit and vegetables tend to be healthier and live longer.
- "Fruit and vegetables reduce the chance of developing cardiovascular diseases such as heart disease or strokes, owing to "hardening of the arteries" (*atheroma*).
- Fruit and vegetables lower your risk of developing obesity and Type 2 Diabetes.
- Fruit and vegetables are filling, but low in calories, so are perfect to manage your weight.

Having a low intake of fruit and vegetables is estimated to cause about 19% of cancers of the digestive system, 31% of heart disease and 11% of strokes. Fruit and vegetables are rich in healthy vitamins and minerals, and they also contain antioxidants such as beta-carotene and vitamin C - thought to protect against damaging chemicals that can infiltrate the body's defences.

Fruit and vegetables contain fibre, which can help to control cholesterol levels, and also to regulate blood sugar levels. Eating fruit and vegetables in preference over foods that are high in fat, salt and sugar, serves to further reduce the risk of diet-related diseases.

So, why are we encouraged to eat at least five portions of fruit and vegetables each day? The World Health Organisation collated evidence, and determined that a minimum of 400 g was required to "meet our nutritional requirements", and to "protect us from diseases such as strokes, heart disease, some cancers, Type 2 Diabetes and obesity".

Five (80g) portions of fruit and vegetables each day is actually the *minimum*. The more fruit and vegetables that we eat, the greater our protection from diet-related diseases. The World Heath Organisation took into account what they believed the nation would realistically be able to consume. If they were to set the target too high, then it would appear to be unrealistic, and might actually serve the opposite effect - that of discouraging people through overwhelm. Not to be confused with fruit, how do you eat an elephant…?

So what constitutes a portion?

- ✓ One large fruit such as an apple, pear, banana, orange, or a large slice of melon.
- ✓ Two smaller fruits such as plums, kiwis, satsumas, clementines, etc.
- ✓ One cup of small fruits such as grapes, strawberries, raspberries, cherries, etc.
- ✓ Two large tablespoons of fruit salad, stewed or canned fruit.
- ✓ One tablespoon of dried fruit.
- ✓ Two tablespoons of any vegetable.
- ✓ One dessert bowl of salad.
- ✓ Three heaped tablespoons of beans, pulses or lentils.

A 150ml glass of fruit juice counts as one of your five a day, even if you have more than one glass. This is because the processing removes most of the fibre, and fruit juice also has a higher sugar content than the natural fruit. Some smoothies may provide two portions, but only if they contain at least 150ml of fruit juice, and 80g of pulped fruit or vegetables. Beans and pulses also count as a maximum of one portion a day, as they contain fewer nutrients when compared with other fruit and vegetables.

Fruit and vegetables add colour, flavour, and texture to any meal or snack. No single fruit or vegetable contains all of the nutrients that you need, so try to include a variety of different colours, indicating different combinations of vitamins, minerals and antioxidants. Juiced, frozen, canned, and dried varieties all count.

Add chopped bananas, pineapples, apples, or dried fruits to your breakfast. Instead of fruit yoghurt, add a dollop of natural low-fat yoghurt to a piece of fruit. Make it a habit to include at least two different vegetables with your main meals. Replace your jars of processed pasta sauces with tomato purée or tinned chopped tomatoes as a "home-made" pasta sauce. When making a *bolognese*, add some red peppers and kidney beans. Add tomato purée or tinned chopped tomatoes to casseroles and stews. This not only benefits your pocket in terms of helping to bulk up meals, but also serve to make them more filling and satisfying – not to mention nutritious.

Nutrients are lost or destroyed during cooking, so try to eat raw fruit and vegetables where possible and try to avoid over-cooking them. Poach, steam or microwave rather than boil, and avoid frying at all costs. If you do boil your vegetables, the water can then be used for stocks, sauces or soups.

Add cucumber, tomato, lettuce, avocado or other alternatives to your sandwiches. Bulk out meals with vegetables, beans and pulses. Fruit is great for snacks. Encourage children to snack on fruit, rather than sweets. Substitute vegetables for crisps with your savoury snacks or dips.

One apple, banana, pear or similar-sized fruit is one portion, as is a slice of pineapple or melon. Two tablespoons of vegetables is another portion. Having a sliced banana with your morning cereal is a quick and convenient way to add another portion. Swap your mid-morning biscuit for a tangerine and add a salad to your lunch. Have a portion (or two) of vegetables with dinner, and snack on dried fruit to effortlessly achieve your five a day.

Your five portions should include a variety of fruit and vegetables. This is because different fruits and vegetables contain different combinations of fibre, vitamins, minerals and other nutrients. Almost all fruit and vegetables count towards your *5 a day*.

One of the first fruits that you will find in the produce aisle of your local supermarket, is bananas. Bananas are "big business" in the UK, which consumes the most in the European Union. (It appears that bananas aren't just *The Minions'*[59] preferred fruit). Each year, "every man, woman and child consumes the equivalent of a forty pound (18.14kg) box". In 2015, 1,160,000 MT (that's 1,160,000,000kg) of bananas were imported into the UK.

---

59   Minions are small, yellow, melodious henchmen, popularised through the "*Despicable Me*" movie franchise.

They are the most popular fruit in the world. Over 100 billion bananas are eaten around the world every year, and over 96% of households in the United States purchase bananas at least once a month.

So, we love bananas, but besides their versatility and popularity, are you aware of the health benefits associated with the *"yellow finger"*? (The word *banana* derives from the Arabic word *"banan"*, meaning finger.)

In *"10 Surprising Health Benefits Of Eating 3 Bananas a Day"*, David K. William writes, "The magic number is three - by eating three bananas per day, you provide your body with about 1500mg of potassium, and loads of health benefits."(Well, at least the following ten…)

1. Bananas lower high blood pressure. "Eating as little as three bananas a day may lower your blood pressure significantly," says William. A medium-sized banana has about 422 mg of potassium and is nearly sodium-free. The high potassium-to-sodium ratio helps to neutralise the harmful effects of sodium in the diet.

2. Bananas improve digestion. Bananas are rich in fibre - both soluble and insoluble - which helps to slow down the rate of digestion. Eating a banana will make you feel full longer and can also help with easing constipation. Incorporating bananas into your breakfast will add energy to your mornings, and keep you satisfied longer.

3. Bananas improve cardiovascular health. A fibre-rich diet has been linked with a reduced risk of both cardiovascular- and coronary heart disease. The soluble fibre in banana is associated with a decreased risk of heart disease.

4. Bananas help create healthy cells. "Bananas are rich in vitamin B6, containing 20% of the recommended daily amount for adults. Vitamin B6 helps produce insulin, haemoglobin and amino acids necessary to create healthy cells. It also helps with the production of antibodies that fight infections." *"A banana a day, keeps the doctor away."*

5. Bananas improve *GI* tract heath. Bananas are relatively easy to digest and are considered non-irritating for the human gastrointestinal (or GI) tract. Bananas are among the first solid foods introduced to babies' diets.
Bananas not only ease digestive strain, but also soothe the digestive tract and help restore lost minerals after diarrhea, as part of the clinical BRAT diet – bananas, rice, applesauce and dry toast.

6. Bananas are rich in Vitamin C. "A full serving of bananas provides 15% of the daily requirement for vitamin C - an important antioxidant that neutralises harmful free radicals in the body. Vitamin C also aids in keeping blood vessels healthy and produces collagen that holds muscles, bones and other tissues together."

7. Bananas improve athletic performance. "Bananas boost the muscles and provide a natural source of antioxidants and other nutrients. According to *The Appalachian State University's Human Performance Lab*, consuming half a banana every 15 minutes during a cycling time trial test was as effective as drinking a carbohydrate matched sports drink. Yohan Blake, the Jamaican Olympics sprinter, reportedly eats 16 bananas a day."

8. Bananas fight anaemia. Bananas are high in iron, which can stimulate production of haemoglobin in the blood and help combat anaemia - a decrease in the number of red blood cells or haemoglobin in the blood. Anaemia can contribute towards fatigue, paleness and shortness of breath. Vitamin B6 present in bananas regulates blood glucose levels, which can also aid people suffering from anaemia.

9. Bananas suppress hunger pangs. "This happens not merely because eating bananas makes you feel full for longer, but also due to their pleasant smell. According to Dr Alan Hirsch of *The Smell and Taste Treatment and Research Foundation* in Chicago, smelling bananas when you are hungry can trick your brain into thinking that you've actually eaten them."

10. Bananas lift mood and help you feel happy. "A medium-sized banana provides about 27mg magnesium, which can help boost your mood and aid a good night's sleep. Men require 420mg, and women 320mg of magnesium per day. If your magnesium levels are low, you're likely to suffer from anxiety, irritability, depression and other disorders."

- ✓ Bananas could help you to feel happier, as they contain tryptophan, a type of protein that the body converts into serotonin, known to promote relaxation and improve mood.
- ✓ The inside of a banana skin can be used to reduce the irritation of a mosquito bite
- ✓ A medium banana contains 95 calories, and provides a quick-but-sustained energy boost in a nutritious and easily digestible form with no fat, cholesterol or sodium
- ✓ Rubbing banana peel on your teeth for about two minutes after you brush can allegedly help to contribute towards a pearly white smile.

From one tropical fruit to another… (I was raised in South Africa, remember.)

A 100 gram serving of raw pineapple is an excellent source of Manganese (44% of RDA) and Vitamin C (58% of RDA), and also includes potassium, copper, calcium, magnesium, beta carotene, thiamine, B6, and folate, as well as soluble and insoluble fibre.

The health and medicinal benefits of pineapples include their ability to improve respiratory health, cure coughs and colds, improve digestion, help you lose weight, and strengthen your bones. Pineapples also improve oral and eye health, reduce inflammation, and help to prevent cancers. They also improve heart health, combat infections and parasites, improve the immune system, and increase circulation.

- ✓ Pineapples Prevent Hair Loss. Vitamin C is not only good for your skin, it is also aids in preventing hair loss, and in thickening hair. "Daily consumption of pineapple can help prevent and ease inflammatory conditions, which affect the scalp, using *Bromelain*, the anti-inflammatory enzyme. It can also offer relief from infections of the scalp."

- ✓ Pineapples Keep Your Skin Flawless and Firm. Vitamin C in pineapples can be used internally as well as externally, as a cure for acne and other inflammatory skin conditions. Pineapple also promotes the synthesis of collagen in your body. The more collagen that is produced, the firmer and more flexible your skin will be. The presence of amino acids and Vitamin C also ensures that damaged cells and tissues are repaired quickly.

Try a pineapple "face mask"… "Apply freshly prepared pineapple juice on your face. Wash off using tepid water after 10 minutes. Or try freshly crushed pineapple wedges to exfoliate your skin and make it look healthier This eliminates dead skin, and accentuates blood flow. Rubbing pineapple on your feet helps to prevent callouses and cracked heels, and will also assist with the inflammation associated with cracks on your feet." (I'm fairly confident that this doesn't count towards your *5 a day*, though…)

- ✓ Pineapples Reduce Symptoms of Arthritis. *Bromelain* – although primarily associated with breaking down complex proteins - also has serious anti-inflammatory effects, and has been positively correlated with reducing the signs and symptoms of arthritis in many test subjects."

- ✓ Pineapples Tackle Digestive Problems. Pineapples are a rich source of fibre, and (like bananas) they contain both soluble and insoluble fibre. "Eating a healthy amount of pineapple can protect you from digestive health conditions, including constipation, diarrhea, irritable bowel syndrome, atherosclerosis, blood clotting, and irregular blood pressure."

- ✓ Pineapples Improve Your Vision. "Macular Degeneration is a condition in which adults lose their vision. The beta-carotene present in pineapple can help improve vision."

- ✓ Pineapples Help Cure Coughs, Colds and Sinusitis. Coupled with vitamin C, *Bromelain* helps to prevent the illnesses that cause phlegm and mucus build-up. If you are already suffering from an illness or infection, *Bromelain* aids in loosening phlegm and mucus, and helping to eliminate them from your body. Eating pineapple can help cure coughs and colds.

- ✓ Pineapples Maintain Your Oral Health. Along with the antioxidant compounds that protect against oral cancer, pineapples also have astringent properties, which help to tighten up tissues and tone the body, as well as strengthening gums and helping to prevent tooth loss. Pineapples are very powerful astringents and are often prescribed as a natural remedy to fix loosening of teeth or the retraction of the gums."

"When it comes to a healthy diet, balance is the key to getting it right. This means eating a wide variety of foods in the right proportions, and consuming the right amount of food and drink to achieve and maintain a healthy body weight."

The NHS suggests that "A diet based on starchy foods such as potatoes, bread, rice and pasta; with plenty of fruit and vegetables; some protein-rich foods such as meat, fish and lentils; some milk and dairy foods; and not too much fat, salt or sugar, will give you all the nutrients you need."

"Most adults in England are overweight or obese", warns the NHS. "Many of us are eating more than we need, and should eat less. And it's not just food: some drinks can also be high in calories. Most adults need to eat and drink fewer calories to lose weight, even if they already eat a balanced diet."

To benefit from a healthy, balanced diet, people should aim to consume:

- ✓ plenty of fruit and vegetables
- ✓ plenty of starchy foods, such as bread, rice, potatoes and pasta
- ✓ some meat, fish, eggs, beans and other non-dairy sources of protein
- ✓ some milk and dairy foods
- ✓ just a small amount of food and drinks that are high in fat and/or sugar

The NHS suggests "to choose a variety of different foods from the four main food groups", but in *balance*. "Most people in the UK eat and drink too many calories, too much fat, sugar and salt, and not enough fruit, vegetables, oily fish and fibre."

So what exactly does the NHS recommend?

It's important to have *some* fat in your diet, but try to avoid foods high in fat. As well as eating at least five portions of fruit and vegetables each day, starchy foods should comprise around one third of everything that we eat.

Potatoes are a great source of fibre. Leave the skins on where possible to retain more of the fibre and vitamins. When eating boiled, or jacket, potatoes, begin to make it a habit to eat the skin too. Try to choose wholegrain or wholemeal varieties of starchy foods, such as brown rice, wholewheat pasta and brown, wholemeal or higher fibre white bread. They contain more fibre (*"roughage"*), and usually more vitamins and minerals than the white varieties.

Meat, fish, eggs and beans are all excellent sources of protein - essential for the body to grow, as well as to repair. They are also good sources of a variety of vitamins and minerals. Meat is a good source of protein, vitamins and minerals, including iron, zinc and B vitamins. It is also one of the main sources of vitamin B12. Try to eat lean cuts of meat and skinless poultry whenever possible to cut down on fat. Always cook meat and poultry thoroughly.

Fish is another important source of protein and contains many vitamins and minerals. Oily fish is particularly rich in Omega-3 fatty acids. The NHS recommends that you "aim for at least two portions of fish a week, including one portion of oily fish. You can choose from fresh, frozen or canned, but remember that canned and smoked fish can often be high in salt."

Eggs and pulses (including beans, nuts and seeds) are also a great source of protein. Nuts are high in fibre and provide a good alternative to snacks high in saturated fat, but they do still contain high levels of fat, so ensure that you eat them in moderation.

Milk and dairy such as cheese and yoghurt are good sources of protein. They also contain calcium, which is essential to keep your bones healthy. Try to avoid full fat varieties, though. "To enjoy the health benefits of dairy without consuming too much fat, choose semi-skimmed, 1% fat or skimmed milk, as well as lower-fat hard cheeses or cottage cheese, and lower-fat yoghurt," suggests the NHS.

Most importantly, consume less fat and sugar... The NHS warns that "most people in the UK eat too much fat and sugar. Fats and sugar are both sources of energy for the body, but when we eat too much of them, we consume more energy than we burn, and this can mean that we put on weight. This can lead to obesity, which increases our risk of Type 2 Diabetes, certain cancers, heart disease and strokes."

Fats play an extremely important role in the structure and function of the body. Do you know that there are two main different types of fat?

- ✗ Saturated fat is found in foods such as cheese, sausages, butter, cakes, biscuits and pies. "Most people in the UK eat too much saturated fat, which can raise our cholesterol, putting us at an increased risk of heart disease."

- ✓ Unsaturated fats, on the other hand, can help to lower cholesterol and provide us with the essential fatty acids needed to help us stay healthy. Oily fish, nuts and seeds, avocados, olive oils and vegetable oils are natural sources of unsaturated fat.

Owing to their differing chemical structures - as a rule of thumb - saturated fats are solid at room temperature, while unsaturated fats tend to be in liquid form at room temperature. The unsaturated ("good") fats are further divided into several categories and include the Omega 3 and Omega 6 groups. In general, the Omega 3's are anti-inflammatory and the Omega 6's are pro-inflammatory.

The Mediterranean diet, for example, is relatively high in Omega 3's and has been shown to reduce rates of cardiovascular disease by 30%. A recent study examined the impact of diet on the mental health of 29 133 male smokers, who recorded their daily meals. The researchers found that greater consumption of processed foods such as margarine, and foods with high levels of saturated fats and relatively low levels of Omega 3 fatty acids, was associated with increased depression, anxiety, and insomnia.[60] "Depression is associated with inflammation and it follows that decreasing inflammation by improving this balance can alleviate symptoms."

Omega 3's also appear to have a direct effect on the brain. Evidence suggests that Omega 3's may prevent the development of dementia and play a role in the treatment of ADHD.

The key is to try to cut down on foods that are high in saturated fat and choose instead smaller amounts of foods that are rich in unsaturated fat. Use just a small amount of vegetable oil or reduced fat spread instead of butter, lard or ghee. When (occasionally) eating meat, choose lean cuts, and trim off any visible fat.

What you eat is just as important as how much you eat. That is why researchers use the acronym CRON - "calorie restriction with optimal nutrition". If you consume fewer calories, for example, you have to make each of those calories count. Certain fatty acids found in fish, for example, make up a large portion of the grey matter of the brain. Research has shown that diets rich in fatty acids can help promote emotional balance and cognitive function, possibly because they are a main component of the brain's synaptic structures.

Research indicates that a calorie-restricted diet is beneficial for both general health, and brain function. Eating wisely helps to regulate your weight, whilst decreasing your risk of heart disease, cancer and strokes. Healthy nutrition also triggers mechanisms to increase the production of nerve growth factors, which are essential to brain function."

In a similar way, studies show that fruit and vegetables can reduce the risk of developing cognitive impairment. This is because "free radicals" play a major role in the deterioration of the brain with age. When a cell converts oxygen into energy, tiny molecules called free radicals are produced.

---

60   Hakkarainen et al. (2004)

In normal amounts, free radicals rid the body of harmful toxins. When they are produced in larger, more toxic amounts, however, free radicals can cause cell death and tissue damage. Vitamin E, Vitamin C and beta-carotene inhibit the production of free radicals. The best natural sources for all of these are in fruits and vegetables. Fish oils, fruits and vegetables are good for you. Fact.

Further dietary advice regarding fats can be found in *"How To Lose Belly Fat Effectively and Healthily"*, "The number one rule in reducing belly fat is DO NOT start by decreasing your fat intake. Not all fats are bad fats. In fact, eating certain fats can help you reduce belly fat. Good fats that you need to add to your eating regime include avocados, olives and other sources of Omega-3".

A study published in *The International Journal of Obesity* found that eating three 140g servings of salmon per week for four weeks as part of a low-calorie diet resulted in approximately 1kg (2.2 lbs) more weight loss than following a diet that didn't include fish.

Dan Mendilow shares some fantastic points on what you need to do to turn your body into a belly-fat burning machine by replacing a few unhealthy foods with healthy foods. Dan goes on to explain the importance of eating certain fats and why you should not be eliminating them in your quest to banish your belly fat:

Studies have shown that drinking diet drinks greatly contributes to belly fat. "Drinking sugar-sweetened beverages which contain excess sugar, mostly due to the large amounts of fructose present, can lead to increased accumulation of fat in the belly", warns Medilow. Apple cider vinegar is a great way to mobilise your metabolism and to bust belly fat. "One theory is that the acetic acid in the vinegar produces proteins that burn up fat," explains Pamela Peeke, Professor of Medicine at The University of Maryland, and author of *"Fight Fat After 40"*.

With stress, and increased levels of cortisol, your body starts to produce more insulin as you age, since your muscle and fat cells simply don't respond as well as they used to. The increase in insulin leads to fat storage, especially around your belly. "A diet high in protein may protect you against insulin resistance, thus decreasing belly fat", claims Medilow.

"Sugar is another nutritional factor that affects our mental and physical well-being. Sugar comes in many different forms, but any form of added sugar is generally unhealthy.[61] Sugar, as glucose, provides our body with a fast source of energy. However, too much sugar causes problems. Sugar leads to direct stimulation of the brain by triggering the release of dopamine. Sugar's effect on the brain has been shown to resemble that of highly addictive drugs like cocaine. This may explain why you crave something sweet when you get stressed.[62]

---

61 Tandel (2011)

62 Barclay (2014)

Consumption of simple sugars triggers a large and rapid release of insulin, which lowers blood sugar levels. This natural response makes you hungrier, slows down your metabolism, and increases your body's storage of fats. Although fruits and vegetables contain sugars, these sugars are complex and are not broken down as quickly and easily.

These complex sugars are also bound to fibre, which slows down their absorption and blunts the insulin response.[63] It's not only Omega 3's which play a role in the treatment of ADHD - research indicates that reducing simple sugar intake can also improve ADHD symptoms.[64]

In order to balance your blood sugar, doctors and nutritionists generally recommend combining healthy sources of protein (meats, eggs, or beans), fats (coconut oil, nuts, or avocado), and carbohydrates (fruits, vegetables, or whole grains) in every meal.[65]

Sugar occurs naturally in foods such as fruit and milk. Sugar is, however, often surreptitiously added to certain food and drinks - a 340ml can of *Coke* is reported to contain 39g of total sugar. Sugar can also be found in seemingly healthy pasta sauces and baked beans.

Most adults and children in the UK consume too much sugar, known collectively as "free sugars". Free sugars are any sugars added to food or drinks - or found naturally in honey, syrups and unsweetened fruit juices.

Sugary foods and drinks can also cause tooth decay, especially if eaten between meals. The longer that the sugar is in contact with teeth, the more damage that it is likely to inflict.

The sugars found naturally in whole fruit are less likely to cause tooth decay, because they are contained within the fibres of the fruit. When fruit is juiced or blended, the sugars are released, and once released, these sugars can damage teeth - especially if you drink juice frequently.

When fruit is dried, some sugars can be released, but dried fruit has a tendency to stick to your teeth. Try to swap dried fruit for fresh fruit. To reduce the risk of tooth decay, dried fruit is best enjoyed as part of a meal, such as dessert, and not as a snack - unless you clean your teeth immediately afterwards.

---

63   Cocate et al. (2011)

64   Johnson et al., (2011)

65   Healthy Eating – Overview (2013)

Free or added sugars shouldn't contribute more than 5% of the energy (calories) that you derive from food and drink each day. That equates to a maximum of 30g of added sugar a day for adults - roughly seven sugar cubes. Children aged 4 to 6 years old should have no more than 19g a day, whilst children aged 7 to 10 years old should consume no more than 24g per day.

Dr. Holly Andersen offers her advice on how to "*Say No To Sugar*", warning that when you eat too much sugar, your body may stop getting the message that it feels full. "Cardiologists pushed everyone to eat low-fat", she claims, "and as a result, food manufacturers have added more sugar to things like crackers and cereals. Focus on protein and healthy fats instead of refined carbohydrates", she suggests.

"I snack on walnuts, almonds, pecans and more", adds Andersen. "They help increase HDL (good) cholesterol, and people who eat nuts seem to live longer with less disease. I proportion them in bags (about a quarter-cup scoop each) so when I get hungry, I won't eat the doughnuts people bring to the office."

"Instead of sugary fizzy drinks or squash, go for water, lower fat milks, or sugar-free, diet and no-added-sugar drinks. Even unsweetened fruit juice is sugary, so limit the amount to 150ml a day. If you prefer fizzy drinks, try diluting fruit juice with sparkling water. If you take sugar in hot drinks, or add sugar to your breakfast cereal, gradually reduce the amount until you can cut it out altogether", recommends Andersen.

"Rather than spreading jam, marmalade, syrup, treacle or honey on your toast, try a lower-fat spread, sliced banana or lower-fat cream cheese instead", Andersen suggests. "Try halving the sugar you use in your recipes - it works for most things except jam, meringues and ice cream. Choose tins of fruit in juice rather than syrup. Choose wholegrain breakfast cereals, but not those coated with sugar or honey".

"Check nutrition labels to help you pick the foods with less added sugar, or go for the lower-sugar version. Look for the "Carbohydrates (of which sugars) figure in the nutrition label", she advises.

- ✗ High – over 22.5g of total sugars per 100g
- ✓ Low – 5g of total sugars, or less, per 100g

The sugar figure in the nutrition label is the total amount of sugars in the food. "Total sugars" describes sugars from all sources (free sugars plus those from milk and those present in the structure of foods such as fruit and vegetables). For example, a plain yoghurt may contain 9.9g total sugars but none of these are free sugars as they all come from milk.

The same applies to an individual portion of fresh fruit salad that might contain around 20g of total sugars, depending on the fruits selected, all of which are naturally present within the cellular structure of the fruit (rather than "free").

This means that food containing lots of fruit or milk will be a healthier choice than one that contains lots of added sugars, even if the two products contain the same total amount of sugars.

Food packaging in the UK has incorporated nutritional information for some time now. Most packaging now also includes the "traffic light" system, and advice on reference intakes (RI) of some ingredients, which generally include sugar. Labels that incorporate the colour-coding system, allow you to determine - at a glance - if the food is high (red), medium (amber) or low (green) in sugar content, for example.

Some labels on the front of packaging will display the amount of sugar in the food as a proportion of the reference intake. Reference intakes serve as guidelines to the approximate amount of particular nutrients and energy required for a healthy diet. The reference intake for total sugars, for example, is 90g a day, including the 30g of "free sugars" mentioned previously.

You can get a rough idea of whether a food is high in added sugars by looking at the list of ingredients. Added sugars must be included in the ingredients list, which is always in descending order – from the highest volume to the lowest. If you find sugar near the top of the list, then that food is almost certain to be high in added sugars.

Beware other words used to describe added sugars, such as "cane sugar, honey, brown sugar, high fructose corn syrup, fruit juice concentrate, corn syrup, fructose, sucrose, glucose, crystalline sucrose, or nectars."

In *"This is what happens to your brain when you give up sugar"*, Jordan Gaines Lewis – Neuroscience Doctoral Candidate at *Penn State College of Medicine* – discusses the neuroscientific effects of sugar, and sugar "addiction".

"In neuroscience, food is something we call a "natural reward". In order for us to survive as a species, things like eating, having sex, and nurturing others must be pleasurable to the brain so that these behaviours are reinforced and repeated," says Gaines Lewis.

"Not all foods are equally rewarding, of course. Most of us prefer sweet, over sour and bitter foods because, evolutionarily, our mesolimbic pathway reinforces that sweet things provide a healthy source of carbohydrates for our bodies", Gaines Lewis proposes. "When our ancestors went scavenging for berries, sour meant "not yet ripe", while bitter meant "alert – poison!"

"Modern diets have taken on a life of their own", warns Jordan. "A decade ago, it was estimated that the average American consumed 22 teaspoons of added sugar per day - an extra 350 calories. A few months ago, one expert suggested that the average Briton consumes 238 teaspoons of sugar each week."

"With convenience more important than ever in our food selections, it's almost impossible to come across processed and prepared foods that don't have added sugars for flavour, preservation, or both", he warns. "These added sugars are sneaky - and unbeknown to many of us, we've become hooked", he claims.

"In ways that drugs of abuse - such as nicotine, cocaine and heroin - hijack the brain's reward pathway and make users dependent, increasing neuro-chemical and behavioural evidence suggests that sugar is addictive in the same way, too," warns Gaines Lewis.

"Like drugs, sugar spikes dopamine release in the *nucleus accumbens*. Over the long term, regular sugar consumption actually changes the gene expression and availability of dopamine receptors in both the midbrain and frontal cortex. Repeated access to sugar over time leads to prolonged dopamine signaling, greater excitation of the brain's reward pathways and a need for even more sugar to activate all of the midbrain dopamine receptors like before. The brain becomes tolerant to sugar - and more is needed to attain the same "sugar high", claims Gaines Lewis.

"In a study by Carlo Colantuoni and colleagues of Princeton University, rats which had undergone a typical sugar dependence protocol then underwent "sugar withdrawal". This was facilitated by either food deprivation or treatment with *naloxone*, a drug used for treating opiate addiction which binds to receptors in the brain's reward system. Both withdrawal methods led to physical problems, including teeth chattering, paw tremors, and head shaking. *Naloxone* treatment also appeared to make the rats more anxious, as they spent less time on an elevated apparatus that lacked walls on either side."

"Similar withdrawal experiments also report behaviour similar to depression, in tasks such as the forced swim test. Rats in sugar withdrawal are more likely to show passive behaviours (like floating) than active behaviours (like trying to escape) when placed in water, suggesting feelings of helplessness."

"A study published by Victor Mangabeira and colleagues in *Physiology & Behaviour*, reports that sugar withdrawal is linked to impulsive behaviour", says Gaines Lewis. "Rats were trained to receive water by pushing a lever. After training, the animals returned to their home cages and had access to a sugar solution and water, or just water alone. After 30 days, when the rats were again given the opportunity to press a lever for water, those which had become dependent on sugar pressed the lever significantly more times than control animals, suggesting impulsive behaviour."

"These are extreme experiments, of course", he reassures. "We humans aren't depriving ourselves of food for twelve hours and then allowing ourselves to binge on soda and doughnuts at the end of the day. But these rodent studies certainly give us insight into the neuro-chemical underpinnings of sugar dependence, withdrawal, and behaviour."

Jordan Gaines Lewis concludes, "Through decades of diet programmes and best-selling books, we've toyed with the notion of "sugar addiction" for a long time. There are accounts of those in "sugar withdrawal" describing food cravings, which can trigger relapse and impulsive eating."

"There are also countless articles and books about the boundless energy and new-found happiness in those who have sworn off sugar for good. But despite the ubiquity of sugar in our diets, the notion of sugar addiction is still a rather taboo topic."

Do you suffer from a sweet tooth? All is not lost.

Why not substitute honey for your sugar kick…? Honey can offer you more health benefits than you might expect, and it has been used for centuries for its acclaimed healing properties.

Despite the fact that honey is essentially a natural form of simple sugar, it's possible to "use it strategically to support a healthy weight and improve your health overall." Published on *Lifehack*, Elise Moreau discusses "*The Amazing Benefits of Honey*":

- ✓ It encourages you to cut down on table sugar. Honey contains about 64 calories per tablespoon, while table sugar contains about 48 calories, claims Moreau. She suggests that although there are more calories in honey than in table sugar, you would generally use less of it than you would if you were to use regular sugar - owing to its sweetness.

- ✓ It may improve brain function. "Raw honey is known to contain naturally active compounds that can enhance memory and lower anxiety", claims Moreau. "In a study on postmenopausal women who were given tualang honey as a supplement, results showed improvements in immediate memory."

- ✓ It helps to regulate your blood sugar. Honey is a simple sugar, but it's better for the body than table sugar. "During the honey-making process, the bees divide the honey molecules into glucose and fructose, which our bodies can absorb directly for a gentler impact on blood sugar levels", proposes Moreau. "With table sugar, our bodies have to work to separate the molecules before using it as energy."

- ✓ It can promote the growth of good bacteria in your gut. "Honey can help to prevent the harmful effects of bad bacteria in the intestine by providing probiotics that increase good bacteria", suggests Elise. "You'll need to select a type of raw honey with the least amount of processing. Heating, filtering and processing honey eliminates the enzymes and nutrients that make it such a functional food for health", she adds.

- It can be used to soothe a sore throat or cough. "Honey has long been used as a popular home remedy for the common cold because of its natural anti-inflammatory and anti-bacterial properties" says Moreau. "In a study conducted on children aged two and over with respiratory tract infections, two teaspoons of honey taken orally before bedtime was shown to have helped reduce night-time coughing and promote better sleep. Honey, however, should never be given to babies (owing to concerns over botulism)."

- It can help you to get a better night's sleep. "If you find that you never quite feel rested when it's time to get up in the morning, try drinking some milk or herbal tea with honey before bed", Elise suggests. "Consuming honey prior to bed will cause a steady rise in insulin along with a mood-boosting release of serotonin, which is then converted into melatonin - the hormone responsible for sleep regulation. Your brain also uses quite a lot of energy when you sleep, so a small amount of honey may help improve your sleep quality", she adds.

- It can give you an energy boost. "Carbohydrates are your body's main source of energy, and at 17g per tablespoon, honey can give you a dense hit of simple carbs when you need it", claims Moreau. "Honey doesn't have protein, fat or fibre, so stick to a very small portion to avoid insulin spikes that could cause you to crash later on", she warns. "It does, however, have as many as 80 valuable nutrients to offer–including vitamins A, C, D, E, K and all the B-complex plus essential minerals like calcium, magnesium, potassium, zinc and others", she adds.

Raw honey is best for its rich nutrition, so when you're shopping, make sure to choose the honey that is darkest in colour. The darker the honey, the less that it has been processed, and therefore the higher its nutritional content and value.

Tilly-Jayne Kidman, in *"This Is What Will Happen When You Start Drinking Honey Water Every Day"*, offers a practical solution to incorporating honey into your diet. "Water is good for you, we all know that. We hear no end that we should be drinking more and more water. After all, water is a vital component for our bodies, let's not forget that we're made up of 80% water!"

"Water basically maintains all of our everyday bodily functions from transporting vital nutrients and oxygen to helping with our day-to-day digestion of food. So we've successfully established that we NEED it", claims Kidman. "Fancy making water even more helpful to your system? Just add honey. This is what will happen if you start drinking honey every day…"

- Your Gas Will Reduce. "If you suffer from bloating, or regularly feel gassy, then a mug of warm honey water will help to neutralise the gas in your system," claims Kidman.

- ✓ You Will Boost Your Immune System. "Honey owns some pretty impressive immune system boosting properties. Be sure to buy raw, organic honey to gain maximum benefit from the bacteria killing assets", adds Kidman. "It's full of enzymes, vitamins and minerals that will protect you against any nasty bacteria."

- ✓ Your Blood Sugar Levels Will Regulate. "The combination of fructose and glucose helps to regulate your blood sugar levels. It's also said to lower cholesterol," she adds.

- ✓ You Will Flush Out Toxins. "Honey and warm water is one of the best combinations to flush waste from your system", suggests Kidman, adding that "adding lemon will improve this even further by helping to increase urination."

- ✓ Your Skin Will Become Clearer. "Honey is a natural anti-oxidant which helps to flush away any waste, and its antibacterial properties help to keep your skin clean and clearer than ever", claims Kidman.

- ✓ You Will Lose Weight. "The natural sugar in honey will help to satisfy your everyday cravings for naughty treats such as cake, sweets, chocolate and cola", claims Kidman. "Swap your sweetener packed drinks for honey water, and you'll be saving up to 64% more calories", she suggests.

- ✓ Your Sore Throat Will Improve. "It can help to soothe a sore throat. Honey is a natural remedy for respiratory infections and the common cough, so next time you have a pesky winter cold, reach for the honey (raw and organic)," Kidman suggests.

- ✓ You'll Be Preventing The Risk Of Heart Disease. "The flavonoids and anti-oxidants in honey are pretty handy at helping to prevent and reduce your risk of heart disease", claims Kidman. "Research has shown that honey slowed down the oxidation process of bad cholesterol in human blood - which can have a harmful effect on your heart, leading to attacks and even a stroke."

Jay Hill, in "*The Most Creative And Funniest Way To Avoid Overeating (Proven By Researchers)*" reinforces that "Habitual overeating is bad for us - it can cause digestive discomfort, leads to weight gain, and makes us feel generally unhealthy. Making minor behavioural changes can work to some extent. For instance, eating food from smaller plates, eating at the table with the TV off, waiting half an hour before going for additional servings, and brushing your teeth as soon as you have finished eating, can all help in cutting down on our food consumption."

Hill proposes "a simple technique that could make all the difference in slowing down your food consumption. Try feeding yourself with your non-dominant hand. It forces you to eat more slowly and this, in turn, gives your stomach more time to signal to your brain that you have reached satiety. Far too many of us eat quickly, and fail to give our brains sufficient time to realise that we are full", she claims.

"There is also a secondary mechanism at work", adds Hill. "Research has shown that our habits exert strong influence on our behaviours, and even subtle changes in cues can have significant knock-on effects when it comes to our actions. When we intentionally disrupt one of our habitual behaviours, it can trigger us to pay more attention to our other actions. In the case of overeating, it appears that the way in which we eat food can cause us to focus more intently on the degree to which it satisfies us. This can result in us ultimately eating less", she claims.

"For example, a paper published in *The Personality and Social Psychology Bulletin* demonstrated the power that eating with the non-dominant hand can have. On two separate occasions, participants were given popcorn to eat whilst watching a film", adds Hill. "When they were allowed to eat with their dominant hands, the amount of popcorn consumed was the same on both occasions, even when the popcorn was stale! When the participants were limited to eating with their non-dominant hand only, they ate up to 30% less food", claims Hill.

"Perhaps the most exciting aspect of these findings is that the participant did not have to intentionally attempt to deprive themselves or limit their consumption - it appeared to happen naturally", Jay suggests. "This is great news for those trying to stick to a diet but discovering that their willpower is dwindling."

"Any technique for reducing overeating that works without requiring huge reserves of willpower has got to be a huge benefit to any dieter", claims Hill. "The next time you find yourself especially hungry, or that extra piece of pizza just seems too tempting, why not try something a bit different? It might seem weird at first but why not give it a go? If you feel awkward doing this in front of other people, just try it when eating alone to begin with. Just be prepared for some slightly messier meals…"

In Her TED talk, "*Why Dieting Doesn't Usually Work*", neuroscientist Sandra Aamodt discusses the merits of "eating mindfully". Here follows an abridged transcript of Aamodt's talk:

"Three and a half years ago, I made one of the best decisions of my life", claims Aamodt. "As my New Year's resolution, I gave up dieting, stopped worrying about my weight, and learned to eat mindfully. Now I eat whenever I'm hungry, and I've lost 10 pounds", she adds.

"At age 13, when I started my first diet", says Aamodt, "I thought I needed to lose weight, and when I gained it back, I blamed myself. And for the next three decades, I was on and off various diets. No matter what I tried, the weight I'd lost always came back."

"As a neuroscientist, I wondered, why is this so hard? Obviously, how much you weigh depends on how much you eat and how much energy you burn", she proposes. "What most people don't realise is that hunger and energy use are controlled by the brain. Your brain does a lot of its work behind the scenes, and that is a good thing, because your conscious mind - how do we put this politely? - it's easily distracted," Sandra claims.

"It's good that you don't have to remember to breathe when you get caught up in a movie" Aamodt proposes. "You don't forget how to walk because you're thinking about what to have for dinner. Your brain also has its own sense of what you should weigh, no matter what you consciously believe. This is called your set point, but that's a misleading term, because it's actually a range of about 10 or 15 pounds", she suggests. (Remember Maltz's "*Psycho-Cybernetics*"?)

"You can use lifestyle choices to move your weight up and down within that range, adds Aamodt, "but it's much, much harder to stay outside of it. There are more than a dozen chemical signals in the brain that tell your body to gain weight, more than another dozen that tell your body to lose it, and the system works like a thermostat, responding to signals from the body by adjusting hunger, activity and metabolism, to keep your weight stable as conditions change."

"That's what a thermostat does. It keeps the temperature in your house the same as the weather changes outside. Now you can try to change the temperature in your house by opening a window in the winter, but that's not going to change the setting on the thermostat, which will respond by kicking on the furnace to warm the place back up," she adds.

"Your brain works exactly the same way, responding to weight loss by using powerful tools to push your body back to what it considers normal. If you lose a lot of weight, your brain reacts as if you were starving, and whether you started out fat or thin, your brain's response is exactly the same", claims Aamodt.

"We would love to think that your brain could tell whether you need to lose weight or not, but it can't. If you do lose a lot of weight, you become hungry, and your muscles burn less energy" she proffers. "Dr. Rudy Leibel of Columbia University found that people who lost 10% of their body weight burned 250 to 400 calories less, because their metabolism was suppressed. A successful dieter must eat this much less than someone of the same weight who has always been thin," she claims.

"From an evolutionary perspective, your body's resistance to weight loss makes sense", claims Aamodt. "When food was scarce, our ancestors' survival depended on conserving energy. Regaining the weight when food was available would have protected them against the next shortage. Over the course of human history, starvation has been a much bigger problem than overeating. This may explain a very sad fact: Set points can go up, but they rarely go down."

"Now, if your mother ever mentioned that life is not fair, this is the kind of thing she was talking about", jokes Aamodt. "Successful dieting doesn't lower your set point".

"Even after you've kept the weight off for as long as seven years, your brain keeps trying to make you gain it back. If that weight loss had been due to a long famine, that would be a sensible response," she adds.

"In our modern world of drive-through burgers, it's not working out so well for many of us", Sandra suggests. "That difference between our ancestral past and our abundant present is the reason that Dr. Yoni Freedhoff of the University of Ottawa would like to take some of his patients back to a time when food was less available, and it's also the reason that changing the food environment is really going to be the most effective solution to obesity", she claims.

"Sadly, a temporary weight gain can become permanent", warns Aamodt. "If you stay at a high weight for too long, your brain may decide that's the new normal".

"Psychologists classify eaters into two groups, those who rely on their hunger and those who try to control their eating through willpower, like most dieters. Let's call them intuitive eaters and controlled eaters", proffers Aamodt. "The intuitive eaters are less likely to be overweight, and they spend less time thinking about food. Controlled eaters are more vulnerable to overeating in response to advertising, super-sizing, and the all-you-can-eat buffet. And a small indulgence, like eating one scoop of ice cream, is more likely to lead to a food binge in controlled eaters. Children are especially vulnerable to this cycle of dieting and then binging," she suggests.

"Several long-term studies have shown that girls who diet in their early teenage years are three times more likely to become overweight five years later, even if they started at a normal weight", she claims, "and all of these studies found that the same factors that predicted weight gain also predicted the development of eating disorders. The other factor, by the way, those of you who are parents, was being teased by family members about their weight. So don't do that", Aamodt warns.

"A study looked at the risk of death over a 14-year period based on four healthy habits: eating enough fruits and vegetables, exercising three times weekly, not smoking, and drinking in moderation. The healthier the lifestyle, the less likely people were to die. The ones that had no healthy habits had a higher risk of death", claims Aamodt, adding that "just one healthy habit pulled overweight people back into the normal range".

"For obese people with no healthy habits, the risk is very high, seven times higher than the healthiest groups in the study," warns Aamodt. "But a healthy lifestyle helps obese people too. If you look at the group with all four healthy habits, you can see that weight makes very little difference. You can take control of your health by taking control of your lifestyle, even If you can't lose weight and keep it off", reassures Aamodt.

"Diets don't have very much reliability", she claims. "Five years after a diet, most people have regained the weight. 40% of them have gained even more. The typical outcome of dieting is that you're more likely to gain weight in the long run than to lose it", she proffers.

"If I've convinced you that dieting might be a problem, the next question is, what do you do about it? My answer, in a word, is mindfulness", she suggests. "I'm not saying that you need to learn to meditate or take up yoga. I'm talking about mindful eating: learning to understand your body's signals so that you eat when you're hungry and stop when you're full, because a lot of weight gain boils down to eating when you're not hungry," claims Aamodt.

"Give yourself permission to eat as much as you want, and then work on figuring out what makes your body feel good", Sandra suggests. "Sit down to regular meals without distractions. Think about how your body feels when you start to eat and when you stop, and let your hunger decide when you should be done. It took about a year for me to learn, but it's really been worth it," she claims.

"I am so much more relaxed around food than I have ever been in my life", claims Aamodt. "I often don't think about it. I forget we have chocolate in the house. It's completely different. I should say that this approach to eating probably won't make you lose weight, unless you often eat when you're not hungry", she says. "Doctors don't know of any approach that makes significant weight loss in a lot of people, and that is why a lot of people are now focusing on preventing weight gain, instead of promoting weight loss," claims Aamodt.

"Let's face it: If diets worked, we'd all be thin already. Why do we keep doing the same thing and expecting different results?" she asks. (That's Einstein's definition of insanity.)

"Diets may seem harmless, but they actually do a lot of collateral damage. At worst, they ruin lives: Weight obsession leads to eating disorders, especially in young kids. In the United States, we have 80% of 10-year-old girls saying that they've been on a diet. Our daughters have learned to measure their worth by the wrong scale," Aamodt suggests.

"Even at its best, dieting is a waste of time and energy", Sandra claims. "It takes willpower which you could be using to help your kids with their homework, or to finish that important project. Because willpower is limited, any strategy that relies on its consistent application is pretty much guaranteed to eventually fail you when your attention moves on to something else."

"What if we told all those dieting girls that it's okay to eat when they're hungry? What if we taught them to work with their appetite instead of fearing it?" suggests Aamodt. "I think most of them would be happier and healthier, and as adults, many of them would probably be thinner. I wish someone had told me that back when I was 13," she laments.

Unhealthy diets and sedentary lifestyles are factors that have been known to drive the obesity epidemic. A study from *The Mayo Clinic* has also linked them to the biology of ageing. "What you eat and how physically active you are directly influences how quickly you age." Tony Robbins, in *"Is Your Lifestyle Aging You?"*, discusses the findings of The Mayo Clinic study.

"Researchers at The Mayo Clinic fed mice either a normal, healthy diet, or a diet that they dubbed the "fast-food diet," - high in saturated fat, cholesterol and sugar. The mice on the fast-food diet showed dangerous changes in health… Their fat mass increased by nearly 300% over four months. What was curious though, is that the researchers found substantial health improvements after introducing exercise to the mice's routine", claims Robbins.

"Half of the mice, a mix between those on the healthy and unhealthy diets, were given exercise wheels. The mice that had been on the fast-food diet, but still exercised, showed an improvement in body weight gain and fat mass" claims Robbins. "Of course, the mice on a normal diet benefited from exercise as well."

"We think at both a biological level and a clinical level, poor nutrition choices and inactive lifestyles do accelerate ageing," says Nathan LeBrasseur, Ph.D., Director of *The Centre on Aging's Healthy and Independent Living Programme* and senior author of the study. "Now we've shown this in very fine detail at a cellular level, and we can see it clinically."

"Those who actively take charge with their bodies and their health, haven't found some new trend, fad or shortcut", concludes Robbins. "They've simply made the decision that they are going to do it. Something just clicked inside their brains, where their *"shoulds"* became their *"musts"*, and better eating habits and enhanced physical activity became an imperative part of their day."

"This study clearly shows the power of diet and exercise. And while that does not mean you need to sign up for a triathlon", suggests Tony, "it does mean that you need to develop healthier habits. Not only will this prevent premature ageing and age-related diseases", proffers Robbins, "it will help you feel better, physically, mentally and emotionally. You can start showing up for yourself, and for others, in a more pro-active, and more conscious way."

In *"5 Ways To Fuel Your Brain"*, Tony proposes that "age is not the only contributing factor to cognitive decline. Our lifestyle also plays a key role. Poor diet, a lack of sleep and exercise, ongoing stress, smoking and environmental pollutants all damage fragile brain cells."

Robbins continues, "The brain is incredibly dynamic and has the potential and the ability to change at any point throughout our entire life. And you have the power to enhance your brain function, protect your brain from damage, and counteract the effects of ageing! It all comes down to your everyday decisions", claims Tony.

He suggests "5 small changes you can make in your life that can mean big differences in your cognitive abilities":

1. Consume more (healthy) fat. "Omega-3 fatty acids offer a number of health benefits, such as improving cognitive performance and warding off mental and mood disorders", says Tony. "They support brain plasticity - your brain's ability to change in response to stimulation demands placed on it, which could then enhance the expression of several molecules related to learning and memory."

    "In one of the largest studies of its kind, researchers analysing the diets of 12,000 pregnant women found that children of those who consumed the least omega-3's were 48% more apt to score in the lowest quartile on IQ tests", warns Robbins. "And in a similar study, 396 children between the ages of 6 and 12, who were given a beverage with omega-3 fatty acids, showed higher scores on tests measuring verbal intelligence and learning and memory after 18 months, compared with a control group of students who did not consume the drink," adds Robbins.

    "A deficiency of omega-3 fatty acids in humans has also been linked to an increased risk of mental disorders such as attention-deficit disorder, dyslexia, dementia, depression, bipolar disorder and schizophrenia. One study found that individuals who consumed more omega-3's had increased volume of the brain's grey matter volume, especially in the hippocampus, the part of the brain associated with self-awareness, compassion and introspection", Tony reveals.

2. Drink green tea. "A rich source of antioxidants, nutrients and minerals, green tea is well known for its ability to protect the body from free radicals and for its power to increase fat burning and boost the body's metabolic rate. But did you know that it has the potential to enhance cognitive function, and, in particular, boost the working memory?" asks Robbins.

3. Walking and stretching. "For decades, researchers have been discovering evidence of the positive relationship between physical exercise and cognitive performance", says Tony. "There are a number of studies that have shown how exercise helps the brain resist physical shrinkage and enhance cognitive flexibility."

    "Studies also concluded that individuals who exercise have healthier brains and perform significantly better on cognitive tests than those who are sedentary", adds Robbins. "Neurologists have found that even moderate exercise, such as walking for just 40 minutes three times a week, can enhance the connectivity of important brain circuits, combat declines in brain function due to ageing and even increase cognitive skills."

    "In another study, half of the participants added stretching and toning to their weekly routine, but changed nothing else about their lifestyles. The other half added moderate aerobic activity to their routine. The aerobic activity unsurprisingly boosted the brain more effectively", claims Robbins, "but those who only stretched and toned still had better results on cognitive performance tests one year into the study, than they had at its onset."

4. Music for the mind. "We listen to music when we exercise because it energises and engages our bodies", claims Tony. "We listen to music when we want to relax because it soothes and calms. But what about listening to music when we want to create a real change in our brain function?" asks Robbins.

    "In a 2011 study, 40 pre-op patients were assigned either to a music group in which they listened to instrumental music, or to a control group in which they listened to a non-musical placebo. Both groups listened to their respective audio stimulus for about two hours before, and then during, their operations. Researchers found that during the surgical process, the patients in the music group exhibited lower propofol consumption and had lower cortisol levels than the control group. Neuroscientists have found that chronic stress and cortisol can trigger long-term changes in brain structure and function", warns Tony.

    "Classical music in particular has also been shown to aid in the development of better concentration levels", adds Robbins. "A study from the University of London's *Institute of Education* found that exposing children to a range of classical music led to enhanced listening skills and the development of increased concentration and self-discipline.

A study from the University of Dayton found that students performed better at spatial and linguistic processing when Mozart was playing in the background."

5. Brain-boosting foods. "The relationship between diet and brain function has been well documented", claims Tony. "Research has shown that children who ate breakfast before school exhibited better memory and acquisition skills while learning. Another study found that individuals who kept healthier diet habits had a reduced risk of cognitive decline as they got older."

"Eating a healthy, balanced diet is only part of the equation", says Tony, adding that "there are some foods that have been shown to improve brain function, protect against age-associated cognitive decline, and encourage focus and clarity":

- ✓ Nuts are a rich source of magnesium - linked to improvements in both short- and long-term memory.
- ✓ Broccoli, rich in vitamin K, enhances cognitive performance and brainpower.
- ✓ Pumpkin seeds provide your body with zinc, which is critical for enhancing memory and thinking skills.
- ✓ Blueberries contain *anthocyanins*, antioxidants that support neuron-to-neuron communication in the brain and may help prevent memory loss.
- ✓ Dark chocolate has been shown to increase brain characteristics of attention and focus.
- ✓ Leafy greens, asparagus, olives, and whole grains are also full of vitamin E, likely to help prevent cognitive decline, especially in elder individuals.

(Strangely, no mention of bananas or pineapples…)

In Yagana Shah's "*5 Ways To Cheat The Aging Process, According To Dietitians*"- Australian dietitian Ngaire Hobbins, author of "*Eat to Cheat Aging*" raises a valuable perspective. "It's not about living forever", she proposes, "it's about ageing so you can live as well as you possibly can. Keep your internal health going and you'll maintain your external health, too", she claims.

Hobbins and fellow dietitian Joan Salge Blake - a clinical professor at Boston University – proposed the following recommendations to "help us all live better, for longer".

1. Make protein a part of every meal. "Protein is an essential part of maintaining your muscles as you get older", says Shah. "We lose muscle mass naturally as we get older, due to lower testosterone levels and also from not being as active. Muscle is important in keeping your body strong, helping you to keep your balance and also for keeping you mobile as you age."

"You can get protein from meats, dairy, eggs, nuts, seeds and legumes, so it's easy to make it part of each meal. Salge Blake, a spokesperson for *The Academy of Nutrition and Dietetics*, says that it's important to spread your protein intake throughout the day, and not just pile it on at one meal."

2. Eat an anti-inflammatory, antioxidant-rich diet. "The food on your plate shouldn't be all one colour", advises Shah. Dietitians suggest different fruits and vegetables from which to source your antioxidants. "Science shows us you need as many different ones as you can get, to get the best benefit."

   "Along with getting antioxidants, from sources like berries, peppers and tomatoes," she adds, "it's important to protect your body from inflammation. The ageing process itself perpetuates more inflammation," she claims, and to fight inflammation, it's important to have a diet rich in omega-3s, like those found in fatty fish, as well as in the rainbow diet. "Extra virgin oil, and oils derived from seeds and nuts are the best way to go", says Hobbins. "Exercise helps immensely with inflammation, too".

3. Don't lose a lot of weight, rapidly. "This includes both accidental weight loss - caused by illness or medications - or weight loss through restrictive dieting. It's important to maintain your muscle tone", Hobbins stresses. "Having a little bit of extra fat on the body can help to reduce the appearance of wrinkles", Salge Blake says, "but, you don't want the extra weight if it's contributing to chronic diseases like high blood pressure or diabetes. If you do have to lose a few extra pounds, the best way to do it is through exercise combined with a healthy, nutritious diet - not just extreme calorie-slashing."

4. Support gut health. "Emerging research says a healthy gut can have a whole slew of wonderful effects on the body," claims Blake. "Just having a healthy gut with a diet that is rich in probiotics would help with a healthy body overall.

   Fermented foods are also good for your gut", she suggests, "along with fibrous vegetables and legumes". Hobbins recommends eating these foods as close to their natural form as possible - with little or no processing - to receive the maximum benefits.

5. Watch your vitamins. "As you age, your skin gets thinner and drier. You're losing some elasticity," says Blake. Compounds called *keratinoids* can help to boost the antioxidant capacity of your skin. Corn, oranges, peppers and egg yolks are some of the best sources of *keratinoids*. Try adding sunflower seeds and almonds to your diet to make sure you're getting adequate amounts."

Here are a few more tips for a more *balanced* diet…

✓ Consult your doctor or a nutritionist to discuss your optimal diet, and potential vitamin supplements. Generally, doctors and nutritionists recommend diets with whole grains and lots of vegetables and fruits with few processed foods or added sugars.

✓ If you need additional Omega 3 Fatty Acids in your diet (consult with your doctor), you can take a supplement, or eat fatty fish once, or two times, per week. Flax and chia seeds are also good sources of Omega 3's.

✓ Regulate your salt intake. Use water-rich foods in salads and soups - like squash, cucumber, lettuce, and tomatoes, to further dilute the sodium in your diet.

✓ Have at least two portions of fresh fruit per day. Most fruits are 90% water and will help to stabilise your electrolytes. They're a good source of fibre and will satisfy your sweet tooth. (Don't forget the vegetables to complete your absolute minimum of *5 a day*!)

✓ Avoid take-aways and processed meals which are brimming with sodium and low water content. They dry out the system and can rapidly increase your levels of dehydration.

✓ Consume less sugar and eat more fibre. Sugar can put excessive strain on the kidneys, while fibre slows down blood sugar levels and holds water in the body.

Back in South Africa in the 1990's, a certain cigarette brand used to heavily promote the slogan, "after action… satisfaction". My suggestion – scrap the nicotine and reach for a watermelon or cucumber after working out. (Somehow, I don't think that's quite what they had in mind…?)

Researchers at the University of Aberdeen Medical School claim that watermelon or cucumber may hydrate your body "twice as effectively as a glass of water". "Water-rich fruits and vegetables also provide you with natural sugars, amino acids, mineral salts and vitamins that are lost in exercise, and furthermore, eating fruits and vegetables high in water content can replenish your body without all the artificial colours and flavours commonly found in sports drinks," *(…or cigarettes!)*

Perhaps the biggest advantage of consuming high water content foods is that they contain minimal calories, yet provide a feeling of fullness. You'll feel satisfied, without overeating or feeling lethargic.

And they also help to raise your levels of hydration…

Water and Hydration:

You need to drink water to survive. Fact. Water is actually more important for your survival than food. Without food, your body can survive for more than a month, but without water, your prognosis would be approximately one week.

Water accounts for approximately 60% of your overall body mass. Your brain is 70-75% water, and your lungs are about 90% water. When you're not properly hydrated, your brain operates on less fuel, and you can feel drained, or experience fatigue or mood fluctuations.

Water nourishes and protects the brain, spinal cord and other tissues. Water regulates the body's temperature, and also helps to remove waste products through the processes of perspiration, excretion, and urination.

Cartilage, which protects and cushions your joints, is composed of up to 80% water. Dehydration of cartilage can cause it to deteriorate and result in joint pain and arthritis. This can also cause spinal pain as spinal discs - composed primarily of water for shock absorption - cannot support your vertebrae as effectively when you do not drink enough water.

Staying hydrated can maintain the health of your lymphatic system - which directly affects how your body fights off infections. Studies have also shown that lack of water in the body – dehydration - can lead to increased cortisol levels, stress, and sickness.

Have I managed to convince you yet? *"H2O is the way to go!"*

Another benefit of drinking water is that you'll most probably also eat less. A study showed that people who drink a glass of water before every meal, lost an average of two kilograms over a three-month period. Water has zero calories, and people also tend to feel more full as a result.

Ancient *Ayurvedic*[66] medicine advocates the health benefits of drinking water on an empty stomach. *Usha Paana Chikitsa* - roughly translated from Sanskrit as "early morning water treatment" claims that the process of drinking water first thing in the morning - on an empty stomach - serves to purify the body's internal system - including cleansing the colon - which enables the body to more effectively absorb the nutrients from food.

---

66 Ayurvedic medicine is one of the world's oldest holistic healing systems. Developed thousands of years ago in India, it is based on the belief that health and wellness depend on a delicate balance between the mind, body, and spirit.

In the 1970's, Dr Fereydoon Batmanghelidj, substantiated these ancient Indian findings through his own research, claiming that "water therapy" can naturally protect us from ailments such as high blood pressure, arthritis, asthma, diabetes and migraines, for example.

According to Dr Batmanghelidj, the body's natural thirst signals are often mistaken for signs and symptoms of other illnesses. "Over our lifespan we gradually become chronically dehydrated. If we treat this root problem, we may be able to avoid unnecessary and invasive procedures and medications," he suggests.

The Japanese Medical Society believes that "water therapy" treatment would help to treat constipation in ten days and combat high blood pressure within thirty days.

- ✓ Drinking at least one large glass of water first thing in the morning, has been shown to increase your metabolism by at least 24% for 90 minutes.

- ✓ After 7-8 hours of sleep, you will wake up dehydrated. Drinking water helps to create new muscle and blood cells and can increase the flow of oxygen.

- ✓ "Your kidneys do an amazing job of cleansing your body of toxins as long as your intake of fluids is adequate," says dermatologist Kenneth Ellner. "Getting fluids into your body right after your wake up will help your body flush out toxins first thing in the morning."

But how much water is enough? There are two main schools of thought…

The *BMJ* - formerly *The British Medical Journal* – suggests that drinking "1.5 to 2 litres of water daily is the simplest and healthiest hydration advice you can give". This advice is to be taken "with a pinch of salt", however – and not literally! "…It is to be emphasised that this conclusion is limited to healthy adults in a temperate climate, leading a largely sedentary existence…"

The other argument is that "Half your body weight in pounds is how many fluid ounces of water you should be drinking on an average day." As with the previous suggestion, the required volume will increase relative to the intensity of activity - and the heat, or humidity of the day, for example.

So, for argument's sake, suppose you weigh 75kg (165.35 lbs) - then half of your weight would be 82.675 pounds. You would need to drink 82.675 fluid ounces of water (or 2.445l, or 4.30 pints) on an *average* day. Simple!

(Probably the best – and simplest - indication as to whether you are drinking enough water is to look at the colour of your urine. If it is a pale straw colour, you are probably drinking enough. If it is dark yellow, then you most probably need to drink more.)

Why not use your phone to remind you to drink a glass of water every hour, or perhaps every ninety minutes? Set a reminder - or there are many apps freely available to download, specifically geared towards gently nudging you towards your new habit of regular hydration.

Lack of water - or dehydration - directly reduces the amount of blood in your body, forcing your heart to pump harder to distribute oxygen-bearing cells to your muscles. Dehydration is also frequently recognised as the underlying cause of symptoms of dementia in elderly people.

In the early stages of dehydration, you can become tired, dizzy, irritable and also experience more frequent headaches. In moderate cases of dehydration, you will become lethargic and begin to lack the energy to move throughout the day. As the degree of dehydration increases, you will become increasingly clumsy and exhausted, and your vision will deteriorate. In the latter stages of dehydration, you may feel nauseous and begin vomiting. Without water, you will eventually enter into a coma, and die…

Still not convinced that *H2O* is the way to go? Matt Duczeminski, on *Lifehack,* lists the following indicators that you're not drinking enough water.

- Your Mouth is Dry - Drinking water lubricates the mucus membranes in your mouth and throat, which continue to keep your mouth moist with saliva.

- Your Skin is Dry - Your skin is your body's largest organ, and dry skin is one of the first signs of dehydration. A lack of water also reduces the amount of sweat that your body can produce - leading to your body's inability to wash away excess dirt and oil which accumulates throughout the day, says Duczeminski.

- You Experience Joint Pain – Remember, our cartilage and spinal discs are comprised of approximately 75% water, to minimise friction, through preventing our bones from grinding against each other with movement.

- Your Muscle Mass Decreases - Your muscles are also comprised mostly of water. Less water in the body therefore simply equates to less muscle mass.

- You Stay Sick Longer - Drinking water allows your body to cleanse, and to continuously flush out toxins. Inadequate water levels reduce the ability of your organs to filter our certain waste products. In a dehydrated body, organs also start to wrest water from areas like your blood, for example.

- Your Eyes Are Dry - A lack of water intake leads to dry, bloodshot eyes. Your tear ducts tend to dry up, causing potential long-term damage to your eyes - especially if you wear contact lenses.

- You're Excessively Thirsty

- You Feel Fatigued and Lethargic - A lack of properly hydrated blood leads to a lack of oxygen being carried around the body, which in turn leads to sleepiness, fatigue, and reduced stamina.

- You Experience Hunger Pangs - When you're dehydrated, your body might start to think it needs some food. This happens throughout the day, and overnight when you wake up craving that midnight snack. However, eating food creates more work for your body, whereas drinking water purifies your organs and supplies your body with the fuel it needs.

- You Experience Digestive Problems - Without proper hydration, the amount - and strength - of mucus in the stomach decreases, allowing stomach acid to rule rampant - commonly referred to as heartburn or indigestion.

- You Experience Constipation - During the process of dehydration, the colon uses up the water that would otherwise have been used by the intestines.

Drinking too much water, however, can also be detrimental to your health. When you drink too much water, you can develop a condition known as *hyponatremia*, in which the excess water floods your body's cells, causing excessive swelling.

Swollen brain cells, for example lead to a wide range of symptoms, including headaches, nausea, cramps, mental confusion, convulsions, fatigue, coma and ultimately death. *Hyponatremia* has resulted in the deaths of many marathon runners, for example.

A BBC publication, *"Why Do We Need Water?"*, states that tea, coffee and fruit juices also count towards your liquid intake, so why not try a cup of tea? Not only does it (allegedly) contribute towards your daily hydration, but white tea, in particular, has been shown to slow down the breakdown of collagen and elastin, helping to prevent ageing of the skin.

Green tea is rich in *polyphenols*, helping to fight off cell damage and ageing. Studies have reported that it may be helpful in preventing a number of conditions including high blood pressure, high cholesterol, and even osteoporosis. One study even found that a *polyphenol* called EGCG in green tea can revive dying skin cells. Green tea also lowers your risk of Type 2 Diabetes, which currently affects about 300 million people globally - through improving insulin sensitivity, and lowering blood sugar levels.

A number of studies have shown that drinking green tea can also speed up your metabolism - most fat-burning supplements now contain green tea. Women who regularly drink green tea are also 22% less likely to develop breast cancer. *Catechins* (a type of natural phenol and antioxidant) in green tea can also slow down the development of harmful bacteria and combat viruses such as Influenza. The selfsame *catechins* also lower your chances of developing Alzheimer's or Parkinson's, through their ability to protect your body's neurons."

The amino acid *L-theanine*, found in green tea, also serves to increase the body's levels of "feel good" dopamine, and stimulates brain activity, helping to focus your brain and increase levels of alertness and concentration. According to *health.com*, every additional cup of green tea that you drink may reduce your risk of coronary artery disease.

Dr. Joseph Mercola, reinforces the benefits of green tea, and *theanine*, in particular. "*Theanine*, an amino acid that crosses the blood-brain barrier and has psychoactive properties, increases levels of *gamma-aminobutyric acid* (GABA), serotonin, dopamine, and alpha wave activity, and may reduce mental and physical stress and produce feelings of relaxation."

One particularly healthy variant of green tea is matcha. To qualify as matcha green tea powder, it has to be extracted from tencha leaves, and undergo a strictly controlled growing process. Matcha is becoming ever increasingly more available - my local coffee shop (*I bow to no sponsor*) now offers matcha. Here are some reasons to choose matcha green tea over coffee - which may also serve to explain its dramatic rise in popularity?

Although matcha only contains about a third of coffee's comparative caffeine content, *L-theanine phytonutrient* - found in matcha green tea - stores the caffeine in the body and releases it at a much slower rate. It can take up to three hours for your body to absorb the caffeine content of matcha, but this has the benefit of energising the body for a longer period of time, without coffee's associated "caffeine spike" - more of a marathon than a sprint, so to speak.

L-theanine phytonutrient also serves to cultivate a calming sensation. While it helps to reduce stress and anxiety, it also increases the alpha brainwaves that can invoke a sense of relaxation without any feeling of drowsiness or sleepiness - none of the nervousness or edginess associated with coffee. Matcha also causes an increase in the secretions of serotonin and dopamine in the body - the neurotransmitters effective in preventing depression and enhancing mood.

Matcha green tea is renowned for its abundance of natural antioxidants - scientifically proven to prevent the growth of cancer cells, and to boost anti-ageing properties. Antioxidants also help to combat skin diseases, whilst protecting against UV radiation. Matcha also contains antibacterial properties that help to clear acne, and contribute towards healthy, radiant skin.

Iron, calcium, protein, potassium, and vitamins A and C are also abundant in matcha, helping to boost your immune system, and to regulate body functions. The high chlorophyll content within matcha, also adds an effective detoxifier to rid the body of toxins and impurities. Matcha has also been shown to burn calories four times faster than the normal rate.

Matcha's antibacterial properties improve general oral health - providing protection to the teeth and preventing plaque build-up - in direct contrast to "coffee breath" and stained teeth.

If wine is more "your cup of tea", then you may be pleased to learn that red wine also contains antioxidants - called *polyphenols* - that protect your blood vessels and arteries. A certain *polyphenol* called *resveratrol*, is believed to help lower the body's levels of LDL (Low-Density Lipoprotein) - or "bad cholesterol".

Studies conducted by Columbia University suggest that *resveratol* protects against skin cancer, owing to its effectiveness in blocking the sun's damaging UVB rays. Research conducted by Texas A&M University found that *resveratrol* also helped to improve learning and memory in rats.

As with all alcoholic beverages, please drink responsibly – moderation is always the key.

Research conducted by Dr Heinz Valtin - published in the *"American Journal of Physiology"*, (controversially?) suggested that caffeinated beverages and mild alcoholic drinks, such as beer – in moderation - can also contribute to the volume of hydration required by your body.

Coffee - like green tea - can lower your risk of Type 2 Diabetes. "Drinking black coffee has been shown to reduce your risk of Type 2 Diabetes by an average of 14% for every daily cup (340ml) of coffee. If you drink two mugs of coffee a day, you'll have a 28% reduced risk of developing Type 2 Diabetes, compared with people who don't drink coffee."

According to a study from *The American Chemical Society*, "those who drink more than four cups of coffee a day reduce their chance of developing Type 2 Diabetes by 50%, with the reduction increasing by an additional 7% with each cup after that."

"Studies have also shown that people who drink four or more cups of coffee a day (approximately 750 ml) may reduce the incidence of cirrhosis of the liver by as much as 80%, and may reduce their risk of developing liver cancer, by as much as 40%."

"Research has also shown that coffee triggers a mechanism in your brain that releases *brain-derived neurotrophic factor* (BDNF), which activates your brain stem cells to convert into new neurons, thereby improving brain health. Research also suggests that low BDNF levels may play a significant role in depression and that increasing neurogenesis has an antidepressant effect."

One Harvard study even found women who drink four or more cups of coffee a day have a 20% lower risk of depression than those who drank little or none. Studies have even shown a link between coffee consumption and a reduced risk of basal cell carcinoma, one of the most common skin cancers.

Another study found that moderate coffee consumption may even boost your rate of metabolism by an additional 11% - caffeine is now also found in virtually all fat burning or weight loss supplements.

In 2013, researchers Shukitt-Hale, Miller, Chu, Lyle, and Joseph conducted a study to "evaluate the ability of coffee supplementation to improve cognitive function in aged individuals and the effect of the individual components in coffee, such as caffeine."

The researchers fed aged rats (19 months) one of five coffee-supplemented diets (0, 0.165, 0.275, 0.55, and 0.825% of the diet) for 8 weeks prior to motor and cognitive behaviour assessment. Aged rats supplemented with a 0.55% coffee diet, equivalent to ten cups of coffee, performed better in psychomotor testing (rotarod) and in a working memory task (Morris water maze) compared with aged rats fed a regular diet.

The rotarod performance test is a test based on a rotating rod with forced motor activity being applied. In the test, the rat is placed on a horizontal, rotating rod suspended above a cage floor, which is low enough not to injure the animal, but high enough to induce avoidance of fall. Rodents naturally try to stay on the rotating rod - or rotarod – in an attempt to avoid falling to the ground. The length of time that the rat can remain on the rotating rod is a measure of their balance, co-ordination and physical condition.

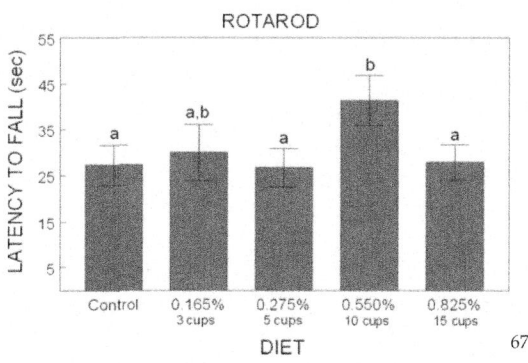

The graph on the previous page reflects the latency to fall (seconds) in the rotarod test for the control and coffee groups. Latency is the time interval between the stimulation and response.

The Morris water maze study placed the rat in a large circular pool, from which it is supposed to find an invisible platform that allows it to escape the water by using various cues.

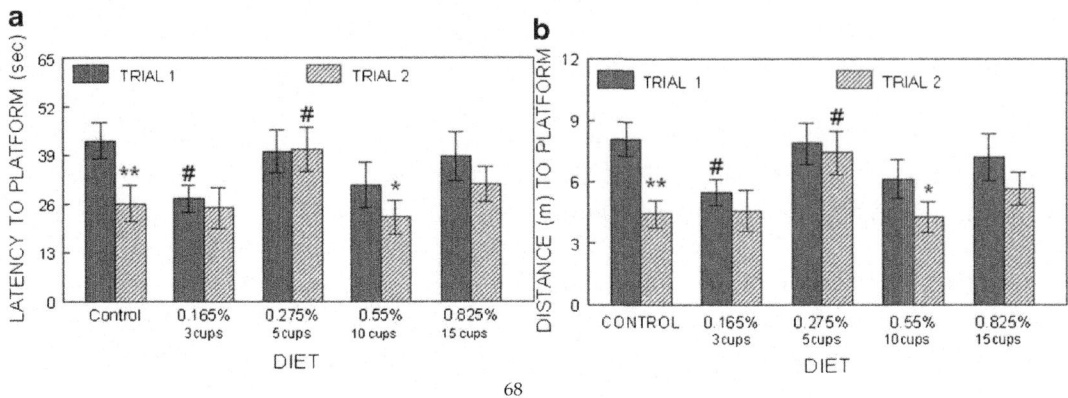

The side-by-side graphs above reflect the Morris water maze performance assessed as latency in seconds (a) and distance in meters (b) to find the hidden platform on days 3 and 4 of testing animals in the control and coffee groups. The asterisks indicate a difference (i.e., an improvement) between Trial 1 and Trial 2 performances.

"In the study, the diet with 0.55% coffee (equivalent to ten cups) appeared to be optimal. The 0.165% coffee-supplemented group (three cups) showed some improvement in reference memory performance in the Morris water maze."

"In a subsequent study, the effects of caffeine alone did not account for the performance improvements, showing that the neuroprotective benefits of coffee are not due to caffeine alone, but rather to other bioactive compounds in coffee. Therefore, coffee, in achievable amounts, may reduce both motor and cognitive deficits in ageing."

"Coffee generally enhances memory, thanks to caffeine's effects on some of the brain's neurotransmitters. By continually enhancing your memory over time, you reduce your chances for dementia and Alzheimer's. Regular coffee drinkers have actually shown to have as much as a 65% reduced risk of developing the world's most common neurodegenerative disease."

---

68   www.ncbi.nlm.nih.gov/pubmed/23344884

"Caffeine is also a psychoactive stimulant. About 30-45 minutes after drinking coffee, the caffeine reaches your brain, and results in increased levels of norepinephrine and dopamine, through impeding the inhibitory neurotransmitter, adenosine - serving to boost your mood, energy, memory and general cognitive functioning."

"Increased levels of dopamine also serve to combat both Parkinson's Disease, and depression. People who drink coffee regularly, have been shown to have a 32-60% reduced chance of developing Parkinson's Disease, whereas drinking four or more cups of black coffee a day (700ml) reduces your chances of becoming depressed by 20%. People who drink four cups of coffee a day are also more than 50% less likely to commit suicide."

According to research conducted at the Seoul National University, even the scent of coffee can have a calming effect, actually changing the composition of a protein in the brain that's associated with stress - specifically stress that has developed as a result of sleep deprivation.

Drinking 680ml to 850ml of black coffee a day, helps to reduce your risk of colorectal cancer by about 15%, and the risk of liver cancer by about 40% - the cancers responsible for the third and fourth most deaths in the world."

"Coffee also reduces your risk of skin cancer - particularly in women - by about 20%. (Researchers at the Brigham and Women's Centre, and Harvard University, found that women who drink at least three cups of coffee per day are less likely to develop skin cancer than women who don't drink coffee at all").

"Regular coffee drinkers also benefit from a 20% lower chance of a stroke, as well as a lower incidence of heart disease."

Coffee is a diuretic - causing increased passing of urine, helping to cleanse your internal system, and flush out bacteria and viruses. Studies suggest that, as a result, drinkers of black coffee generally tend to be healthier as they tend to get sick less often.

It is important to note, however, that an excessive intake of caffeine can actually dehydrate the body. A caffeine intake in excess of 500 milligrams per day can actually be counter-productive to your goal of hydration.

The human body has been shown to absorb more nutrients from coffee than it does from other popular sources of antioxidants such as fruits and vegetables. If you drink coffee, it is your single largest source of antioxidants, containing important nutrients such as vitamins B2, B3, and B5, Manganese, Magnesium, and Potassium. (Although, it does not contribute to your *5 a day*!)

Powerful stuff, coffee - but did you know that caffeine has even been linked with honesty? *Honestly…*

In a study, published in 2011, Barnes, Schaubroeck, Huth, & Ghumman, sought to examine "the relationship between sleep deprivation, depletion, and deceptive behaviour". For the study, half of the students had been kept awake overnight in a lab, the remaining 100 students were well-rested. Half of the students were given standard chewing gum, and the other half were given chewing gum containing 200mg of caffeine - the equivalent of a 340ml cup of coffee.

The students were then instructed that they would be sharing money with someone else in the study. They could choose to send either an honest or deceptive message (about the amount of money that they would be sharing) to the person with whom they thought they would be sharing the money.

The 100 sleep-deprived students were far more likely to send a deceptive message than their 100 well-rested counterparts. And among the sleep-deprived students, those who had been given the caffeine-enriched chewing gum were less likely to send the deceptive message than those participants who had received the standard chewing gum.

A further study, published in 2010, suggested that caffeine may even "protect against increased risk-taking propensity in those who are sleep deprived". 25 Adults (21 men, and 4 women) completed two different risk-taking scales - Balloon Analog Risk Task (BART) and Evaluation of Risks (EVAR) - at regular intervals during 75 hours of continuous sleep deprivation.

Roughly half were given caffeine during the study, whilst the control group were given only a placebo. The placebo group showed significant increases in risk-taking propensity and behaviour, over the 75-hour observation, whereas the caffeinated group did not. "3 nights of total sleep deprivation led to a significant increase in behavioural risk-taking but not self-reported perception of risk-propensity. Overnight caffeine prevented this increase in risky behaviour".

It is also important to note, however, that the increased cerebral and cognitive activity, and the increase also in energy levels that are produced by coffee consumption is, however, only a temporary effect and the body may actually begin to feel even more tired than before. To maintain the (temporary) energy boost, the body will - over time - begin to crave more caffeine.

Studies have also shown that a sudden increase in caffeine creates havoc to the psychological state of mind and may also cause users to become nervous and edgy. Coffee intake has also been linked with skin disorders and can cause acne outbreaks. Drinking an excessive amount of caffeine has also been linked with an increased risk of heart complications. The results of a 2014 study linked an excessive intake of energy drinks with angina, irregular heartbeat, and even death.

If coffee is not quite "your cup of tea", then why not drink a smoothie for breakfast? It's a great way to boost your water intake and has the added benefit of also providing essential fibre, which aids water retention, and also uses the water to "keep you regular". (And a smoothie does count towards your *5 a day*.)

If you're looking to boost your levels of antioxidants, alongside your hydration requirements, then look no further than a refreshing glass of pomegranate juice - one of the most potent fruit juices in terms of its concentration of *polyphenols*. A Spanish study found that pomegranate can actually slow down the natural wear and tear on your cellular DNA. Subjects given pomegranate extract pills, showed a reduction in cell damage - a cause of ageing - in just one month.

Pomegranate juice is also an excellent source of vitamin C, which plays an important role in the skin's collagen production and is known also for its properties of repairing and preventing skin damage caused by the sun. Pomegranate, however, can also interfere with certain medications, so please check with your doctor before embarking on a pomegranate regime.

It's important to remember that, whatever you're drinking, please take the time to check the ingredients for added sugar, or other "hidden" additives. Sugar serves to raise your body's level of triglycerides - fat in the blood, used to provide energy to the body. If unused, these triglycerides are then stored as fat. High levels of triglycerides have been linked to an increased risk of heart disease.

And more food for thought… A recent study of female rats and their offspring found that the production of a gene associated with the growth of nerves was diminished by increased levels of both sugar and stress.

Hydration is essential to your overall well-being, but please be mindful of "the oil that you choose to lubricate your machine". You honestly do not "need" to add that little extra *something* to your water.

Please beware excessive levels of sugar, caffeine and additives. The answer lies in the use of the term "excessive" - as with most things in life, moderation is the answer.

Exercise:

"Take care of your body. It's the only place you have to live." *Jim Rohn.*

According to the NHS, "It's the miracle cure we've all been waiting for. It can reduce your risk of major illnesses, such as heart disease, strokes, Type 2 Diabetes and cancer, by up to 50% and lower your risk of early death by up to 30%. It's free, easy to take, has an immediate effect and you don't need a GP to get some. Its name? *Exercise*".

"Whatever your age, there's strong scientific evidence that being physically active can help you lead a healthier and even happier life." People who engage in regular activity have a lower risk of many chronic diseases, such as heart disease, Type 2 Diabetes, strokes, and some cancers. Physical activity can also boost self-esteem, mood, sleep quality, and energy, as well as reducing your risk of stress, depression, dementia and Alzheimer's disease.

"If exercise were a pill, it would be one of the most cost-effective drugs ever invented," says Dr Nick Cavill, a health promotion consultant. "Given the overwhelming evidence, it seems obvious that we should all be physically active. It's essential if you want to live a healthy and fulfilling life into old age."

It has been medically proven that people who partake in regular physical activity have:

- up to a 35% reduced risk of coronary heart disease and strokes
- up to a 50% reduced risk of Type 2 Diabetes
- up to a 50% reduced risk of colon cancer
- up to a 20% reduced risk of breast cancer
- a 30% reduced risk of early death
- up to an 83% reduced risk of osteoarthritis
- up to a 68% reduced risk of hip fracture
- up to a 30% reduced risk of depression
- up to a 30% reduced risk of dementia"

It has been suggested that "there is a significant association between exercise and improved mood and mental well-being". The question remains, however, does exercising generate a more positive mood and enhanced mental well-being, or are "happier people" simply more inclined to engage in regular exercise?

"Researchers studying exercise have consistently found that it has a positive impact on mood. It has been proven that physical activity stimulates the release of endorphins - the "feel-good" chemicals in the brain.[69] Some researchers argue that exercise acts as a diversion from negative thoughts.[70] Others argue that exercise improves mood by virtue of the personal growth and goal attainment that results from efforts to master a physical skill.[71]

Furthermore, research indicates that the social interaction involved in certain kinds of exercise (such as team sports) contributes to personal satisfaction and consequently, mood enhancement."[72]

Exercise has been studied as an alternative therapy to the traditional antidepressant medications used in the treatment of depression. Based on accumulated evidence, The Cochrane Review concluded that exercise has a "large clinical impact on depression".

Blumenthal et al. studied the effect of exercise on adults suffering from clinical depression. They compared exercise with a commonly prescribed anti-depressant and found that exercising was just as effective as the anti-depressant, in reducing depressive symptoms.

In Kathleen Mulpeter's *"These Are the Best Exercises for Anxiety and Depression"*, Ben Michaelis, PhD is quoted as saying that "The body is the mind and the mind is the body. When you take care of yourself, you are helping the whole system."

"Needless to say, you should always consult with your doctor about your treatment options," says Michaelis. "But it can't hurt to incorporate exercise, of any kind, into your routine. Research suggests that these three activities in particular could help alleviate symptoms of depression or anxiety."

1. Running. Running burns calories, reduces food cravings, and lowers your risk of heart disease. "Running for just five minutes a day might even help you live longer, but it's also been shown to improve mood in a variety of ways," says Michaelis. "Running causes lasting changes in our "feel good" neurotransmitters serotonin and norepinephrine, both during and after exercise," he explains. "The repetitive motions of running appear to have a meditative effect on the brain. The mental benefits can be especially powerful for people who suffer from depression."

---

69   Fox (1999)

70   Smith (2006)

71   Ströhle (2009)

72   Stubbe (2007)

"In a 2006 review published in *The Journal of Psychiatry & Neuroscience*, researchers found evidence to suggest that "exercise can work in a similar way to antidepressants, alleviating major depressive disorder by promoting the growth of new neurons in the brain." "Running may make it easier for you to fall asleep at night," says Michaelis, "which benefits your overall mental health by improving memory, lowering stress levels, and protecting against depression."

2. Hiking. "There is evidence that being around plants, trees, and especially decaying trees can help reduce anxiety because these plants emit chemicals to slow down the process of their decay, which appears to slow us down as well," suggests Michaelis.

A study published in *Environmental Health and Preventive Medicine* found that participants who had taken a 20-minute walk in the woods had "lower stress hormone levels than participants who had been in a city". A recent study revealed that when young adults went on a 50-minute nature walk, they "felt less anxious and had improved memory function".

Marilyn Rogers agrees. On *Lifehack*, Rogers writes that "Those who focus too much on negative thoughts about themselves can exhibit anxiety, depression, and other issues, such as binge eating or post traumatic stress disorder. In a recent study, researchers found that hiking in nature decreases these obsessive, negative thoughts."

Research also found that "those who walked for 90 minutes in a natural environment reported lower levels of rumination and also had reduced neural activity in the subgenual prefrontal cortex, which is associated with mental illness. Those who walked through an urban environment didn't enjoy these benefits"…

Our world is becoming increasingly more urban, and that urbanisation "is linked to depression and other forms of mental illness. Simply removing us from an urban environment to spend time outdoors where there are fewer mental stressors, less noise, and fewer distractions can be advantageous for our mental health."

According to a study by Ruth Ann Atchley and David L. Strayer, "creative problem solving can be improved by disconnecting from technology and reconnecting with nature. Participants hiked while backpacking in nature for approximately four days and they were prohibited from using technology. They were asked to perform tasks requiring creativity and complex problem solving. They found that those immersed in the hiking excursions had increased performance on problem-solving tasks by 50%".

Hiking can also burn 400 to 700 calories an hour, depending on the intensity of the hike. Hiking isn't as stressful on our joints, when compared with running, for example. "It's astonishing that a physical activity as simple and low-cost as hiking can provide so many mental health benefits."

According to *WebMD*, "more and more doctors are writing "nature prescriptions" or recommending "ecotherapy" to reduce anxiety, improve stress levels, and to curb depression. Plus, nature prescriptions are becoming more accepted by traditional health care providers as more research shows the benefits of exercising and spending time in nature."

3. Yoga. In a study published in *Evidence-Based Complementary and Alternative Medicine*, "all of the study's participants who had taken yoga classes experienced "significant" reductions in depression, anger, anxiety, and neurotic symptoms."

"The research suggested yoga as a "complementary treatment for depression". A series of studies, conducted in 2012, examined the effects of yoga on anxiety and stress. "In 25 out of the 35 studies, subjects experienced a significant decrease in stress and anxiety symptoms after starting yoga."

"The great thing about yoga is that besides the stretching and core strengthening, there is a tremendous focus on breathing, which helps to slow down and calm the mind," says Michaelis. "Experts believe that yoga's focus on the breath is especially beneficial for your mental health because it's difficult to be anxious when you're breathing deeply."

In *"The Best Exercise For Your Age"*, published in *The Huffington Post*, Alice Oglethorpe suggests that "some workouts can be more beneficial than others at different points in your life." Oglethorpe suggests the different types of exercise which she believes are the most beneficial to the following different age groups:

> ***The 20's:*** "Your current cardiovascular fitness level can help predict how healthy you'll be later", suggests Oglethorpe. In a study published in *JAMA Internal Medicine*, people in their 20's were subjected to a treadmill test in which researchers gradually increased the speed and incline, and measured how long the participants could endure. "When the researchers followed up with the subjects years later, in midlife, they found that those who lasted at least 10 minutes had a 50% lower risk of death and 40% lower risk of cardiovascular disease compared with those who could only complete 6 minutes of the test." The researchers recommended 30 minutes of moderate cardiovascular exercise (such as a brisk walk, including hills) 5 days a week, or 25 minutes at a greater intensity, 3 times a week.

Yoga. "Today's graduates are faced with very few job opportunities, and most of them are also burdened with the debt of their student-loans", adds Oglethorpe. "We see a lot of students in their 20's who don't know how to relax," says Jay Gupta, a co-founder of YogaCaps, a non-profit organisation that works with hospitals and community organisations to teach yoga to those with chronic diseases.

"Chronic stress is linked to sleeplessness, depression, a weaker immune system and even digestive issues. Learning healthy ways to cope with stress will benefit you now and in the long term. Research suggests that yoga might help to regulate stress responses in the body, such as elevated cortisol levels and high blood pressure. Gupta says practicing a little yoga every day would be ideal, but 2 sessions per week is a good start."

> **The 30's:** *Add intervals to your cardiovascular workouts.* "This is the decade when your metabolism starts to slow down, but you may not realise how important it is to counteract the decline", warns Oglethorpe.

"Due to the slower metabolism, you could gain up to 2 pounds of fat every year," says Mike Siemens, director of exercise physiology at Canyon Ranch Health Resort, in Arizona. "Interval training helps your body keep burning calories after you stop exercising. The effect continues for 10 to 12 hours after an interval workout, compared with 4 or 6 hours after a regular one."

Siemens suggests that you "Push yourself to an 8 or 9 on the exertion scale (you shouldn't be able to continue a conversation), then lower to a 6 or 7 (you can say 10 words or so without being out of breath), and then repeat. Alternate between those two levels for 20 to 40 minutes, 2 to 3 days a week. Start with whatever ratio of work time to recovery time works best for you and progress from there", he suggests.

"Around the age of 30, you start to lose up to one-third of a pound of muscle a year - that's why most people get weaker as they age," suggests Siemens. "You might think that anything that works your muscles is enough to build muscle back up, but those activities only maintain your muscle mass", he warns. "Lifting weights can help rebuild what you've lost. You want a weight heavy enough that you can't do more than 8 to 12 repetitions in a row. Focus on your chest, legs, back and shoulders, doing 2 to 3 sets of moves that work those areas a few times a week."

> **The 40's:** *More exercise - any kind will do.* "It will help to protect your telomeres, the stretches of DNA on the ends of our chromosomes that get shorter with age and leave cells vulnerable to damage", says Oglethorpe. A study in *Medicine & Science in Sports & Exercise* showed that the more "physically active people were during middle age, the lower their risk for shortened telomere length and the healthier their cells stayed as they aged."

- ***The 50's:*** *Tennis, dancing, hiking.* "Weight-bearing exercises help you to maintain bone density, which generally starts to drop once women enter menopause", suggests Oglethorpe.

  "Bone is living tissue, and it only keeps itself as strong as it needs to be," suggests Elizabeth Matzkin, MD - chief of women's sports medicine at Brigham and Women's Hospital in Boston. "If you regularly stress your bones, they'll maintain greater strength to keep up with your activities."

  "Aim for 30 minutes of daily weight-bearing activity. If that doesn't work with your schedule," Matzkin says, "you can get the same benefit with fewer but longer workouts, as long as you lengthen your workouts slowly to avoid injury."

  A recent study in Gerontology suggests that the more powerful your legs are, the better your brain will age. Researchers studied female twins with an average age of 50, and found that "within the pairs, the twin with stronger legs had a brain that aged better (both structurally and functionally) over a 10-year period." One theory suggests that "when our muscles are put to work, they release neurochemicals that stimulate brain cells, and since leg muscles are among the largest muscles in the body, they may release more of these neurochemicals."

- ***The 60's, and beyond:*** *Regular strength training.* "You'll give your brain a lift. Women in their 60's and 70's who lifted weights twice a week had fewer white matter lesions on their brains, a warning sign of cognitive decline that is also connected to a higher risk of dangerous falls, according to a study in *The Journal of the American Geriatric Society*. Those who strength-trained only once a week did not see the same benefits."

  "Using medium-heavy weights (you should be able to do 10 repetitions of each move before you need a break), do a variety of moves that work your whole body for 40 minutes, twice a week." Try also to engage in "light" activities such as walking and gardening. "Find an activity that gets you up and moving regularly, and try to commit to 30 minutes of it every day."

The NHS recommends the following exercise requirements "to stay healthy, or to improve health". As above, the recommendations are separated into suggested age groups...

Five to Eighteen Years Old

The NHS recommends that to maintain a basic level of health, children and young people aged 5 to 18 need to engage in "at least 60 minutes of physical activity every day - this should range from moderate activity, such as cycling and playground activities, to vigorous activity, such as running and tennis".

"On three days a week, these activities should involve exercises for strong muscles, such as push-ups, and exercises for strong bones, such as jumping and running. Many vigorous activities can help you build strong muscles and bones, including anything involving running and jumping, such as gymnastics, martial arts and football." Children and young people should reduce the time they spend sitting watching TV, playing computer games and traveling by car when they could walk or cycle instead.

"Moderate activity raises your heart rate and makes you sweat. One way to tell if you're working at a moderate level is if you can still talk, but you can't sing the words to a song", such as

- ✓ walking to school or walking the dog
- ✓ playing in the playground
- ✓ riding a scooter
- ✓ skateboarding or rollerblading
- ✓ cycling on level ground or ground with few hills

"Vigorous activity is linked to better general health, stronger bones and muscles, as well as higher levels of self-esteem. There is good evidence to suggest that vigorous activity can bring health benefits over and above those of moderate activity. A rule of thumb is that one minute of vigorous activity provides the same health benefits as two minutes of moderate activity.

Vigorous activity makes you breathe hard and fast. If you're working at this level, you won't be able to say more than a few words without pausing for a breath.

Muscle strength is necessary for daily activities, and to build and maintain strong bones, regulate blood sugar and blood pressure, and help maintain a healthy weight. For young people, muscle-strengthening activities are those that require them to lift their own body weight or work against a resistance, such as lifting weight.

Adults (19 to 64 years old)

"To stay healthy, adults aged 19-64 should try to be active daily and should do at least 150 minutes of moderate aerobic activity such as cycling or fast walking every week, and strength exercises on two or more days a week that work all the major muscles (legs, hips, back, abdomen, chest, shoulders and arms). Also, adults aged 19-64 should engage in 75 minutes of vigorous aerobic activity, such as running or a game of singles tennis every week, and strength exercises on two or more days a week that work all the major muscles.

The NHS recommends "a mix of moderate and vigorous aerobic activity every week. For example, two 30-minute runs plus 30 minutes of fast walking equates to 150 minutes of moderate aerobic activity, and strength exercises on two or more days a week that work all the major muscles."

For a moderate to vigorous workout, the NHS has created a programme, "*Couch to 5K*", a nine-week running plan, designed specifically for beginners.

Muscle-strengthening exercises are counted in repetitions and sets. A repetition is one complete movement of an activity, like a bicep curl or a sit-up. A set is a group of repetitions. The NHS recommends that for each strength exercise, you try to do at least one set, and eight to 12 repetitions in each set. To get health benefits from strength exercises, you should do them to the point where you struggle to complete another repetition.

The NHS has also created "*Strength and Flex*", a 5-week exercise plan for beginners to improve strength and flexibility. You can do activities that strengthen your muscles on the same day or on different days as your aerobic activity – whatever works best for you. Muscle-strengthening exercises are not an aerobic activity, so you'll need to do them in addition to your 150 minutes of aerobic activity.

<u>Older Adults (65 and over)</u>

"Older adults aged 65 or older, who are generally fit and have no health conditions that limit their mobility, should try to be active daily and should do at least 150 minutes of moderate aerobic activity such as cycling or walking every week, and strength exercises on two or more days a week that work all the major muscles. Also, "older adults aged 65 or older, who are generally fit and have no health conditions that limit their mobility", should try to engage in 75 minutes of vigorous aerobic activity such as running or a game of singles tennis every week, and strength exercises on two or more days a week that work all the major muscles.

Again, the NHS recommends "a mix of moderate and vigorous aerobic activity every week.

"You should also try to break up long periods of sitting with light activity, as sedentary behaviour is now considered an independent risk factor for ill health, no matter how much exercise you do. Older adults at risk of falls, such as people with weak legs, poor balance and some medical conditions, should do exercises to improve balance and co-ordination on at least two days a week. Examples include yoga, tai chi and dancing."

"Moderate activity will raise your heart rate and make you breathe faster and feel warmer. Daily chores such as shopping, cooking or housework don't count towards your 150 minutes, because the effort isn't enough to raise your heart rate, but they are important nonetheless, as they break up periods of sitting."

Vigorous activity makes you breathe hard and fast. If you're working at this level, you won't be able to say more than a few words without pausing for breath.

The NHS is quick to bemoan what it terms a "modern problem". "People are less active nowadays, partly because technology has made our lives easier. We drive cars or take public transport. Machines wash our clothes. We entertain ourselves in front of a TV or a computer screen. Fewer people are doing manual work, and most of us have jobs that involve little physical effort. Work, house chores, shopping and other necessary activities are far less demanding than for previous generations."

We move around less and burn off less energy than previous generations used to. Research suggests that many adults now spend more than seven hours a day sitting down - at work, on transport, or in their leisure time. People aged over 65 spend 10 hours or more each day sitting or lying down, making them the most sedentary age group.

The Department of Health describes inactivity as a "silent killer". Evidence is emerging that sedentary behaviour, such as sitting or lying down for long periods, is bad for your health. Not only should you try to raise your activity levels, but you should also reduce the amount of time you and your family spend sitting down.

Common examples of sedentary behaviour include watching TV, using a computer, using the car for short journeys and sitting down to read, talk or listen to music – and such behaviour is thought to increase your risk of many chronic diseases, such as heart disease, strokes, and Type 2 Diabetes, as well as weight gain and obesity."

"We have to find ways of integrating activity into our daily lives," proffers Dr Nick Cavill, a health promotion consultant. "Whether it's limiting the time babies spend strapped in their buggies, or encouraging adults to stand up and move frequently, people of all ages need to reduce their sedentary behaviour. Each of us needs to think about increasing the types of activities that suit our lifestyle, and can easily be included in our day," suggests Dr Cavill.

"To keep the body in good health is a duty, otherwise we shall not be able to keep our mind strong and clear." *Buddha*

"Champions aren't made in gyms. Champions are made from something they have deep inside them - a desire, a dream, a vision. They have to have the skill, and the will. But the will must be stronger than the skill." *Muhammad Ali.*

Rest and Recuperation:

The Mental Health Foundation suggests that "30% of adults in the UK are severely sleep deprived, putting them more at risk of mental health and relationship issues." Approximately 33% of Americans (roughly 83 million) receive less than the recommended amount of sleep.

"Lack of adequate sleep has been linked to a host of adverse effects on our physical and mental health, including obesity, diabetes, high blood pressure, strokes, and depression. It also wreaks havoc on our cognitive abilities and work performance by impairing memory and learning, judgment, and critical thinking. And insufficient sleep is associated with a higher rate of accidents, injuries, and medical and occupational errors." A number of historical disastrous *accidents* have been linked with sleep deprivation, including:

- The Chernobyl nuclear disaster, 1986.
- The space shuttle Challenger explosion, 1986.
- The Exxon Valdez Oil Spill, 1989.
- American Airlines Flight 1420 Crash, 1999.

Research conducted at the University of Chicago revealed that sleep improves memory retention and learning new tasks.[73] Another study examined the effects of sleep on well-being. The study consisted of 68 418 participants, including children and adolescents, who were asked to complete journal entries and questionnaires. The researchers found that "inadequate sleep was associated with family issues, school troubles, physical problems, and depressive symptoms".[74]

Studies of sleep deprivation in healthy young adults indicate that it is associated with up to a 40% reduction in memory, thinking speed, reaction time, and cognitive ability.[75] Sleep deprivation is also linked with with mood instability, and has been shown to lead to over-reactions and impairment of judgment.[76]

There is a vast amount of research which supports that exercise, good nutrition, and sleep are associated with improved mental well-being and, in some cases, reduced depression and anxiety. Again, the conundrum is, do sleep, exercise and nutrition actually improve mental well-being, or are those with greater mental well-being generally more inclined to exercise, sleep well, and maintain a balanced diet?

---

[73] Harms (2013)

[74] Smaldone et al. (2007)

[75] Killgore (2010)

[76] Motomura et al. (2013)

Our increasingly fast-paced society and high-pressure school environments make it more challenging for us to get the recommended amount of sleep each day. In 1960, *The American Cancer Society,* determined that the average amount of sleep was 8 hours. Since 2008, this number has decreased to an average of 6.7 hours.

While there is a long-standing belief that we should rest between six and eight hours every night, *The Surrey Sleep Research Centre* is claiming that it is the quality of sleep that is important rather than the quantity. Moreover, the ideal amount of sleep will vary for each individual, and relative to contributing factors. The average length of time is recommended to be between five and nine hours in total.

So just how much *quality* sleep should you be aiming for ?

"*Your Guide to Healthy Sleep*", published by The National Institutes of Health, recommends the following "Average sleep needs by Age"... Remember, it's all about the *quality* of your sleep, which can skew the recommended *quantities*...

- Newborn to 2 months old: 12 - 18 hours
- 3 months to 1 year old: 14 - 15 hours
- 1 to 3 years old: 12 - 14 hours
- 3 to 5 years old: 11 - 13 hours
- 5 to 12 years old: 10 - 11 hours
- 12 to 18 years old: 8.5 - 10 hours
- Adults (18+):   7.5 - 9 hours

Remember also that there is a massive gap between the amount of sleep that you can "get by on" and the amount that you need to perform at your best. "Sleep is a necessity, not a luxury," says Helpguide. "The quality of your sleep directly affects the quality of your waking life, including your productivity, emotional balance, creativity, physical vitality, and even your weight. No other activity delivers so many benefits with so little effort."

When you sleep, your body doesn't shut down. It is during sleep – particularly the deep sleep cycles – that your body repairs and restores, performing the diverse "biological maintenance" required to keep your body operating at its peak. Just as your car requires regular servicing to run smoothly and to peak performance, your "machine" requires regular servicing too. Would you pass your "MOT"?

Without enough hours of restorative sleep, you won't be able to work, learn, create, and communicate at a level even close to your true potential. "Sleep deprivation has a wide range of negative effects that go way beyond daytime drowsiness. Lack of sleep affects your judgment, co-ordination, and reaction times. Sleep deprivation can affect you just as much as being drunk."

"A growing body of research points to the fact that skimping on sleep can lead to weight gain, an increase in injuries and a decrease in testosterone levels, which is often associated with depression and bone density loss."

How many times have you reached for "the cookie jar", or that sweet "midnight snack" when you've felt tired? A recent study revealed that people who sleep less than six hours a day were almost 30% more likely to become obese, than those who slept between seven and nine hours. An independent study even suggests that sleeping less than seven hours a night may cause you to eat an additional 385 calories a day, adding 0.45kg (1lb) to your waistline every week.

Not only does sleep fatigue stimulate your appetite, it unfortunately appears to specifically stimulate cravings for high-fat, high-carbohydrate foods to satisfy a quick energy boost. If you find yourself reaching for the mid-afternoon coffee, energy drink, or that bar of chocolate, it might mean one of two things. You either need to look at your diet, or your (lack of) deep sleep...

It is during deep sleep that the body's muscles recover, repairing tissue torn during workouts, and the brain creates memories and clears out toxins. The most harmful effects of sleep deprivation arise from a lack of *deep* sleep - critical to "maintaining your health, stimulating growth and development, repairing muscles and tissues, and boosting your immune system."

"Sleep is all about recovering. So if you're not sleeping, you're not recovering. And if you're going to break your body down a lot, you better find ways to build it back up. And the only way to do that is get a lot of sleep." *Tom Brady*, five times Superbowl-winning Quarterback for The New England Patriots.

"Many people think that you build (muscle) in the gym, but you actually build when you sleep," Chirjeev Sawhney - a personal trainer and fitness manager at a Gold's Gym in Arlington - told *The Washington Post*. "It's when you repair that broken tissue that you get stronger," Sawhney stresses.

To wake up feeling refreshed and energised, it is essential to benefit from *quality* deep sleep.

In *"6 Ways to wake up early and not feel tired"*, *Lifehack* suggests:

- ✗ Avoid drinking coffee, red wine, and consuming chocolate prior to sleep
- ✓ Go to the toilet just before you aim to sleep
- ✓ Ensure that your room reflects the core principles of Feng Shui
- ✓ Focus on something happy and exciting when you stir in the morning
- ✓ Create a manageable exercise regime for the morning
- ✓ Get your hydration right when you first stir

Brendon Burchard, in his blog, *"How to wind down"*, discusses the merits of creating a new evening routine - and following it regularly - if "you have difficulty winding down at the end of a busy day". Brendon proposes the following four ideas...

1. Transition from the busy day. After work, Brendon suggests that you do something to help you to release the stress from the day. "Meditating, exercising, stretching, or taking a nap or short walk are all great options to transition. Whatever it is, have a transition routine that tells you that the busy day is over and it is time to wind down."

2. Don't get stuck in social media or in front of screens. "Social media and entertainment fires off dopamine in your brain and also increases anxiety, preventing you from winding down", warns Brendon. "Avoid all screens in the hour before bed", he stresses.

3. Have a gratitude practice. Brendon recommends that every day, you write down all of the things that you are thankful for, your accomplishments, and the new things that you have learned. He then suggests that you write down what you need to do the following day "so you can free your mind and relax. Making lists help you relax", he suggests.

4. Use your home environment. "Dim the lights, play calming music, light candles, and lower the temperature to 20°C before bed. Make sure your room is pitch back when you go to bed. And before you fall asleep, generate gratitude."

If you can successfully wind down at the end of each day, Brendon proposes that you'll be fully energised the following morning – as long as you've benefited from *deep* sleep – which, to be honest, is far more likely when you approach the night in an already relaxed state.

Similarly, in "*5 Ways To Empty Your Mind Before Bed*", Naomi Goodlet explores five suggestions to clear your head before bedtime.

1. Write down your thoughts. To prevent your thoughts from keeping you awake all night, try to write them down", suggests Goodlet.

2. Visualisation. If you want to calm your mind before bed, Goodlet suggests "imagining your thoughts escaping your head into a basket, ready to be picked up when you wake the next morning."

3. Meditation. Meditation has many benefits, including a calmer mind and improved sleep.

4. Make a promise to continue your thoughts when you wake. "Your mind is very persistent. It will keep throwing around thoughts, ideas and worries as long as you let it", claims Goodlet. "Make a promise to continue these thoughts in the morning. This closure can help you to get to sleep".

5. Switch off. "95% of people use some type of electronics in the hour leading up to bed.

Artificial light from the screens increases the brain's level of alertness, and suppresses the release of the hormone melatonin by up to 22% – negatively affecting sleep, performance and mood."

In *"7 Reasons you feel so tired that have nothing to do with sleep"*, Leigh Weingus suggests that there might be other reasons behind a sense of tiredness, which may actually have nothing to do with a lack of sleep…

- Too much sugar. Weingus suggests that "too much sugar makes your energy levels plummet. Although sugar provides a spike of energy when you first consume it, within half an hour it will leave you totally exhausted and craving more," he warns.
- You're depressed. Exhaustion is one of the symptoms of depression.
- You're not exercising enough. Regular exercise fights exhaustion and boosts energy.
- You're dehydrated. According to Dr. Roger Henderson, "Other symptoms of dehydration appear before people start to feel thirsty, including fatigue and tiredness, headaches and poor concentration," reports Weingus.
- You're not getting enough iron. Iron deficiency is when there are not enough red blood cells to distribute oxygen throughout your body, leading to exhaustion.
- You're burned out. Dedicating at least an hour of "*me*" time every day is important if you want to keep your energy levels high - not to mention your personal happiness", suggests Weingus.
- Your space is cluttered.

"Sleep is that golden chain that ties health and our bodies together." *Thomas Dekker.*

"Sleep is the best meditation." *The Dalai Lama*

Stress:

Stress actually plays an important role in our lives. Stress is essentially your reptilian brain's response to any perceived threat, or danger. As part of your self-preservation system, your "stressed" brain releases adrenaline and cortisol which serve to increase your heart rate and blood pressure, to prepare you for the imminent "fight or flight". It's perfectly natural, but this burst of hormones is intended to be just that – a "burst"; a short "spike" for immediate response. The problem lies in prolonged periods of stress – chronic stress – where these levels remain constantly elevated...

Dr. Mercola, in *"How Stress Affects Your Body"*, suggests that we "may be marinating in corrosive stress hormones around the clock, and this can have serious consequences, from adding stubborn fat to your belly, to elevating your blood pressure and triggering a heart attack".

Dr. Mercola continues, "When stress becomes chronic, your immune system becomes increasingly desensitised to cortisol, and since inflammation is partly regulated by this hormone, this decreased sensitivity heightens the inflammatory response and allows inflammation to get out of control. Inflammation, in turn, is a hallmark of most diseases, from diabetes to heart disease, and cancer."

"Elevated cortisol levels also affect your memory by causing a gradual loss of synapses in your prefrontal cortex," adds Dr. Mercola. Chronic stress has also been heavily linked with the onset of dementia. In one study, detailed by Dr. Mercola, 72% of Alzheimer's patients had "experienced severe emotional stress during the two years preceding their diagnosis".

Dr. Mercola adds that stress alters the way in which fat is deposited, owing to the specific hormones and chemicals that your body produces when you're under the influence of stress. "Recent research shows that chronic stress stimulates your body to produce *betatrophin* - a protein that blocks an enzyme that breaks down body fat," warns Dr Mercola. "What's worse", he adds, is that "stress-induced weight gain typically involves an increase in belly fat, which is the most dangerous fat for your body to accumulate as it increases your risk for cardiovascular disease."

Dr. Mercola concludes with the offer of a glimmer of hope... "suffering ill effects from stress is not an inevitable fact. A lot depends on how you respond to these day-to-day stresses. As you learn how to effectively decrease your stress level, your health will improve as well."

The key, according to Dr. Mercola, is to find out which stress reduction technique works best for you, and to stick to a daily stress-reduction programme.

Dr. Mercola's key recommendation is to ensure that you get enough sleep. (Remember, it's the *quality* that counts.) "Sleep deprivation dramatically impairs your body's ability to handle stress and is yet another risk factor for heart attack. Besides that, other stress management approaches include the following:"

- ✓ Regular physical activity
- ✓ Meditation, and Mindfulness training
- ✓ Yoga
- ✓ Social connectedness
- ✓ Laughter and levity (the treatment of a serious matter with humour)
- ✓ Spending time in nature
- ✓ Listening to music
- ✓ Scheduling time to have fun
- ✓ Aromatherapy

Not only does chronic stress increase the risk of depression, hypertension, and some cancers, but as discussed by Emma Haak, in *"5 Things Stress Is Doing To Your Body"*, there are also other damaging effects that prolonged stress has on your body.

"Roughly 25% of people say that stress gives them an upset stomach or indigestion, according to a survey by *The American Psychological Association*", says Haak. "Prolonged anxiety slows digestion as your nervous system directs its energy toward the organs and muscles most critical to survival. This, in turn, can cause nausea, constipation, cramping, and bloating."

Melanie Greenberg PhD. - in *"6 Proven Ways To Recover From Stress"*, writes that "stress, whether large and small, is a fact of life". "Whatever your stress, you need coping tools", she suggests. She proposes six "proven ways to reduce stress or recover more quickly":

1. Slow Things Down. Greenberg suggests taking 5- or 10-minute mental breaks throughout your day, to check for any signs of tension or worry, adding that "this is an easy and quick way to bring mindfulness into your life".

2. Exercise. Aerobic exercise has many stress-relieving benefits. "It can improve your mood, help you sleep better, improve your focus and mental alertness, and make you feel fitter and more confident", proffers Greenberg.

3. Get outside. In addition to the numerous benefits of spending time outdoors, Greenberg cites a study of students who were deliberately subjected to stress. The students had to sit a maths exam and were then given the feedback (regardless of their actual results) that they were performing below average. The participants were then allocated to one of two groups that either saw pictures of empty pathways and trees, or pictures of urban scenes. The participants that saw the pictures of trees had "faster cardiovascular recovery from stress".

4. Try to See Your Stress as a Challenge. Remember, it's not what happens to you that shapes you, it's what you think about what happens to you; the meaning that you give it.

   Greenberg reinforces this theory through discussing a study by Harvard and Yale researchers. "The researchers showed one of two brief video clips to managers at a large, multinational banking firm, then measured their mood and work performance in subsequent weeks. These managers had high-pressure jobs with quotas they had to meet.

   One group saw a clip showing the negative effects of stress while the other group saw a clip about seeing stress as a positive challenge. "The group that saw the clip about the positive aspects of stress actually felt less stressed", claims Greenberg. "They engaged more at work and were happier and healthier. They also reported a 23% decrease in stress-related physical symptoms, compared to the group whose members saw the negative video."

5. Stand Upright. (Remember Amy Cuddy's "Fake it 'til you make it" power pose?

6. Smile. Amy Cuddy revealed that changes in your physiology cause small chemical reactions in your body. Tony Robbins talks about changing your "state". A study by Tara Kraft and Sarah Preston at *The University of Kansas* showed that "smiling can help your body resist stress", adds Greenberg.

In Kelly McGonigal's "*The Upside of Stress: Why Stress Is Good for You and How to Get Good at It*", McGonigal proposes that your brain actually "grows stronger from psychological challenges". "The idea that we grow through adversity is not new. It's present in the teachings of every major religion and many philosophies. It's even become a cliché to say, "Whatever doesn't kill you makes you stronger", claims McGonigal.

(The following text was adapted from "*The Upside of Stress: Why Stress Is Good for You and How to Get Good at It*" - a *TED* Talk by Kelly McGonigal, and "*How To Make Stress Your Friend*", originally published on *ideas.ted.com*.)

McGonigal continues, "You know that the stress response gives you energy by flooding your body with adrenaline. But the stress response doesn't end when your heart stops pounding. Other stress hormones are released to help you recover from the challenge." These stress-recovery hormones include DHEA and nerve growth factor, both of which increase neuroplasticity. They help your brain learn from experience."

"DHEA is classified as a neurosteroid; in the same way that steroids help your body grow stronger from physical exercise, DHEA helps your brain grow stronger from psychological challenges."

"For several hours after you have a strong stress response, the brain is rewiring itself to remember and learn from the experience," suggests McGonigal.

"Stress leaves an imprint on your brain that prepares you to handle similar stress the next time you encounter it. Psychologists call the process of learning and growing from a difficult experience stress inoculation. Going through the experience gives your brain and body a kind of stress vaccine," claims McGonigal.

"This is why putting people through practice stress is a key training technique for NASA astronauts, Navy SEALS, emergency responders and elite athletes, and others who have to thrive under high levels of stress", she claims.

"But stress inoculation doesn't just transfer to similar stress situations; getting good at one kind of stress often helps in unfamiliar challenges", claims McGonigal. For example, "when people were asked how they are coping with the biggest source of stress in their lives, 82% said that they were drawing on strengths and confidence developed from past stressful experiences."

"Not every stressful situation creates the kind of learning that helps us thrive under future stress", claims McGonigal. "Stress can also be paralysing, draining and traumatising. Sometimes what we learn from stress is fear, not courage, or self-doubt instead of self-confidence," she adds.

"One thing does seem to predict whether a stressful experience is strengthening, is the biology of your stress response," says McGonigal. "The ratio of hormones you release plays a role in determining whether a stressful experience leads to positive or negative outcomes. Higher levels of cortisol have been associated with worse outcomes, such as impaired immune function and depression."

"In contrast, higher levels of DHEA have been linked to reduced risk of anxiety, depression, heart disease, neurodegeneration and other diseases we typically think of as stress-related. The ratio of DHEA to cortisol that you release during stress is sometimes referred to as the growth index of your stress response."

"A higher growth index - meaning more DHEA - is associated with thriving during and after stressful experiences", says McGonigal. "It's associated with better performance, greater learning, and fewer post-traumatic stress symptoms during military survival training", adds McGonigal. "It's even been shown to predict recovery from extreme trauma, such as childhood abuse."

"An important question, then," asks McGonigal, is: "How do you influence your own - or somebody else's - growth index?"

"One strategy is to choose a more positive mindset toward stress," she claims, suggesting to "make a conscious choice when you're stressed to view stress as helpful, and the experience as an opportunity to learn and grow."

"This mindset can actually shift your stress physiology toward a state that makes such a positive outcome more likely, for example by increasing your growth index and reducing harmful side effects of stress such as inflammation."

"I learned this first-hand when I participated in a mock study at Columbia Business School to better understand the findings of stress mindset researcher Alia Crum (now a professor at Stanford University). In the study, Crum put people through a stressful mock job interview that included strongly negative feedback, which the participants were expected to act on immediately."

"Before the job interview, every participant was randomly assigned to view one of two videos about stress. The three-minute video that I watched, opened with the message, "Most people think that stress is negative … but actually research shows that stress is enhancing," says McGonigal.

"The video went on to describe how stress can improve performance, enhance well-being, and help you grow. The other video - which the other half of the participants in the study watched - opened with the ominous announcement, "Most people know that stress is negative... but research shows that stress is even more debilitating than you expect," adds Kelly. "The video went on to describe how stress can harm your health, happiness and performance at work."

"Crum found that people who were asked to view stress as enhancing released more DHEA during the interview, resulting in a higher growth index."

"Other studies confirm that viewing a stressful situation as an opportunity to improve your skills, knowledge or strengths makes it more likely that you will experience stress inoculation or stress-related growth", says McGonigal. "Once you appreciate that going through stress makes you better at it, it gets easier to face each new challenge. And the expectation of growth sends a signal to your brain and body: get ready to learn something, because you can handle this."

"People who are good at stress allow themselves to be changed by the experience of stress. Embracing our natural capacity for growth can help us change in positive ways, even in circumstances we would never choose," concludes McGonigal.

In a subtle nod to the "WAIT" acronym for mindfulness, Chris Charyk has proposed a (not dissimilar) acronym - "STOP" - "for dealing with stressful situations", as he terms it.

In *"The Mental Trick You Can Use to Get Through Any Stressful Situation"*, Charyk claims that STOP is "a powerful, yet surprisingly basic strategy that helps you to be focused, alert, relaxed, and at your emotional best when a big moment presents itself in your life".

"It's a four-step mental checklist to use anytime you want to add a burst of fresh energy, creativity, or insight to whatever is going on", claims Charyk. "By taking a very brief break - even less than one minute - you can determine the very best action to take in the moment", he suggests.

- *Stop.* "Stop what you are doing: Press the pause button on your thoughts and actions", suggests Charyk.

- *Take.* "Take a few deep breaths to centre yourself and bring yourself fully into the present moment," says Charyk.

- *Observe.* Observe what is going on with your body, your emotions and your mind. Charyk asks "What assumptions are your making about your feelings? What is the story you're telling yourself about why you are having them?"

- *Proceed.* "Proceed with whatever you were doing, making a conscious, intentional choice to incorporate what you just learned", Charyk concludes.

"Tension is who you think you should be. Relaxation is who you are." Chinese proverb

"The greatest weapon against stress is our ability to choose one thought over another." *William James.*

"God will never give you anything you can't handle, so don't stress." *Kelly Clarkson.*

Anxiety, Depression and Fear:

In 2013, it was estimated that 615 million people were suffering from depression or anxiety worldwide.[77] Each year in Britain, an estimated one in four adults will experience at least one diagnosable mental health problem.

According to *The Mental Health Foundation*, 70 million workdays are lost every year in the UK due to mental illness - including anxiety, depression and stress related conditions - making mental illness the leading cause of sickness and absence from work. According to *Digitaldetox*, 60% of people say that even a holiday does not relieve their stress levels.

"Anxiety is considered one of the most common mental health problems in the western world". In 2013 there were 8.2 million cases recorded in the UK. Interestingly, studies show that it is more commonly seen in women. In England, women are almost twice as likely to be diagnosed with anxiety disorders than men." It is yet to be determined whether this is a biological factor, or due to the fact that women are generally more likely to seek help.

Nearly half a million workers in the United Kingdom suffered from work-related stress, anxiety or depression in 2016. Statistics released by The Health and Safety Executive reveal that for the year 2016, stress, anxiety and depression in the workplace accounted for

- 11.7 million lost working days
- 24 working days lost per case (on average)
- 37% of all work-related ill-health cases
- 45% of all working days lost due to ill health

In 2014/2015, the estimated annual cost of work-related stress, anxiety and depression in Great Britain was £5.2 billion.

Research has shown that depression is a kind of brain damage, which supports the fact that it's not something people can just "cure" or "get over". Dealing with depression means navigating a vicious cycle of sadness and hopelessness. It can leave you with an absence of motivation and energy, which are essential for you to take the steps that you need to take, to pull yourself out of the mire.

In *"The Ultimate Guide: Self-Help Tips To Deal With Depression"*, Jenny Marchal suggests "manageable steps you can do on a daily basis that can help you self-manage your depression".

---

77 World Health Organisation, 2016

"They are by no means an attempt at a cure," she writes, "but they can help alleviate the feelings of despair and darkness that seem to take over so easily. It's important to acknowledge that you may be suffering from depression and taking some steps towards a lighter path will help with your overall outlook on life", she suggests.

Marchal proffers that "the first step is to recognise that you are suffering from depression. Admitting that you're suffering from depression does not make you a weak person; in fact it's the opposite", she stresses. "Accepting that you have depression will allow you to be able to do something about it. Hiding it away or putting it down to a bad phase in your life will only allow it to spiral out of control. Having depression is not something to be ashamed of and the sooner you realise this and admit that you may have it, the sooner you can deal with it," she reassures.

"It's important to establish that your actions will help you with your depression," she says. "You have the power to control what happens to you. Breaking actions down into small daily steps can seem less less daunting and greatly relieve symptoms of depression," she adds. "Plus they don't always need a lot of time or effort to achieve. Keep that belief that every little step is helping you in a positive way." (How do you eat an elephant?)

Marchal also recommends the therapeutic benefits of exercise. "You can find it hard to motivate yourself to get out of bed let alone think about exercising but exercise is crucial for helping you deal with depression," says Marchal. "Exercise has been found to be as effective as antidepressant medication as it increases energy levels and decreases tiredness."

Marchal also suggests establishing a healthy diet. "Sugar and carbohydrates are common foods to reach for when we need comfort. Cakes, biscuits and breads are full of refined sugar and carbohydrates, which can leave us feeling lethargic, which can add to other symptoms of depression. It can also lead to a crash in mood as our blood-sugar levels drop dramatically," she warns.

"There are certain foods that help with boosting our mood, including bananas, nuts, omega-rich fish, brown rice and spinach. Complex carbohydrates such as whole-grain foods can boost serotonin levels without the crash that we get with simple carbohydrates," she adds. "Consider taking extra vitamins and supplements including complex B-vitamins and folic acid. Vitamin B deficiency in particular can trigger depression or alternatively you can eat foods rich in vitamin B like eggs, green leafy vegetables and chicken."

Marchal also recommends eating at regular intervals, adding that "going for too long without food can cause irritability and low blood sugar levels which can cause mood swings. Make sure you try to eat a healthy meal or snack every 3-4 hours," she advises.

In support of Jenny Marchal's hypothesis that "depression is actually a kind of brain damage", David Erichsen in *"Depression Isn't A Choice, It's A Kind Of Brain Damage"*, writes that "persistent depression causes brain damage, and not the other way around".

Erichsen continues, "Neurologists previously had hypothesised that brain damage was a predisposing factor for chronic depression, but a new study published in *Molecular Psychiatry* sheds a different light. The study, which consisted of 9 000 individual samples, collected from the ENIGMA group, showed evidence of hippocampus shrinkage in 1 728 patients diagnosed with chronic depression compared to the 7 199 healthy individuals partaking in the study."

Erichsen concludes that "In the past, depression has often been thought of as a lifestyle that people are just too weak to climb out of. Other people might incorrectly assert that depression is a sign of mental weakness. This could not be further from the truth", he stresses. "Whether depression is a disorder or disease doesn't matter. The fact remains that depression is a debilitating condition that drastically affects the lives of millions of people all over the world."

"Depression is not just sadness, nor is it is symptom of weakness. It isn't discriminatory against race, gender or ethnicity. Most importantly, depression is not a choice." Jenny Marchal also offers advice in dealing with anxiety. In *"The Ultimate Guide: Self-Help Tips To Deal With Anxiety"* published on *Lifehack*, she suggests the following self-help tips:

- ✓ Get Perspective On Your Worries. "Your beliefs are only in your head. Most of what's going on in our minds isn't reality," says Marchal. "If you have fears and doubts they only exist because you've allowed them to. That doesn't mean they're real on the outside. Curbing anxiety starts with the mind, your perspective and the way you choose to see everything", proposes Marchal. Remember also Einstein's advice, "We cannot solve our problems with the same thinking we used when we created them."

- ✓ Ask Yourself "Is It Possible To Solve The Problem"? "Instead of worrying, try intentionally thinking of a solution. If you find a solution then you diminish the worry you created in the first place," proffers Marchal.

- ✓ Challenge Your Anxious Thoughts. "What evidence is there that makes this thought true or not true? Is there a better way to perceive this problem - a more positive one?" She asks. "Really try to challenge your thoughts and get your mind to think differently about them."

- ✓ Yoga And Mindful Walking. "Yoga incorporates mediation with stretching positions beneficial for your mind and body. Being mindful and relaxed helps to calm your thoughts and worries," says Marchal.

- ✓ Relax At Home. Marchal stresses the importance of "creating a haven where you can relax and escape from your worries and anxieties. Taking time out to sit quietly and do the things you love and make you happy, will have a great effect on calming your mind," suggests Marchal.

- ✓ Create an Exercise Routine

- ✓ Eat Healthily. "Make sure that you avoid alcohol, caffeine and sugar which are anxiety-inducing, and can increase periods of worry," she advises. "Many foods high in anti-oxidants help enhance your mood - especially cranberries, blueberries and blackberries. Also include any food high in magnesium as lack of magnesium can trigger anxiety – oily fish, nuts, seeds and leafy green vegetables are a great addition. Caffeine-free tea like Oolong contains GABA which is an amino acid that helps with calming the nervous system and promotes sleep. It's important to get a wide variety of healthy foods and supplements that promote a nutritious body and mind that will help you deal with anxiety more efficiently," she recommends.

- ✓ Practice Meditation. "Regular mediation practice has been found to calm the body and the mind, reducing blood pressure, improving immune systems, enhancing mood and therefore reducing depression", claims Marchal. "Meditation will train your brain to focus, which is a great skill to develop when you suffer from anxiety; it will reduce the stress you feel around problems and allow you to see problems more clearly" she claims.

- ✓ Breathing Techniques. "When we're stressed and anxious we tend to make shorter and sharper breaths, which results in an imbalance of oxygen and carbon dioxide in the body," suggests Marchal. "When we breathe deeply and calmly, we are sending more oxygen to the brain which allows us to relax, calm down and see things more clearly."

- ✓ Repeat Your Worry. "This may seem counterproductive", claims Marchal, "but experts say that repeating your worry will cause you to get bored of it. When we adapt to something we become more comfortable with it, so when you find yourself feeling anxious about something, then deal with it head-on by thinking about it and thinking about it! Eventually your brain will get sick of it or bored and the thought will start to become less and less."

- ✓ Set Aside A Particular Time To Worry. "Try to set up a particular time to process your worries - preferably at the end of the day," she suggests. "Write them down when they come up and set it aside to think about later. The beauty of this is that you'll find a lot of your worries won't exist anymore by the end of the day – and if they still do then your worry time can deal with it," she adds.

- ✓ Making Peace With Time. "Try to make peace with time in that most of our worries either never materialise or float away eventually.

Remember how many times a problem never turned out to be a problem; that emergency was never an emergency. Stop and ask yourself if you're really going to be worrying about this in the next hour, day, month or year? By doing this you can put less significance and importance on what's causing you the anxiety."

"I've had a lot of worries in my life, most of which never happened." *Mark Twain.*

In *"5 Tips To Avoid Unnecessary Negativity"*, Sam Austin offers a few tips to prevent thinking negatively…

- Avoid presumption and mind-reading. Austin writes, "Thinking negatively stops us relaxing with the uncertain." He calls this "mindreading" - "They haven't liked me on Facebook; they don't like me!" or "They only said that to make me feel better, they don't really think that!"

   According to Austin, these are "emotional presumptions made by the "primal mind". Austin proposes that "avoiding the assigning of meaning to something before you have any real evidence is a key part of overcoming negative thinking. These are ambiguous situations where any presumed conclusion will be inaccurate." You'll also be able to consider all possible reasons you can think of, not just the negative ones. Every presumable answer is as plausible as the other, so try to avoid this unnecessary thinking. Which leads us to…"

- Consider opposing perspectives. "The guy in the car in front has cut you up. Now the "primal brain" will seek revenge. Even if it's just to vent your anger. There may be occasions where you've accidentally cut someone up in the past, everyone makes mistakes. Consider that may be he didn't check his mirrors or that he misinterpreted the space between you.. Then consider this" says Austin: "Holding on to anger is like grasping a hot coal with the intent of throwing it at someone else; you are the one who gets burned." *Buddha.*

   Your anger is not felt by them, but, it may well ruin the rest of your day. So, overall, how has this issue affected you're overall journey, you might now arrive at your destination 10-15 seconds later than you would have? Is it worth it?" he asks.

   "All thoughts and perceptions are filtered through your unique belief system, and it's this filter that causes negative thoughts. Consider other perspectives and your filter won't be so tight with accepting only what you think is the right way of doing things. From there, it is still your choice whether you pursue the negative thought or not – always."

- Take note of what you watch/read and listen to. "Who we spend our time with, the material we choose to watch and read is a powerful influence on our cultural references," suggests Austin. "If, for example, you watch TV soaps/dramas daily, just watch closely how often positive interactions occur versus unnecessary negative ones and consider the impact that may have when you're involved in a similar situation."

- Try not to play the victim. "You cannot control other people's actions, you can only control your reaction to those actions." Accept this as fact and it will make a huge difference in your overall well-being," says Austin. "You may not be able to change the boss at work who is always putting you down or the family member that is always complaining, but you can control the way their actions make you "feel" and how you are reacting to them." Remember "living from the inside-out"?

In *"The Five Truths About Fear"*, Susan Jeffers, Ph.D. - bestselling author of *"Feel The Fear And Do It Anyway"* discusses five essential truths about fear.

1. The fear will never go away as long as you continue to grow! "Every time you take a step into the unknown, you experience fear," she suggests. "There is no point in saying, "When I am no longer afraid, then I will do it." You'll be waiting a long time. Fear is part of the package."

2. The only way to get rid of the fear of doing something is to go out and…do it! "When you do it often enough, you will no longer be afraid in that particular situation," suggests Jeffers. "You will have faced the unknown and you will have handled it. Then new challenges await you, which certainly add to the excitement in living."

3. The only way to feel better about yourself is to go out and…do it! "With each little step you take into unknown territory, a pattern of strength develops. You begin feeling stronger and stronger and stronger," says Jeffers. (Remember the "confidence-competence loop"?)

4. Not only are you afraid when facing the unknown, so is everyone else! "This should be a relief", she says. "You are not the only one out there feeling fear. Everyone feels fear when taking a step into the unknown. All those people who have succeeded in doing what they have wanted to do in life have felt the fear - and did it anyway. So can you!"

5. Pushing through fear is less frightening than living with the bigger underlying fear that comes from a feeling of helplessness! "This is the one truth that some people have difficulty understanding. When you push through the fear, you will feel relief as your feeling of helplessness subsides. You will wonder why you didn't take action sooner. You will become more and more aware that you can truly handle anything that life hands you."

In *"How To Spend Less Time Living In Fear And More Time Living Free"*, Joseph Pennington suggests that "Most people live in a constant state of fear and worry without even knowing it. So many factors affect our emotional state that it can be difficult to know what neutrality feels like."

Pennington believes that these influences can be either external or internal. "When thinking about external influences, media outlets are the main players, bombarding our lives with fear-mongering stories about terrorism, health epidemics, natural disasters, and global warming. Their purpose is not to inform us of the latest events and information, but to ensure maximum drama, and therefore maximum ratings and sales," he says.

"Internal influences include how the brain is hardwired," adds Pennington, "the environment we grew up in, and the experiences we've had. Together, internal and external influences unconsciously shape how we think about and respond to fear in our daily lives."

"A man who fears suffering is already suffering from what he fears." *Michel De Montaigne*

An acronym which I like to use to describe FEAR - False Expectations Appearing Real. Ask yourself, how much of your "F.E.A.R." can be attributed to your reptilian brain projecting "worst-case scenarios" or "catastrophising" past events – or the *meaning* you gave them - onto your predicted future event?

Again, it all boils down to perception - the *meaning* that we give it. Most sources of negativity stem from a memory of a recent event or the exaggerated imagination of a potential future event.

"...The only thing we have to fear is...fear itself - nameless, unreasoning, unjustified terror which paralyses needed efforts to convert retreat into advance..." *Franklin D. Roosevelt*

"I learned that courage was not the absence of fear, but the triumph over it." The brave man is not he who does not feel afraid, but he who conquers that fear." *Nelson Mandela*

"The boat is the safest when it is in port, but that is not what boats were built for." *Paulo Coelho*

"Your results will never exceed what you are willing to tolerate." *Tony Robbins*

"Life is found in the dance between your deepest desire and your greatest fear." *Roger Hamilton*

"Don't let the fear of losing be greater than the excitement of winning." Robert Kiyosaki

Productivity, And Time Management:

Stephen Covey, author of *"The 7 Habits of Highly Effective People"*, said that "Time management is a misnomer. The challenge is not to manage time, but to manage ourselves. The key is not to prioritise what's on your schedule, but to schedule your priorities."

Perhaps the best advice that I have ever encountered with regards to "~~time management~~" - rather prioritisation, was found within the pages of *"Eat That Frog! 21 Great Ways to Stop Procrastinating and Get More Done in Less Time"*, penned by Brian Tracy.

"Procrastinators, be advised", warns Tracy, "Success is not a magical combination of genetics and fashion sense. Rather, it is a series of time management behaviours which must be practiced on a regular basis."[78] The essence of the book is distilled below, but I strongly recommend that you get hold of a copy and read it in full, for yourself…

Mark Twain once said that if the first thing you do each morning is to eat a live frog, you can go through the day with the satisfaction of knowing that that is probably the worst thing that is going to happen to you all day long. From a productivity perspective, your "frog" is your biggest, most important task - the one you are most likely to procrastinate on if you don't do something about it.

"If You Have To Eat Two Frogs, Eat The Ugliest One First" - if you have two important tasks before you, start with the biggest, hardest, and most important task first. Discipline yourself to begin immediately, and then to persist until the task is complete before you go on to something else.

"If You Have To Eat A Live Frog At All, It Doesn't Pay To Sit And Look At It For Very Long". The key to reaching high levels of performance and productivity is to develop the lifelong habit of tackling your major task first thing each morning. You must develop the routine of "eating your frog" before you do anything else and without taking too much time to think about it.

Successful, effective people are those who launch directly into their major tasks and then discipline themselves to work steadily and single-mindedly until those tasks are complete. Or, as Napoleon Hill wrote, "Men who succeed reach decisions promptly, and change them, if at all, very slowly. Men who fail, reach decisions, if at all, very slowly, and change them frequently, and quickly. Indecision and procrastination are twin brothers."

---

78   "Eat That Frog!", Brian Tracy. Originally published 2001.

Another publication that I would have no hesitation in recommending is Stephen Covey's "*7 Habits of Highly Effective People*". Again, I recommend that you read the book – cover to cover - but in the interests of (your) time, here follows a brief synopsis...

1. Be pro-active. Acknowledge that it's up to you to take control of your own life.
2. Begin with the end in mind. Knowing what you want is the first step to achieving it.
3. Put first things first. "Urgent" vs "Important". Being busy is different to being effective
4. Think win/win. It's not about competition. We are all winners when we work together.
5. Seek first to understand, then to be understood
6. Synergise. We are most effective when we utilise our own strengths and encourage others to do the same.
7. Sharpen the saw. Spend time on developing your talents. Work smarter, not harder.

Tony Robbins suggests that "Leaders make the decisions that no one else can – or will – make. The best ones use a system to ensure they are choosing the best possible option and reducing any potential downside. Trying to be perfect when it comes to decision-making is insane", claims Robbins. "You've got to stop being fearful; you've got to stop worrying about failure. The only failure is failing to decide, putting off what inevitably you know you need to do", he adds.

"When I make tough decisions, I use a six-step process that not only helps me make the best possible decision, but also reduces the downside of any decision", adds Tony, "because we all know that decisions have power. The system is called OOC/EMR". Tony recommends using paper, so that "you don't get stuck "looping" through potential scenarios".

- *Outcomes*. "What is the result you are after? Why do you want to achieve it? You must be clear about your outcome and its importance to you. Remember, reasons come first, answers come second," suggests Tony.

- *Options*. "Write down all of your options, including those that initially may sound far fetched. Remember, One option is no choice. Two options is a dilemma. Three options is a choice. Write down ALL options whether you like them or not," says Tony.

- *Consequences*. "What are the upsides and downsides of each option?" asks Tony. "What do you gain by each option and what would it cost you?"

> *Evaluate* your options.. "Review each of their upsides and downsides (consequences). Ask yourself:

i. What outcomes are affected?
ii. How important (0-10) is each upside/downside in terms of meeting your outcomes?
iii. What is the probability (0-100%) that the upside/downside will occur?
iv. What is the emotional benefit or consequence if this option were to actually happen?

(After completing this stage, you will be able to eliminate some options from your list...)

> *Mitigate* the damage. "Review the downside consequences for each of your remaining options. Then, brainstorm alternative ways to eliminate or reduce those downsides," suggests Tony.

> *Resolve*. "Based on the most probable consequences, select the option that provides the greatest certainty that you will meet your desired outcomes and needs."

i. Select your best option and strengthen your resolve to make it work.
ii. Resolve that, no matter what happens, this option will give you a win.
iii. Design your plan for implementation and then take massive action.

In conclusion, Tony suggests that "it's better to make a decision and monitor to see if you need to shift your approach than to remain paralysed in indecision". (Analysis paralysis)

In "*The Life-Changing Power of Discipline*", my mentor, Bob Proctor – discusses the merits of discipline. He begins, "Ray Stanford, my first mentor, told me something critical during one of the first conversations we ever had. He said, "You need only one quality to succeed. You must have discipline."

"I didn't want to have discipline. I thought discipline meant punishment," says Bob. "The truth is discipline is the ability to give yourself a command and then follow it. It didn't take long for me to figure out that Ray was right, you will never develop anything of consequence if you are not disciplined. However, if you are disciplined, you can have anything you seriously want."

"This is so basic, it's so simple, yet it's so misunderstood. People who make it in life, whether that's becoming really rich, running a successful business, or living life on their own terms, have all developed the skill of self-discipline," adds Bob.

"Don't worry if you currently lack discipline," says Bob, reassuringly. "It's something you can develop with practice, and the more you practice, the better you'll become at it." Bob suggests three things to develop discipline:

1. "Realise that if you want something different in life, you're going to have to do things differently. Then, command yourself to do what you know has to be done," he suggests.

2. "Begin scheduling your day - from the time you get up until the time you go to bed. If you have a schedule", Bob recommends, "you're more apt to do more of the things you really need to do to get where you want to go."

3. "Hold the image of being successful at what you want to do. Envision a complete shift. And proceed to let that vision unfold every day," suggests Proctor.

Bob concludes, "It won't be easy at first; however, you'll get stronger and stronger. And then you'll be able to do what you want, instead of just what you think you can do." Sandy Gallagher - Bob's partner at The Proctor Gallagher Institute - in "*10 Ways To Beat Procrastination*", suggests ten things you can do "to beat procrastination and enjoy a happier, more fulfilling life:"

1. Make a decision. "Decision is the opposite of procrastination," says Gallagher. "Just like right and left, up and down, hot and cold, there's procrastinate and decide. To become more decisive, get "*Think and Grow Rich*", she suggests, "and read the chapter on decision every day for 30 days. This will go a long way in helping you act quickly on your ideas."

2. Write it out. Sandy suggests following this three-step process:

    a) "Get a sheet of paper and write out how you currently feel about procrastination", Sandy suggests. "Elaborate on how you procrastinate - what you do, when you do it"

    b) "Take out a second sheet and ask yourself, "What would be the exact opposite of that?" Then, on the top of the page, write "I am so happy and grateful now that…" and below it write out detailed statements that are the opposite of the things you wrote on the first sheet. When you are finished, burn or shred the first sheet of paper," recommends Gallagher.

    c) "Read and rewrite what you wrote on the second sheet every day until you notice that you're no longer procrastinating," says Sandy.

3. "Chop it up. Sometimes we procrastinate because we don't know where to begin. Break large projects into milestones, and then into small, actionable steps", she suggests. (How do you eat an elephant?)

4. Quiet your mind. Sandy suggests that "Meditation is one of the most effective ways to get rid of self-sabotaging behaviour, including procrastination."

5. Stop trying to be perfect. "Perfectionism is an illusion that slows you down and prevents you from reaching your goal", says Sandy. "Act quickly, doing the best that you can."

6. Partner up. "Find an accountability partner so that you can help each other commit to, and follow through on, the things you each need to do to move toward your goals and dreams," she suggests.

7. Take a closer look. "Revisit what you're putting off, and ask yourself why you have it on your list. Be honest with yourself." (Do It or Ditch It!)

8. Put it on your gratitude list. "Write down how grateful you are that you started the project and that it's going well. Write it in the present tense, and feel like you have already achieved it," says Sandy.

9. Reward yourself for taking action. "When you accomplish something you want to put off, reward yourself. Do whatever will make you feel good about overcoming the procrastination," she recommends.

10. Adjust your attitude. "Procrastination stops you from winning and realising many great joys in life. But even a small shift in your attitude can make a big difference in your results," says Sandy. "So every day ask yourself, "What environment do I want to create for my life to really thrive?" Procrastination can't survive in an environment like that."

In *"11 Practical Ways To Stop Procrastination"*, Celestine Chua offers practical advice to ditch procrastination, and get going…

1. Break your work into little steps. How do you eat an elephant?

2. Change your environment. Different environments have different impact on our productivity," says Chua. Does your environment make you want to work? If not, consider changing your workspace."

3. Create a detailed timeline with specific deadlines. "Just one deadline for your work is an invitation to procrastinate. We get the impression that we have time, and keep pushing everything back, until it's too late. Break down your project then create an overall timeline with specific deadlines for each small task," recommends Chua. "This way, you know you have to finish each task by a certain date. Your timelines must be robust, too – for example, if you don't finish this by today, it's going to jeopardise everything else you have planned after that. It creates the urgency to act."

4. Eliminate your procrastination pit-stops. Eliminate distractions.

5. Hang out with people who inspire you to take action.

6. Get a buddy. "Having a companion makes the whole process much more fun," says Chua. "Both of you will hold each other accountable to your goals and plans."

7. Tell others about your goals. Multiple accountability buddies!

8. Seek out someone who has already achieved the outcome. "Go seek them out and connect with them. Seeing living proof that your goals are very well achievable if you take action, is one of the best triggers for action," she suggests.

9. Re-clarify your goals. (Do It, or Ditch It!)

10. Stop over-complicating things. Remember, there's never a perfect time…

Chua concludes, "Get a grip, and just do it. It boils down to taking action. You can do all the strategising, planning and hypothesising, but if you don't take action, nothing's going to happen. I have never heard anyone procrastinate their way to success before", she says.

In *How To Solve Your Biggest Barrier To Start*, Cynthia Tripathi – in keeping with the philosophy that "it's the start that stops most people" - suggests that "We often create so many barriers. Barriers to start. Barriers to achieve what we truly want. We complicate things and overthink it. So we make it complex in order to excuse ourselves from starting," she proposes.

"We decide if I just had this, or if things were this way, then I would start. What if you could make the process of taking action more simple and exciting? Do you think taking action could change your life? Is there a way to entice action instead of avoid it?" she asks.

"Humans like novelty. Ask any woman who has a closet full of clothes and still feels she has "nothing to wear," she jokes. "We like new. We like the novelty of something we haven't seen before. Enter consumer psychology," she adds. "Even if we already have an item at home that works perfectly fine, we still want the latest and greatest. There is a better way to use this innate psychology to actually help us achieve our goals."

Tripathi suggests that this "novelty mentality" can be used as a strategy to get you started. "Ask yourself what novelty item you can invest in, that will get you excited about taking action," she suggests. "Sometimes all you need is the right gear to give you that extra push."

"Have you ever gotten something new and didn't hesitate to use it?" she asks. "You stopped creating these barriers because the novelty overcame them. You were so excited about your new running shoes, or that new song, and you couldn't wait to get outside and go for a jog. It forced you to take action on your goals."

"I encourage you to invest in something new that can help you to take action. Our willpower alone is never enough. We need to have a reason to get started, and getting the right gear will often give you the strategy to overcome your initial barriers." Tripathi concludes by asking, "What have you been putting off? What can you invest in that will spark action?"

In his blog, "*4 Steps To Avoiding Overwhelm*", Brendon Burchard suggests "4 big ideas for you on how to avoid being overwhelmed:"

1. Start your day organised. "Randomness is the mother of overwhelm. Don't just wake up and plunge into the inbox, which starts your day in reaction, versus strategy. Before responding to anyone, plan the day ahead. Know what you will focus on, and you'll feel more purposeful," Burchard suggests.

2. Transition well. "Take time to transition from one project to another," he suggests. "Create time in between things to reset, and to set an intention and timeline for the next activity. No matter how awesome you are, your brain needs a break to bring back full focus and creativity. Take a nap, meditate or go on a short walk between activities."

3. Catch up. "At the end of each day, give yourself time to catch up on all the important things that need to be closed before bedtime," he recommends. "Try a 30-minute catch-up period right before, or after, dinner and make that time law – no matter what, that's your time to catch up, and your family should know about it."

4. Be more mindful. "Develop the ability to deal with uncertainty and unforeseen chaos by meeting them with full awareness, and choice to be the best you can be," says Brendon. "Life doesn't get any more peaceful if you don't." Ask, "How can I meet the demands on my plate from a place of peace and enthusiasm? How can I be grateful for what is put before me because I know it's helping me grow?"

We all know about the benefits of getting a good night's sleep – and the damaging consequences of sleep deprivation. But, according to Sean Kim in "*7 Morning Habits to Increase Your Productivity For the Day*" "the biggest bottleneck that few of us attempt to improve is our morning habits. "If you want to become more productive and effective during your day, then you need to optimise your morning habits.

How we structure and spend the first few hours of each day will determine how the rest of our day will play out, and how effective we can be in our lives," suggests Kim. As Brendon Burchard suggests, "Win the mornings!"

Kim recommends the following "simple and easy-to-implement habits that you can do today to increase your productivity for the day, and for the rest of your life:"

1. Wake up next to sunlight. "Studies have shown that those lacking sleep and suffering from insomnia is mostly due to artificial light confusing our internal clocks," says Kim.

2. Meditate. "Studies have shown that after a 20-minute meditation session, our brains are more focused and less distracted, which allows us to remove multi-tasking, achieve our goals for the day faster, and become a top performer," says Sean.

3. Automate your decisions. "We only have so much willpower in a typical day", reinforces Kim. "In order to effectively use our willpower towards the tasks that matter, it's better to minimise the number of decisions we make in the morning. Most of us go through the same routines in the morning, but there are always routines we can automate."

    Kim suggests "picking out your outfit before bedtime, eating the same breakfast each morning, and waking up earlier to avoid route changes," as examples. "You'll be surprised how morning automation can provide you the flexibility to be more productive and spontaneous throughout the rest of your day," he adds.

4. The "One Thing" According to Gary Keller, author of "*The One Thing*", the best way to prioritise, is to pick "the Domino Effect" - when a task that you complete, or an action that you take, will make everything else on your list easier to complete or even unnecessary," suggests Kim

5. Do the hardest thing first ("Eat That Frog"). Kim reveals that "A study on the human brain showed that our prefrontal cortex, the part of the brain responsible for creativity, is the most active when we wake up. This explains why creatives, such as writers or designers, do their best work early in the morning, upon waking up."

Zig Ziglar suggests "*5 Ways to Get Twice as Much Done Every Day (Without working any longer or any harder)*":

1. Get organised. Zig suggests that to "start preparing for your day the night before. Write down the things you have to get done tomorrow. Set your goals, then organize them in the order of their importance. Get the difficult and disagreeable things out of the way first. Free your mind to concentrate on the rest. You're accepting responsibility. You're making commitments."

2. Show commitment. "When you hit the wall - not if... when you hit the wall - if you've made the commitment, your first thought is, How do I solve the problem? If you haven't made the commitment, your first thought is, How do I get out of this deal? When you make a commitment, things happen," says Zig.

3. Build integrity. "When you do the right thing, you have nothing to feel guilty about," says Ziglar. "With integrity, you have nothing to fear because you have nothing to hide. With guilt and fear both removed from your back, doesn't it just make sense that you can function more efficiently? You will be freer to do the right thing, always. Emerson said, "If you would lift me up, you've got to be on higher ground.""

4. Stay positive. "The 1828 Webster's Dictionary does not have the word pessimist in it," claims Ziglar. "It only has the word optimist. The good news is if you are a natural-born pessimist, you definitely, emphatically, positively can change. You are a pessimist by choice, because you are what you are, and where you are, because of what's gone into your mind. You can change by changing what goes into your mind. When you're enthusiastic and highly motivated, you decisively move from one task to another."

5. Cut the chitchat. "Have you noticed that people who have nothing to do want to do it with you?" he asks. "When you finish one task, move with purpose to another one. And people will not block you for that five-minute gossip session. I am absolutely convinced that the listener has more to do with the gossiping than the speaker, because if you don't listen, they're not going to talk to you. When you move with purpose, people will step aside and let you go," he suggests.

"I will absolutely guarantee that you will save a minimum of an hour a day in two, three, and five-minute increments. An hour a day is five hours per week, which is 260 hours per year. That is six weeks of your life - will you use it or waste it? Zig asks. "What could you do with six extra weeks every year?"

Tony Jeary proposes "strategic planning" using what he terms the MOLO principle - to "prioritise your activities, and your life". The process is pure simplicity... Draw a line down the centre of a piece of paper. On one side, simply write "More Of..." and on the other "Less Of..."

"What do you want more of? What do you want less of?" asks Jeary. "Give yourself more time to do the things you love, and reach even more of your goals faster than ever before."

In *"Overthinking Everything? Use This Strategy to Get Out of Your Head"*, Mel Robbins suggests that "The project or business doesn't start until you do". "Our subconscious drives 95% of our decisions, according to Gerald Zaltman, a Harvard Business School professor emeritus. How you feel about the decision stalls your progress. If you feel uncertain about choosing, guess what? You'll just keep thinking about it," says Robbins.

Robbins suggests that "the first step is taking control."

"Despite what you might think, you are always ready to start. If you make the wrong decision at some point, you can adjust. You don't have to know all of the answers, you just have to start and then you'll figure them out." Robbins suggests that Richard Branson is a great example of someone taking action. "He had never flown a plane and didn't know anything about engineering them, but he started an airline regardless."

Mel recommends asking yourself what your idol would do. "Early in my career, as I was trying to break into the business, and build a platform from scratch, I was constantly uncertain. I devised a simple strategy that helped me ignore my feelings of self-doubt, so I could make important calls. I picked someone I admired and thought about what she would do in my situation."

"I chose Martha Beck, an author and Oprah Winfrey's life coach. I wanted to build a business and media platform similar to hers, write a magazine column, and build a training company. Whenever I was faced with a choice and I doubted myself, I asked, What would Martha Beck do? as a way to help me make decisions based on what I wanted, not how I felt. Asking this question is a form of cognitive restructuring," Robbins continues.

"By stopping your thoughts and asking yourself a question, you interrupt your emotions, and focus your mind." "What would your hero do? No thinking. No reconsidering. No uncertainty - just push yourself. Trust me, you'll figure it out from there."

Another tip from Robbins, "When in doubt, flip a coin. My Martha Beck strategy uses logic, but flipping a coin taps into your heart and soul. If you must choose between two things, label them Choice A (heads) and Choice B (tails). As the coin flies in the air, you'll secretly root for one or the other. That's how you'll know what you truly want," claims Robbins.

You might think that it's more productive to take lunch at your desk. "The working lunch" is more the norm than the exception these days. Kate Bratskeir - Food and Health Editor of *The Huffington Post* – suggests that "62% of professionals typically dine *"al desko"*.

Besides the "keyboard hygiene", Kate believes that there are several health reasons why you shouldn't be eating lunch at your desk. In *"Eating At Your Desk Is Terrible For You And Your Work"*, she lists three reasons that she advocates are "serious enough to convince you to take full advantage of your lunch break":

1. You'll prevent weight gain. Mindless eating leads to increased calorie consumption, and therefore weight gain. When you're not paying attention to how much you are eating, you'll soon begin to notice the calories totting up. If you stay in your chair, you're also not "changing your state", nor allowing yourself to potentially benefit from some exercise, fresh air, or even sunlight!

2. You might get on better with your colleagues. "Workplace satisfaction is so much higher if you eat with your colleagues," says Brian Wansink, Director of *Cornell University's Food and Brand Lab*. "Also, the benefits of socialising are that your stress and blood pressure levels tend to decrease, and you usually feel happier than before you started," adds Kate.

3. You'll be more productive. "Researchers have found that employees who socialise are actually more productive than those who don't. And you're probably spending more time on Facebook than meeting a deadline, while you're lunching at your desk," claims Kate.

Kate concludes, "Taking a break is exactly what helps you manage your time. Physical movement and new visual stimulation gives your brain a break, and the chance to reboot, meaning that, by the time you get back to your desk, you'll be a better employee with a fresher perspective. And, very likely, have a satisfied appetite."

Just to satisfy your curiosity, *Lifehack* published their list of the 8 top barriers to productivity - "The top 8 time wasters (in no particular order)"

- ✘ Trying to please everyone
- ✘ Perfectionism
- ✘ Worrying about how others see you
- ✘ Lack of priorities
- ✘ Repeating the same mistakes
- ✘ Doing everything by yourself without asking for help
- ✘ Comparing yourself with others
- ✘ Complaining, instead of making changes

How many are you guilty of?

Similarly, *Lifehack* also listed "How to stop procrastination and get things done:"

- ✗ Stop being a perfectionist
- ✓ Break your task down to lessen the sense of overwhelm
- ✓ Set a specific deadline for your task
- ✗ Eliminate distractions around you
- ✓ Create a stress-free work environment
- ✓ Ask for help to tackle challenges that deter you from getting started
- ✓ Remind yourself of the end goal
- ✓ Come up with a reward you will receive to get motivated
- ✓ Tell others about your goal
- ✓ Think positively

According to *Digitaldetox*:

- ✗ The average employee spends 2 hours a day recovering from distractions
- ✗ One third of people would rather clean their toilets than their email inbox
- ✗ The average employee checks 40 websites a day, switching activities 37 times an hour, changing tasks every two minutes

Only 2% of people can actually multi-task without a decline in performance. I also read a statistic the other day which suggested, that for every distraction, it takes 20 minutes, on average, to return to what you were doing before being distracted. In other words, it is suggested that it will take (on average) 20 minutes to "repair the damage" of the distraction – to return to the state (and level of productivity) that you were at, at the time of the distraction.

No discussion on productivity would be complete without the inclusion of "The Pareto Principle". "The principle was suggested by management thinker Joseph M. Juran. It was named after the Italian economist Vilfredo Pareto, who observed that "80% of income in Italy was received by 20% of the Italian population".

The principle presupposes that the majority of your results (averaged at 80%) will be driven by a relatively small proportion (20%) of your efforts – and vice versa. So, in essence, focus on – and prioritise – the 20% of your efforts which are returning 80% of your results, rather than spending 80% of your time chasing after the 20%…

Remember what Stephen Covey said, "The key is not to prioritise what's on your schedule, but to schedule your priorities."

"Leave nothing for tomorrow which can be done today." *Abraham Lincoln*

"My Way": Regrets, and Lessons in Living...

There is no failure, only feedback. And what better feedback than those who have lived life, in the "sunset of their lives?" Before you read the following pages, take the time to reflect. Ask yourself, *Have you lived? Have you loved? Have you mattered?*

Bronnie Ware, a nurse working in palliative care, spent many years tending to people who were literally on their deathbeds. From her experience with her terminally ill patients, she compiled a list of the five most common regrets of the people that she had cared for over the years...

The following passage has been distilled from her website, *bronnieware.com*, where Bronnie listed the following "Regrets of the Dying..."

Bronnie writes, "For many years I worked in palliative care. My patients were those who had gone home to die. Some incredibly special times were shared. I was with them for the last three to twelve weeks of their lives. People grow a lot when they are faced with their own mortality. I learnt never to underestimate someone's capacity for growth. Some changes were phenomenal. Each experienced a variety of emotions, as expected, denial, fear, anger, remorse, more denial and eventually acceptance. Every single patient found their peace before they departed though, every one of them."

"When questioned about any regrets they had or anything they would do differently, common themes surfaced again and again. Here are the most common five:"

1. *I wish I'd had the courage to live a life true to myself, not the life others expected of me.* "This was the most common regret of all. When people realise that their life is almost over, and look back clearly on it, it is easy to see how many dreams have gone unfulfilled."

   "Most people had not honoured even a half of their dreams, and had to die knowing that it was due to choices they had made, or had not made", says Bronnie. "It is very important to try and honour at least some of your dreams along the way. From the moment that you lose your health, it is too late. Health brings a freedom very few realise, until they no longer have it."

2. *I wish I didn't work so hard.* "This came from every male patient that I nursed", said Ware. "They missed their children's youth, and their partner's companionship. Women also spoke of this regret. But as most were from an older generation, many of the female patients had not been breadwinners. All of the men I nursed, deeply regretted spending so much of their lives on the treadmill of a work existence," she says.

"By simplifying your lifestyle, and making conscious choices along the way, it is possible to not need the income that you think you do. And by creating more space in your life, you become happier and more open to new opportunities, ones more suited to your new lifestyle," she adds.

3. *I wish I'd had the courage to express my feelings.* "Many people suppressed their feelings in order to keep peace with others", claims Ware. "As a result, they settled for a mediocre existence, and never became who they were truly capable of becoming. Many developed illnesses relating to the bitterness and resentment they carried as a result."

"We cannot control the reactions of others. However, although people may initially react when you change the way you are by speaking honestly, in the end it raises the relationship to a whole new and healthier level. Either that or it releases the unhealthy relationship from your life. Either way, you win," suggests Ware.

4. *I wish I had stayed in touch with my friends.* "Often they would not truly realise the full benefits of old friends until their dying weeks, and it was not always possible to track them down. Many had become so caught up in their own lives, that they had let golden friendships slip by over the years."

"There were many deep regrets about not giving friendships the time and effort that they deserved", Bronnie laments. "Everyone misses their friends when they are dying. It is common for anyone in a busy lifestyle to let friendships slip. But when you are faced with your approaching death, the physical details of life fall away."   "People do want to get their financial affairs in order if possible. But it is not money or status that holds the true importance for them. They want to get things in order more for the benefit of those they love. Usually though, they are too ill and weary to ever manage this task. It all comes down to love and relationships in the end. That is all that remains in the final weeks, love and relationships," claims Bronnie.

5. *I wish that I had let myself be happier.* "This is a surprisingly common one. Many did not realise until the end that happiness is a choice", reveals Ware. They had stayed stuck in old patterns and habits. The so-called "comfort" of familiarity overflowed into their emotions, as well as their physical lives. Fear of change had them pretending to others, and to their selves, that they were content. When deep within, they longed to laugh properly and have silliness in their life again."

"When you are on your deathbed, what others think of you is a long way from your mind. How wonderful to be able to let go and smile again, long before you are dying."

"Life is a choice. It is *YOUR* life. Choose consciously, choose wisely, choose honestly. Choose happiness." *Bronnie Ware.*

Sam Austin, co-founder of *LiveLearnEvolve*, asks, "What can we learn from dying?" He explores this concept in *"Twelve Life Lessons from Man Who's Seen 12,000 Deaths"*. "In Varanasi, India there is a guesthouse where people check-in to die. For 44 years, Bhairav Shukla has been the manager of the *Mukti Bhawan* guesthouse, where he's witnessed both the rich and the poor take refuge, as they await death and hope to find peace in their final days."

1. *Resolve all conflicts before you go.* Bhairav has seen this story replay in many forms over the years. "People carry so much baggage, unnecessarily, all through their life only wanting to drop it at the very end of their journey. The trick lies not in not having conflicts but in resolving them as soon as one can", advises Bhairav.

2. *Simplicity is the truth of life.* "People stop eating indulgent food when they know they are going to go. The understanding that dawns on many people in their final days is that they should've lived a simple life. They regret that the most," suggests Bhairav. "A simple life, as he explains, can be attained by spending less. We spend more to accumulate more, and thus create more need. To find contentment in less is the secret to having more", he adds.

3. *Filter out people's bad traits.* Bhairav maintains that every person has shades of good and bad. "Instead of dismissing "bad" people, we must seek out their good qualities. Harbouring bitterness for certain people, comes from concentrating on their negatives. If you focus on the good qualities though, you spend that time getting to know them better or, maybe even, loving them", he suggests.

4. *Be willing to seek help from others.* "To know and do everything by yourself might feel empowering, but it limits one from absorbing what others have learned. Bhairav believes we must help others, but more importantly, have the courage to seek help when we're in need. Every person in the world knows more than us in some respect. And their knowledge can help us, only if we're open to it. We must help others, but more importantly, have the courage to seek help when we're in need."

5. *Find beauty in simple things.* Mukti Bhavan plays soulful bhajans and devotional songs three times a day. "Some people", he says, "stop and admire a note or the sound of the instruments as if they have never heard it before, even if they have. But that's not true of everyone", he adds. "People who are too critical or too proud, are the ones who find it hard to find joy in small things, because their minds are preoccupied with "seemingly" more important things."

6. *Acceptance is liberation.* "Most people shirk away from accepting what they are going through. Only once you accept your situation, is when you become free to decide what to do about it.

When you are not in denial of a problem, you have the strength to find a solution." Bhairav believes that indifference, avoidance, and denial of a certain truth cause anxiety; they develop a fear of that thing in the person. Instead, accept the situation so you are free to think what you want to do about it, and how. Acceptance will liberate you and empower you," proffers Bhairav.

7. *Accepting everyone as the same makes service easier.* "Categorisation leads to complication and one ends up serving no-one well.

   "The day that you treat everyone the same, is the day that you breathe light and worry less about who might feel offended or not. Make your job easier," he says.

8. *If/when you find your purpose, do something about it.* "To have awareness about one's calling is great, but only if you do something about it. A lot of people, Bhairav says, know their purpose but don't do anything about realising it, bringing it to life. Simply sitting on it is worse than not having a calling in the first place. Take action on what truly matters" suggests Bhairav.

9. *Habits become values.* Bhairav recommends "cultivating good habits to be able to house good values. And building good habits happens over time, with practice. "It's like building a muscle; you have to keep at it everyday."

10. *Choose what you want to learn.* "In the vastness of the infinite amount of knowledge available to us, it is easy to get lost and confused. "The key lesson here is to be mindful of choosing what you deeply feel will be of value to you", he says. "People might impose subjects and philosophies on you because it interests them, and while you must acknowledge their suggestions, the wise thing to do is delve deeper into what rejoices your own heart and mind", recommends Bhairav.

    "In the last days of their life a lot of people can't speak, walk or communicate with others with as much ease as they could earlier. So, they turn inwards. And start to remember the things that made their heart sing once, things that they cared to learn more about over the course of their life, which enriches their days now," claims Bhairav.

11. *You don't break ties with people; you break ties with the thoughts they produce.* "You can seldom distance yourself from people you have truly loved or connected with in some way. However, in any relationship, along the way, certain mismatch of ideologies causes people to stop communicating. This never means you are no longer associated with that person. It simply means that you don't associate with a dominant thought that person brings with them, and to avoid more conflict you move away. The divorce, Bhairav affirms, is with the thought and never with the person. To understand that is to unburden yourself from being bitter and revengeful."

12. *10% of what you earn should be kept aside for Dharma.* Bhairav doesn't define *Dharma* as something religious or spiritual. Instead, he says it is associated more with doing good for others and feeling responsible about that. A simple calculation of his is to keep 10% of your income for goodwill. Many people donate, or do charitable acts, towards the end of their life because death is hard on them. In their suffering, they begin to empathise with others' suffering."

"He says those who have the companionship of loved ones, the blessings of unknown strangers, and an all-encompassing goodwill of people, exit peacefully and gracefully. That is possible when you don't cling on to everything you have and leave some part of it for others."

In *"Powerful Advice From a Dying Man"*, Seth M. asks, "What truly matters to you in this life? Many of us spend hours and hours in deep self-reflection hoping to find answers that will give us peace, but it seems that once your entire being becomes jeopardised, the answers become all too clear. We're only on this planet for a blink of an eye. Life isn't about how long you live, it's about what you do while you're living."

Seth reproduces the letter of a dying 24-year-old man, in the hope that it will encourage you to "realise that you want your life to be shaped by the choices you had the courage to make, not the ones you didn't". The essence of the letter is reproduced below.

"I am only 24 years old, yet I have already chosen my last tie. It's the one that I will wear on my funeral a few months from now… The cancer diagnosis came too late to give me at least a tenuous hope for a long life, but I realised that the most important thing about death, is to ensure that you leave this world a little better than it was before you existed, with your contributions."

"When I learned how much time I had left, however, it became clear which things are really important. So, I am writing to you for a selfish reason. I want to give meaning to my life by sharing with you what I have realised:

- ✗ Don't waste your time on work that you don't enjoy. It is obvious that you cannot succeed in something that you don't like. Patience, passion, and dedication come easily only when you love what you do.

- Take control of your life. Take full responsibility for the things that happen to you. Limit bad habits and try to lead a healthier life.

- It's stupid to be afraid of others' opinions. Fear weakens and paralyses you. If you let it, it can grow worse and worse every day until there is nothing left of you, but a shell of yourself. Listen to your inner voice and go with it. Some people may call you crazy, but some may even think that you're a legend.

- Most of all, don't procrastinate. Let your life be shaped by decisions you made, not by the ones you didn't.

- Appreciate the people around you. Your friends and relatives will always be an infinite source of strength and love. You shouldn't take them for granted.

"We care so much about the health and integrity of our body that, until death, we don't notice that the body is nothing more than a box - a parcel for delivering our personality, thoughts, beliefs and intentions to this world. If there is nothing in this box that can change the world, then it doesn't matter if it disappears."

"You can float through a life created by circumstances, missing day after day, hour after hour. Or, you can fight for what you believe in, and write the great story of your life. I hope you will make the right choice."

"Leave a mark in this world. Have a meaningful life, whatever definition it has for you. Go towards it. The place we are leaving is a beautiful playground, where everything is possible. Yet, we are not here forever. Our life is a short spark in this beautiful little planet that flies with incredible speed to the endless darkness of the unknown universe. So, enjoy your time here with passion. Make it interesting. Make it count!"

On a lighter note, from regrets of the dying, to regrets of the "not flying…"

A British Airways survey of 2 000 Americans, aged 55 and over, showed that - for the generation born between 1946 and 1961 - "a fifth of all respondents said that not traveling enough was their biggest regret in life".

The survey, published by *The Huffington Post*, also revealed that:

- 17% of male respondents said that working too much was their biggest regret
- 22% of women said not traveling enough was their biggest regret
- 8% of women respondents said working too much was a regret
- 26% of respondents said losing contact with friends was their biggest regret
- 17% of men said not spending enough time with their children was their biggest regret

"Travel is fatal to prejudice, bigotry, and narrow-mindedness, and many of our people need it sorely on these accounts. Broad, wholesome, charitable views of men and things cannot be acquired by vegetating in one little corner of the earth all one's lifetime." *Mark Twain*

"*Take it away, Frank*"…

"And now, the end is near
And so I face the final curtain
My friend, I'll say it clear
I'll state my case, of which I'm certain

I've lived a life that's full
I've traveled each and every highway
But more, much more than this
I did it my way

Regrets, I've had a few
But then again, too few to mention
I did what I had to do
And saw it through without exemption

I planned each charted course
Each careful step along the byway
And more, much more than this
I did it my way

Yes, there were times, I'm sure you knew
When I bit off more than I could chew
But through it all, when there was doubt
I ate it up and spit it out
I faced it all and I stood tall
And did it my way

I've loved, I've laughed and cried
I've had my fill my share of losing
And now, as tears subside
I find it all so amusing

To think I did all that
And may I say - not in a shy way
Oh no, oh no, not me
I did it my way

For what is a man, what has he got
If not himself, then he has naught
To say the things he truly feels
And not the words of one who kneels
The record shows I took the blows
And did it my way.

Yes it was my way."[79]

---

[79] "*My Way*", performed by Frank Sinatra, written by Claude Francois, Gilles Thibaut, Jacques Revaux, Paul Anka • Copyright © BMG Rights Management US, LLC, Songs Music Publishing

Inspirational Quotes...

"There are no secrets to success. It is the result of preparation, hard work, and learning from failure." *Colin Powell.*

"Develop success from failures. Discouragement and failure are two of the surest stepping stones to success." *Dale Carnegie.*

"95% of your emotions are determined by the way you talk to yourself." *Brian Tracy.*

"Only those who attempt the absurd can achieve the impossible." *Albert Einstein.*

"Strength does not come from winning. Your struggles develop your strength." *Arnold Schwarzenegger.*

"In a gentle way, you can shake the world." *Mahatma Gandhi.*

"The only person you are destined to become, is the person you decide to be." *Ralph Waldo Emerson.*

"Failure is nature's plan to prepare you for great responsibilities." *Napoleon Hill.*

"In order to do something you've never done, you have to become someone you've never been." *Les Brown.*

"Everyone can rise above their circumstances and achieve success if they are dedicated to, and passionate about, what they do." *Nelson Mandela.*

"It's never too late to be what you might have been." *George Eliot.*

"Your life only gets better when you get better." *Brian Tracy.*

"Being the richest man in the graveyard doesn't matter to me. Going to bed at night knowing we've done something wonderful matters to me." *Steve Jobs.*

"Do just once what others say you can't do, and you will never pay attention to their limitations again." *James R. Cook.*

"The ultimate source of happiness is our mental attitude." *The Dalai Lama.*

"If you don't like something, change it. If you can't change it, change your attitude." *Maya Angelou.*

"You may not control all the events that happen to you, but you can decide not to be reduced by them." *Maya Angelou.*

"A Roman general in the time of Caesar had a motto - "If it is possible, it is done. If it is impossible… it will be done." And that is what I live by." *Evel Knievel.*

"It always seems impossible until it's done." *Nelson Mandela.*

"…The people who are crazy enough to think they can change the world are the ones who do." *Steve Jobs.*

"You already have everything you need to succeed locked up inside you. Reading and studying simply draws out and develops what's already within. It empowers you to be your best self." *Bob Proctor.*

"The future belongs to those who believe in the beauty of their dreams." *Eleanor Roosevelt.*

"My job was to make everyone understand that the impossible was possible. That's the difference between leadership and management." *Sir Alex Ferguson.*

"Keep your words positive,
because your words
Become your behaviour.

Keep your behaviour positive
Because your behaviour
Becomes your habits.

Keep your habits positive
Because your habits
Become your values.

Keep your values positive
Because your values
Become your destiny."   *Mahatma Ghandi.*

Addendum: Sensory Preference Questionnaire:

To determine whether you exhibit a predominantly Visual, Auditory (Hearing) or Kinaesthetic (Feeling) sensory preference, please read each question, and select the letter which applies the _**most**_ to you - A, B, or C... There are no right or wrong answers...

1. _I make important decisions based on:_

C) My gut feeling
B) Which way sounds best to me
A) Which way looks best to me

2. _How would you know that you have had a good day?_

B) A productive meeting, or good news over the telephone
A) A clear desk, or "To Do" list with everything marked as completed
C) An "inner glow", a smile, and a feeling of deep satisfaction

3. _Which would you prefer for a celebratory treat?_

B) A personal dedication on the radio
A) A weekend break to somewhere you have never visited before
C) Your favourite meal, with good wine, and good company

4. _It is easiest for me to:_

B) Find the ideal volume and settings on my iPod
C) Select the most comfortable furniture
A) Select rich, attractive colour combinations

5. _Which magazines would you be most likely to read?_

C) DIY, Sports, or Creative Crafts
B) Music, or Current Affairs
A) _National Geographic_ or _Vogue_

6. _Which activity would you prefer on holiday?_

C) Lazing on a sun-drenched beach, occasionally swimming to cool off
B) Attending a concert, or a lecture on local culture and history
A) Seeing the sights and local culture, visiting a museum or art gallery

7. Which of the following pastimes most appeals to you?

A) Cinema, Photography, Art, Interior Design
C) Sport, Sculpture, Cookery, Gardening
B) Playing a musical instrument, Listening to music or an audiobook, Singing

8. I ...

B) am very attuned to the sounds of my surroundings
C) am very sensitive to the way that clothing feels on my body
A) have a strong response to colours and presentation

9. During a disagreement, I am most likely to be influenced by:

B) The other person's tone of voice
A) Whether I can see the other person's point of view or not
C) Whether I am in touch with the other person's feelings or not

10. What do you look for, to believe that a person is telling you the truth?

A) The way that they look at - or avoid looking at - you
B) Their tone of voice
C) The feeling you get about their sincerity

11. If you were to show your appreciation to someone, which would you choose?

B) Telephone them
C) Give them a bottle of their favourite drink/box of chocolates
A) Write them a "Thank You" note

12. Which of the following careers do you find most appealing?

A) Artist, or Designer
B) Lecturer, Telesales, or Customer Liaison
C) Gardener, Nurse, or Counsellor

13. Which programme would you prefer to watch?

C) Wildlife/Nature
A) Painting or Art
B) Popular music/Classical concert

14. Which would be your preferred method of relaxation?

A) Look into something relaxing, such as a candle's flame
C) An aromatherapy massage
B) Talk with a friend

15. I most easily express myself by:

A) The way that I dress and look
C) The feelings that I share
B) My tone of voice

Mostly A's =   Your sensory preference is **Visual**
Mostly B's =   Your sensory preference is **Auditory**
Mostly C's =   Your sensory preference is **Kinaesthetic**

As with DiSC personality profiling, it is possible to share many of the characteristics of different sensory profiles, and, like DiSC, it may change with external environments. Listen to people talking - including yourself - notice what you notice... The biggest reveal is in your language, such as "I see," "I feel," or "I hear" - it's really that simple!

If you can communicate in the other person's preferred sensory preference, then the core meaning of your message will be better received by that person - not being subjected to their distortion of "translation"...

People who exhibit a visual sensory preference, tend to prefer seeing what they are experiencing - pictures, images, graphs, and colours will help their understanding better than an explanation, or reading simple text. They prefer visual cues - meaningful symbols, colours and graphics.

People who exhibit an auditory sensory preference, tend to prefer the spoken word. You may need to hear the sound of your own voice to process information, or rely on audiobooks and recordings rather than simple text. They may also choose to join a community, or group, wherein they can discuss their development, or shared interests.

People who exhibit a kinaesthetic sensory preference, tend to prefer physically completing tasks, and gaining knowledge through the practical experience. They prefer movement, activity, and getting "hands on" - interacting with different materials and engaging in role plays.

Printed in Great Britain
by Amazon